There is no more urgent question than that of why and how western political systems have become saturated by the concern for security. Yet the more govenments pursue security the more they subvert the freedoms they claim to secure. The more also they render the world dangerous.

Mark Neocleous is amongst the most acute observers of this lethal paradox. Returning to it here, by interrogating the complicity that also obtains between security, freedom and capital, Neocleous asks who gets what, where, when, and how when security operates as the generative principle of formation for our political and economic orders. Detailing also how emergency powers derived from martial law in a process that has progressively militarised social and political relations he provides a powerful counter-weight to abstract arguments about states of emergency.

Challenging and accessible, this book opens up new political questions as it describes the new ways in which life has become more comprehensively securitized.

Professor Michael Dillon, Politics and International Relations,
Lancaster University

D1586644

CRITIQUE OF SECURITY

Mark Neocleous

Edinburgh University Press

Edinburgh University Press Ltd
22 George Square, Edinburgh

Typeset in Palatino Light by
Norman Tilley Graphics Ltd, Northampton,
and printed and bound in Great Britain by
CPI Group (UK) Ltd, Croydon, CR0 4YY

A CIP record for this book is available from the
British Library

ISBN 978 0 7486 3328 9 (hardback)
ISBN 978 0 7486 3329 6 (paperback)

CONTENTS

ACKNOWLEDGEMENTS

The font used on the cover of this book is demi-dingbat, part readable, part pictorial. It was compiled by Keith Bates in a Pop Art fashion using images trawled from internet searches, entering various expressions relating to 'Security' and aiming to reflect the theme intuitively and eclectically. Its appearance derives partly from children's spelling books or alphabet cards, and partly from its ancestors, the Mailart Typeface and Mailart Graphics font. It received a Commendation in the 2005 FUSE typeface competition. I am grateful to Keith for his permission to use it.

As the arguments in this book have been developed they have been tried out in various venues. A paper on 'Liberty, Security and the Myth of Balance', at University of Glasgow School of Law, November 2004, allowed me to try out some of the ideas in Chapter 1; I am grateful to Adam Tomkins and Lindsay Farmer for the invitation. The main thrust of the arguments that run through Chapters 2 and 3 was tried out in Tel-Aviv University School of Law, January 2006, at the invitation of Roy Kreitner, Yishai Blank and Shai Lavi; Glasgow Film Theatre, February 2006, at the invitation of the Glasgow School of Fine Art and Ross Birrell; Nanjing University, November 2006, at the invitation of the Centre for the Study of Marxist Philosophy; and at the University of Buffalo Law School, May 2007, at the invitation of Markus Dubber.

For reading or commenting on parts or all of the argument I am grateful to Ross Birrell, Stuart Elden, Nasser Hussain, Olena Kobzar, George Rigakos and Guillermina Seri. For smiling through various stages of the writing I am, as ever, heavily in debt to Debbie Broadhurst.

INTRODUCTION

The forces of law and order have to be reminded about life and its sanctity. Don't let the bastards off the hook. They try to act like we arenay real live human beings. They arenay trained in seeing us properly, us people I am talking about, these Security fuckers man it is trained out of them.

James Kelman, *You Have to Be Careful in the Land of the Free* (2004)

On 4 August 1999, the *Atlanta Journal* reported that a flight from Atlanta to Turkey the previous day had been prevented from taking off by the FBI, with all 241 passengers forced to leave the plane. A huge 'security operation' then ensued: passengers questioned; luggage unloaded and matched to passengers; the plane searched by humans and dogs; one man detained. The reason for all this was that the detained man was thought to be 'a potential threat to national security'. And the reason he was thought to be a potential threat to security was that the man, who was eventually released, had paid for his ticket in cash. A few years later, following the introduction of yet more stringent 'security measures' as part of the global 'war on terror', a woman was arrested under the UK Prevention of Terrorism Act for walking on a public cycle path in the harbour area of Dundee. The official reason given for the arrest was that 'the woman was in a secure area which forbids people walking', and so she was 'seen as a security risk',[1] although the authorities conceded that if she had been on a bike security would not have been threatened. Bizarre as it may seem, the woman's arrest was probably consistent with the more general advice given to businesses and universities by the British security service MI5 on how they might help in the 'war on terror'. The advice included 'ensuring that everything has a place and that items are returned to that place', and 'pruning all vegetation and trees, especially near

1

entrances'.[2] If the security of global order is to be pursued with some good caretaking and orderly gardening, then the woman's arrest is perhaps not so bizarre, since by walking on a cycle path she was clearly 'out of place': 'disorderly', no less, and so a threat to security.

Well before 11 September 2001, Michael J. Shapiro suggested that in the modern period talk about security is wholly intelligible, and proposed that we ask after the conditions of this intelligibility.[3] In fact, the examples suggest that talk about security is often *unintelligible*. Take, as another example, the 2003 House of Commons Research Paper on the law of occupation in Iraq. Describing one of the main tasks during the 'war on terror' as overcoming the resistance of the Iraqi security forces, it also suggests reforming those same security services. This is 'to demonstrate to the Iraqi people that our quarrel is not with them and that their security and well-being is our concern'. At the same time, the Report suggests that the task is to secure the sites of 'weapons of mass destruction' and to 'provide for the security of friendly forces'.[4] Taken in a literal sense – that is, if we remove for a moment the politics behind the Iraq debacle – the argument seems to be: security forces must be removed in order to improve security; something that does not exist (the weapons of mass destruction) must be secured; that which must also be secured we must first partially destroy; that which is called security is not security. The whole thing is unintelligible.

So if, as it seems, talk about security is often unintelligible, then perhaps we need to ask after the conditions of this unintelligibility. This is not an easy task, since our whole political language and culture has become saturated by 'security'. Nearly all political disputes and disagreements now appear to centre on the conception of security, and nothing seems to advance a policy claim more than to be offered in the discourse of security.[5] But it is not just formal politics at issue here. The contemporary social and political imagination is similarly dominated by the lexicon of security and the related idea that we are living in an increasingly insecure world. Everywhere we look a 'need' for security is being articulated: a discussion of the effect on UK academics of the Fixed-Term Employees (Prevention of Less Favourable Treatment) Regulations 2002 is called 'Security Alert'; a group of farmers aiming to halt what it sees as a perceived decline in UK food production calls itself Food Security Ltd; the potential extinction of tigers sees the Wildlife Conservation Society, the World

Wildlife Fund and the Smithsonian National Zoological Park demand that 'now more than ever, tigers need homeland security'.[6] Just three examples, but they make clear the extent to which the paradigm of (in)security has come to shape our imaginations and social being. 'Security consciousness' is the new dominant ideology; every day is Security Awareness Day.[7]

This saturation of the political and social landscape with the logic of security has been accompanied by the emergence of an academic industry churning out ideas about how to defend and improve it. Security has been defined[8] and redefined.[9] It has been re-visioned,[10] re-mapped,[11] gendered,[12] refused.[13] Some have asked whether there is perhaps too much security,[14] some have sought its civilisation,[15] and thousands of others have asked about how to 'balance' it with liberty. Much of this redefining, re-visioning, re-mapping, and so on, has come about through a more widespread attempt at widening the security agenda so as to include societal, economic and a broad range of other issues such as development or the environment. These moves have sought to forge alternative notions of 'democratic' and 'human' security as part of a debate about whose security is being studied, the ontological status of insecurities and questions of identity, and through these moves security has come to be treated less as an objective condition and much more as the product of social processes. At the same time, a developing body of work known as 'critical security studies' has emerged.

This range of research – now quite formidable, often impressive and sometimes drawn on in this book – has a double lack. First, for all its talk about discourse, processes and the need for a critical edge, it still offers a relatively impoverished account of the different ways in which security and insecurity are imagined.[16] To speak of different 'security fields' such as the environment, migration, energy, and so on, often fails to open up the analysis to the ways in which spaces and places, processes and categories, are imagined through the lens of insecurity and in turn appropriated and colonised by the project of security. Given the centrality of the state to the political imagination, to imagine the whole social order through the lens of insecurity is to hand it over to the key entity which is said to be the ground of security, namely the state.[17] This is related to the second lack, which is that for all the critical edge employed by the authors in question, the running assumption underpinning the work is that security is still a *good thing*, still *necessary* despite how much we interrogate it. The assumption seems to be that while we might engage in a critical interrogation of security, we could never quite be against it. 'Why we might want "security" after all' is how one of the most influential essays in this area ends.[18] As Didier Bigo points out, how to *maximise* security always seems to remain the core issue.[19] And so there is a danger that these approaches do not quite manage to shake off the managerialism prevalent in more traditional security studies: the desire to 'do' security better. The common assumption remains that security is the foundation of freedom, democracy and the good society, and that the real question is how to improve the power of the state to 'secure' us.

But what if at the heart of the logic of security lies not a vision of freedom or emancipation, but a means of modelling the whole of human society around a particular vision of order? What if security is little more than a semantic and semiotic black hole allowing authority to inscribe itself deeply into human experience? What if the magic word 'security' serves merely to neutralise political action, encouraging us to surrender ourselves to the state in a thoroughly conservative fashion?[20] And what if this surrender facilitates an ongoing concession to authority and the institutional violence which underpins the authority in question, and thus constitutes the first key step in learning how to treat people not as human beings, but as objects to be administered? In other words, what if the major requirement of our time is less an expanded, refined, or redefined vision of security, and nothing less than a *critique of security*? Corey Robin points out that when a particular idea routinely accompanies atrocities then some real critical engagement with the idea would seem to be in order.[21] And since there is a clear and not particularly long line linking the idea of security and the atrocities being carried out in Guantánamo, Abu Ghraib and the other 'security centres' at which people are currently being held, never mind the long history of states slaughtering millions in the name of security, then the time must be right for a critique of security.

The starting point of the critique is to see it not as some kind of universal or transcendental value, but rather as a mode of governing, a political technology through which individuals, groups, classes, and, ultimately, modern capital is reshaped and reordered. As a principle of formation, as Mick Dillon calls it,[22] security is a technique of power; a political enactment deployed and mobilised in the exercise of power. Extending an argument I have made elsewhere,[23] I want to show the extent to which security has facilitated a form of liberal order-building, and to develop a critique of the constant re-ordering of politics and reshaping of society in the name of security. In so doing I aim to challenge the ways in which security has become the master narrative through which the state shapes our lives and imaginations (security risks here, security measures there, security police everywhere), producing and organising subjects in a way that is always already predisposed towards the exercise of violence in defence of the established order. As such, the critique of security is part and parcel of a wider critique of power. This requires taking on the thinkers, groups and classes which have accepted and peddled the security fetish: security-obsessed politicians and policy wonks, the security and intelligence services, the security industry and security intellectuals; the 'security Fuckers', as James Kelman calls them.

Such a critique must stand at a critical distance from critical security studies (and thus act as a kind of 'critique of critical criticism', in the sense in which Marx meant it in 1845). This 'school' of thought argues that security has to be oriented around the notion of emancipation. Ken Booth has argued that since 'security' is the absence of threats and 'emancipation' is the freeing of people from human and physical constraints, 'security and emancipation are two sides of the same coin. Emancipation, not power or order, produces true security. Emancipation, theoretically, is security'. He adds that this equation can be sustained empirically: 'emancipation, empirically, is security'.[24] This seems to me to be as about as mistaken as one can possibly be about security; as we will see in Chapter 1, it is in fact far closer to classical liberalism than it is to critical theory.[25] Part of the argument here is that security and *oppression* are the two sides of the same coin.

Any argument of this kind needs to go well beyond the places in which security is usually studied. 'Security studies' as such has tried a little too hard to understand itself as a discipline, and in so doing has tended to replicate the various schools or positions found in the study of international relations, offering up its own version of the narrow and deeply disciplinary 'name, school and subfield' approach without which most academics seem lost. And yet the proliferation of work aiming to expand security has quickly run into difficulties of definition. For example, the United Nations tells us that 'human security' has two aspects: 'first, safety from chronic threats such as hunger, disease and repression' and, second, 'protection from sudden and hurtful disruptions in the patterns of daily life – whether in homes, in jobs or in communities'.[26] Whatever logic the first aspect may have, the second aspect appears to turn all human being and social interaction into a security problematic (neatly handing them over, of course, to the institutions which like to claim the power and right to secure). At the same time, one finds people working on security and yet seemingly talking about very different things. The extent to which 'security' has been 'disciplined' over the years[27] has been used to 'discipline' people in turn, encouraging intellectuals to retreat so far into their fields of expertise that, for example, people working on 'social security' have absolutely no contact with people working on 'national security' (just one of the many instances in which the division of intellectual labour in the university reflects nicely the desire of the state to keep these things apart, to draw a veil over the unity of state power). Rather than seek to be part of a discipline or school centred on security – of the traditional, critical, or expanded type; of the national or social kind – the critique of security ranges widely and wildly through and around security studies and international political economy; history, law and political theory; international relations and historical sociology, in a seriously ill-disciplined manner which will no doubt annoy the Guardians of Discipline and Professors of Good Order (the 'security guards' of the modern academy). Academic disciplines are part of a much broader problem of the compartmentalisation of knowledge and division of the intellect against which critical theory must struggle. This book is therefore not even meant to be an inter-disciplinary text; rather, it is anti-disciplinary. It is a work of critique.

Marx once described *Capital* as 'a critique of economic categories or, if you like, a critical exposé of the system of bourgeois economy'.[28] He saw critique as a method for simultaneously unmasking ideas and rooting them within the context of class society and the commodity form. This book is an attempt at a critique of one of the key political categories of our time, as a simultaneous critical exposé of the system of bourgeois politics. In that sense it is meant as an unmasking of the ideology and a defetishising of the system of security. One of the features of ideology is that it imposes an obviousness or naturalness on ideas without appearing to do so – a double victory in which the obviousness of the ideas in question is taken as a product of their 'naturalness', and vice versa: their obviousness is obvious because they are so natural.[29] This is nowhere truer than with security, the necessity of which appears so obvious and natural, so right and true, that it closes off all opposition; it has to remain unquestioned, unanalysed and undialectically presupposed, rather like the order which it is expected to secure. And if opposition to security is closed off, then so too is opposition to the political and social forces which have placed it at the heart of the political agenda. I want to write against this ideology by writing about the ways in which security has been coined, shaped and deployed by political, commercial and intellectual forces. The book is therefore written against the security-mongering – in the literal sense of the 'monger' as one who traffics in a petty or discreditable way – that dominates contemporary politics. I will perhaps be charged with not taking insecurity seriously enough. But to take security seriously means to take it critically, and not to cower in the face of its monopolistic character. This is to hold true to the idea of critique as a political genre that aims to resist the course of a world which continues to hold a gun to the heads of human beings.[30]

Foucault defines critique as the 'art of not being governed quite so much'.[31] If, as seems clear, this art now requires a critique of security, then it also requires an understanding of the history of security as an idea and ideal. In other words, 'critique is not a matter of saying that things are not right as they are. It is a matter of pointing out on what kinds of assumptions, what kinds of familiar, unchallenged, unconsidered modes of thought the practices that we accept rest'.[32] This is an approach which takes as its starting point one or more of the contemporary rituals of power and asks how its central terms and concepts have historically functioned: 'a critique of our own time, based upon retrospective analyses'.[33] This book aims at a critique of security in our time, based on some retrospective analyses of some key moments in its history and development. The historical enquiry is meant to resonate with contemporary debates concerning security and, relatedly, war and violence.

We begin by exploring the place of security in classical liberalism. The argument is that liberalism's key concept is not liberty, but security, and this is so because security is the supreme concept of bourgeois society. My aim here is to further an argument I first made in *The Fabrication of Social Order* about the centrality of insecurity to liberal thinking. Here, I trace security politics back into Locke's account of prerogative and then expand this into a wider set of claims about liberalism and security. The prerogative power is important in this context because it is said to be necessary for moments of crisis: states of exception in which necessity must prevail in the interest of good order. In these conditions, the space is created for the exercise of emergency powers in the name of security. This then opens door for an examination of the ideological circuit between emergency powers and security in Chapters 2 and 3.

Much has been made recently of the idea that we have moved into a permanent 'state of emergency' following 9/11. My argument is that what is needed is less an analysis of the 'state of emergency' and much more an interrogation of the ways in which emergency powers became normalised through the twentieth century. As well as undermining any distinction between the 'normality' of the rule of law on the one hand and the 'exception' of the violence exercised through emergency powers on the other, this argument points us to the permanence of emergency well before 9/11. The permanence of emergency created the platform for security to become the central category of liberal order-building in the twentieth century. To make this argument I trace the idea of 'national security' as it emerged in the late-1940s back to earlier debates about 'social security' in the 1930s. Introduced through the use of emergency powers, security created the grounds for a new liberal order-building domestically via social security and internationally via national security. Security could thus be used as a political technology on both the domestic and the international front, the basis of which was a particular vision of economic order.

Chapter 4 then takes up the ways in which the political technology of security could mobilise citizens around a particular vision of the nation. By tracing an intimate connection between national identity and the politics of loyalty as these were played out in the early national security state,[34] I come to argue for a recognition of what I call the security–identity–loyalty complex. This complex is a crucial mechanism for deploying loyalty as a political technology of security and identity, coming to shape social behaviour in all sorts of ways thought to be important to social order.

Finally, Chapter 5 has two targets. First, it takes up the current debate about the 'privatisation' of security in both the domestic and international fields. Contra the logic of privatisation, which makes absurd claims about the 'hollowing-out' of the state, I argue that what is taking place is the commodification of security, at the heart of which is a security industry working hand-in-hand with the state rather than undermining it, thriving on but also peddling security as the fetish of our times. This fetishism, I suggest, is also shared by my second target: those security intellectuals so in thrall to both the security state and the security industry that they have allowed their work, indeed their disciplines, to be shaped and ordered by the security state.

A final introductory word on fascism. A number of writers have noted that there is a real Schmittian logic underpinning security politics: that casting an issue as one of 'security' tends to situate that issue within the logic of threat and decision, of friend and enemy, and so magnifies the dangers and ratchets up the strategic fears and insecurities that encourage the construction of a certain kind of political reason centred on the violent clampdown of the moment of decision.[35] 'Speaking and writing about security is never innocent', says Jef Huysmans, 'it always risks contributing to the opening of a window of opportunity for a "fascist mobilisation"'.[36] Events since 11 September 2001, bear witness to this. It seems abundantly clear that any revival of fascism would now come through the mobilisation of society in the name of security.[37] This potential for fascist mobilisation underlines once more that far from being a distinct political force outside of liberalism and capital, fascism is in fact liberal capitalism's doppelgänger. The lesson of the twentieth century is that the crises of liberalism, more often than not expressed as crises threatening the security of the state and the social order of capital, reveal the potential for the rehabilitation of fascism; thriving in the crises of liberalism, the fascist potential *within* liberal democracy has always been more dangerous than the fascist tendency *against* democracy.[38] The critique of security being developed here is intended as a reminder of the authoritarian, reactionary and fascist potential within the capitalist order and one of its key political categories.

To this end, the aim of the critique of security is not a set of proposals for democratising security, humanising security, balancing security with liberty, or any other policy proposal to improve the wonderful world of security. There are more than enough security intellectuals for that. The aim is to play a part in freeing the political

imagination from the paralysis experienced in the face of security –
to free ourselves from security fetishism by provoking and intriguing
others to try and think politics without security. It is often said that
security is the gift of the state; perhaps we ought to return the gift.

Chapter 1

'THE SUPREME CONCEPT OF BOURGEOIS SOCIETY': LIBERALISM AND THE TECHNIQUE OF SECURITY

═══════

> It's on the market, You're on the price list
> It's on the market, You're on the price list
> It's on the market, You're on the price list.
> Gang of Four, 'Return the Gift' (1979)

There's a question much loved by political theorists, widely used in trying to get their students into political theory, and it usually goes like this: 'Liberty and Equality: Must they Conflict?'. If you put it to students now, they might think there's something just a little odd about this question. Surely, if there is any question to be asked, it is whether liberty and security must conflict. Shifting the question this way would be a reasonable reflection of the extent to which security has come to the fore as perhaps the pre-eminent issue. One can now go for weeks or months without encountering the question 'liberty versus equality' in everyday debate; one can hardly say the same about 'liberty versus security'. Likewise, one can go for days without reading in the newspapers about issues pertaining to equality, but one can barely turn a page (or a corner, for that matter) without coming up against the question of security.

So if these are bad days for equality, then they are also bad days for liberty. For any claim to liberty in the contemporary world quickly runs up against the (counter-)demand for security. Much of the discussion concerning the theory and practices surrounding security centres on the relationship between these and their consequences for liberty. Either explicitly or implicitly, the assumption is that we must forego a certain amount of liberty in our desire for security. The general claim is

11

that in seeking security, states need to constantly limit the liberties of citizens, and that the democratic society is one which has always aimed to strike the right 'balance' between liberty and security. The follow-on from this is that recent changes in international order, not least the attacks on the World Trade Center but also a more general sense or feeling of political instability, require us to rethink the balance much more towards security and thus away from liberty. Contemporary newspapers and periodicals are saturated with articles on the 'balance' between liberty and security, governments have latched on to this ideological trope when presenting proposals for new security measures,[1] and it constitutes one of the animating ideas in judicial discussion. In this chapter I want to first unpick some of the underlying tensions in this set of assumptions. More explicitly, I want to suggest that the key assumption involved – that liberty and security are antonyms and that we must somehow find a 'balance' between them – is desperately misplaced. The obvious tactic to achieve this might appear to be to focus on a range of key areas: recent 'anti-terrorism' legislation, the political implications of the perpetual 'war on terror' and the ideological interpellation of all sorts of activities as 'terrorist', questions around ID cards, new forms of surveillance technology, and so on. But not only is this now rather well-trodden ground, but also virtually all the commentaries on these issues accept to some degree the need to find a 'balance'.

I will therefore take a very different approach by suggesting that the question of balance is an essentially liberal one. Ronald Dworkin and Andrew Ashworth have shown that the notion of balance is a rhetorical device of which one must be extremely wary. Aside from lacking any empirical evidence and often involving the giving-up of the liberties of others, usually minorities, the whole approach based on 'balancing' presupposes that 'balance' is self-evidently a worthy goal – hence 'balance of powers', 'balance of trade', and so on – and thus acts as a substitute for real argument.[2] I want to push this further and show that the idea of balance doesn't just act as a substitute for real argument, but in fact functions as a mechanism for working any argument into a fundamentally liberal mode of thought. And behind this liberal mode of thought lies a set of fundamentally illiberal justifications for a range of extreme and dangerous 'security measures'. Thus rather than take what has fast become the standard approach of criticising security measures in terms of their threat to liberty, or of asking 'how much liberty are we willing to sacrifice in the search for security?', I suggest that what is needed is an exploration of the ways the liberal project of 'liberty' is in fact a project of security.

Because liberalism has situated itself as the ideology, movement or party of liberty, and because it is so often reiterated in these terms, a common assumption is that if anyone should be defending liberty against security, it is liberals. The classic formulation of this view is found in Benjamin Franklin's claim that 'they that can give up essential liberty to obtain a little temporary safety deserve neither liberty nor safety', a claim that has been repeated so many times in the twenty-first century that to list all references would be a research task in itself. This chapter suggests that there's a certain myth-making going on when people talk of the search for the right 'balance' between liberty and security, and that this myth-making obscures some of the real history of liberalism. For while it may be that 'the *moral* instinct of the liberal is typically to give some special status . . . to the protection of basic liberties, which means that they cannot be traded away',[3] the *political* instinct lies firmly in the direction of security. So, building on one of Marx's insights and on a key theme within Foucault's work, I argue that rather than resist the push to security in the name of liberty, liberalism in fact enacts another form of political rationality that sets in place mechanisms for a 'society of security'.[4] 'Security' here straddles law and economy, police power and political economy, and becomes the dominant mode of what Foucault calls 'governmental rationality'. Taking these ideas, I want to suggest that in encouraging an essentially liberal mode of thought, the myth of a 'balance' between security and liberty opens the (back) door to an acceptance of all sorts of authoritarian security measures; measures which are then justified on liberal grounds. This argument is developed through a critical historical analysis of the relationship between security and liberty in the liberal tradition, which will then open the door to a wider discussion of security, emergency powers and liberal order-building in the chapters which follow.

SECURITY, SOVEREIGNTY, PREROGATIVE

Modern political thought is often understood as beginning with the clash of positions exemplified by the 'absolutist' Hobbes and the 'liberal' Locke, a clash in which the story of sovereignty is said to be told in terms of either security or liberty. By beginning with a conjectured state of nature, both writers highlight the insecurities which serve to generate the social contract and the sovereign body. For Hobbes, humans are so driven by their desire for pride, revenge and natural passions that no covenant is secure in the state of nature. A power is thus needed 'great enough for our security' and for which an authoritarian state is necessary:

> The only way to erect such a Common Power, as may be able to defend them from the invasion of Forraigners, and the injuries of one another, and thereby to secure them . . . is to conferre all their power and strength upon one Man, or upon one Assembly of men, that may reduce all their Wills, by plurality of voices, unto one Will.[5]

The search for security is thus the driving force behind the creation of absolute sovereignty, derived in turn from the supposed absolute liberty of the individual in the state of nature. The peace achieved via the social contract compared to the condition of war in the state of nature is 'peace' in the sense that it indicates a certain security – of both sovereign and subjects and in terms of both physical protection and a psychological confidence about the future. Without these there is no industry, culture, communication, transport: 'no Building . . . no Knowledge . . . no account of time; no Arts; no Letters, no Society'. The insecurity would, famously, render life nasty, brutish, and short.

In terms of contemporary politics, then, Hobbes's position pushes the 'balance' overwhelmingly in the direction of security; his mutual exchange of obedience for protection is equally an exchange of liberty for security. For Locke, in contrast, the state of nature is a state of 'perfect liberty' with no 'Absolute or Arbitrary Power', but which is still full of anxiety, fear and insecurity.[6] The aim is to supposedly find a society in which such liberty can be secured, and in which the citizens have a right to dissolve the Government should it be thought to be undermining liberty.[7] In this way it is generally said that Locke establishes a political position in which the balance is shifted towards liberty and the protection of that liberty against the demands of arbitrary power. I want to suggest that, contrary to this traditional image, Locke might in fact be thought to inaugurate less a tradition of 'liberty' and much more a *liberal* discourse on the *priority of security*.

The key to my argument lies in Locke's account of prerogative.[8] Locke's political thought appears to revolve around the power of the people to constitute for themselves a government. In so doing they appear to place political supremacy in the legislature; the legislature is supreme because it assures the rule of law, protects life, liberty and property, and prevents any exercise of arbitrary power. And yet Locke concedes that there must also be scope for discretion, since the public good – the protection of life, liberty and property – may sometimes require immediate action. Locke therefore concedes that 'the good of the Society requires, that several things should be left to the discretion of him, that has the Executive Power'. Events may occur where 'strict and rigid observation of the laws may do harm'. Law-making is often too slow, too 'numerous' and cannot deal with 'Accidents and Necessities' that may concern the public. Locke here plays on 'executive power', a term which he introduces not in relation to the body politic, but in relation to the state of nature and which he concedes is a 'strange doctrine': 'That *in the State of Nature, every one has the Executive Power* of the Law of Nature'. For 'the *Execution* of the Law of Nature is in that State, put into every Man's hands . . . For the Law of Nature would, as all other Laws that concern Men in this World, be in vain, if there were no body that in the State of Nature, had a *Power to Execute* that Law'.[9] It is this executive power – note: a *strong* executive power – which both allows and encourages men to construct political power, a part of which is a new form of executive power standing alongside the legislative.

The power to act at moments which require immediate action or where the legislature is slow is what Locke understands by prerogative: 'This Power to act according to discretion, for the publick good, without the prescription of the law, and sometimes even against it, *is* that which is called *Prerogative*'. Through prerogative the people permit their Rulers to act 'of their own free choice', not only where there is no clear legal position ('where the Law was silent') but sometimes where they might feel the law insufficient or unimportant ('against the direct letter of the Law').[10] Prerogative therefore grants to the sovereign discretionary powers not bound by law and which might even be used against the law. This is 'an Arbitrary Power', Locke comments in parenthesis, as though it were a minor point which might be passed over and which allows him to ignore the fact that arbitrary power is precisely the kind of power his constitution was designed to prevent – 'we do but flatter ourselves, if we hope ever to be governed without an arbitrary power', says Robert Filmer, one of Locke's key targets.[11] Prerogative, then, grants rulers powers which are legally indeterminate at best. At worst, prerogative serves to place rulers beyond law. The only requirement is that prerogative is exercised in the interests of the 'safety of the people' and the 'public good'. The principle of *Salus Populi Suprema Lex* (the safety of the people is the supreme law), so central to Hobbes, is for Locke also 'so just and fundamental a Rule that he who sincerely follows it, cannot dangerously err'. In other words, prerogative 'is, and always will be just' so long as it is exercised in the interest of the people.[12]

Now, Locke's initial intention appears to restrict the exercise of prerogative to foreign affairs and the conduct of war and peace, since this is the field in which events can least easily be predicted, subject as they are to the actions of other states. He distinguishes between the internal exercise of power concerning the relations between the individuals within civil society, and the external exercise of power concerning the 'defence of the Common-wealth from Foreign Injury'. Internal affairs ('the Society *within* itself') are the province of the Executive power; external affairs ('the *security and interest of the publick without*') are the province of the Federative power. Yet Locke comments that these two powers 'are hardly to be separated' and 'are always almost united'.[13] Sheldon Wolin points out that the casual, unargued quality of such a comment conceals an important move,[14] though this is perhaps being kind to Locke: as Harvey Mansfield has pointed out, 'Locke casual is Locke furtive'.[15] For the unity of the two powers allows civil society to be governed according to the same principle governing external affairs. Because external affairs must ultimately be governed according to the public good and protected from the designs of foreigners, 'it is much less capable to be directed by antecedent, standing, positive Laws . . . and so must necessarily be left to the Prudence and Wisdom of those whose hands it is in'. In other words, the Federative Power is equivalent to 'the Power every Man naturally had before he entred into Society', and thus somehow retains the very power that man was expected to forego in establishing the contract, namely the right to defend oneself and enforce the law of nature.[16] But if the Federative power retains the power of man in natural society, and the Executive and Federative powers are always almost united, then the prerogative meant to be used by the Federative power to govern external relations is easily transposed onto the Executive power. In a move we will see become one of the most common tropes of security politics, the distinction between external and internal affairs of state is obliterated and the Executive is given the power to act according to discretion in 'emergency situations' and on the grounds of security, without the prescription of law and sometimes against the law. That is, onto the Executive is transposed the undisputed power deemed necessary for the maintenance of the state, the security of order and the safety of the people. Suddenly Locke's apparently casual use of the phrase 'mighty *Leviathan*' to describe the body created from the original compact does not sound so casual after all.[17] Indeed, in this as in many other ways he is closer to adopting some of Hobbes's claims and categories rather than refuting them, and we are reminded that in the early 1690s many people suspected Locke of leaning in a Hobbesian direction.[18]

What Locke achieves in these moves is to import into his argument a space for the exercise of prompt and flexible action outside the 'normal' legal and constitutional limits placed on the state: the magistrate may 'command or forbid [actions] so far as they tend to the peace, safety, or security of his people', on the grounds of 'necessity of state and the welfare of the people'.[19] Pre-empting the standard defence of prerogative peddled by modern politicians and judges ever since, the superficial reason why such prerogative must exist appears to be the empirical complexity of political activity – there are simply too many occasions when Executive action cannot be adequately prescribed by laws and rules, and Legislatures are often too slow to respond. And this is most notably the case when society is thought to be most at risk. As John Dunn points out, it is because the sorts of political action which cannot be adequately prescribed by laws or general rules are characteristically those in which the ends of political society are most at risk and which demand the deployment of force that there *has* to be such a power.[20] In chapters to follow we will see that this is precisely at the heart of 'states of emergency' and the basis of powers exercised in the name of security. For the moment, however, we should note that this notion was first found in the doctrine of reason of state.

The doctrine of reason of state holds that besides moral reason there is another reason independent of traditional (that is, Christian) values and according to which power should be wielded, not according to the dictates of good conscience or morality, but according to whatever is needed to maintain the state. The underlying logic here is order and security rather than 'the good', and the underlying basis of the exercise of power is necessity. The doctrine is thus founded on principles and assumptions seemingly antithetical to the liberal idea of liberty – in either the moral or the legal sense. Courses of action that would be condemned as immoral if conducted by individuals could be sanctioned when undertaken by the sovereign power. 'When I talked of murdering or keeping the Pisans imprisoned, I didn't perhaps talk as a Christian: I talked according to the reason and practice of states'.[21] Hence for Machiavelli, Romulus deserved to be excused for the death of his brother and his companion because 'what he did was done for the common good'.[22] The doctrine of reason of state thus treats the sovereign as *autonomous* from morality; the state can engage in whatever actions it thinks right – 'contrary to truth, contrary to charity, contrary to humanity, contrary to religion'[23] – so long as they are necessary and performed for the public good. But this is to also suggest that the state might act beyond law and the legal limits on state power so long as it does so for 'the common good', the 'good of the people' or the 'preservation of the state'.

In being able to legitimate state power in all its guises the doctrine of reason of state was of enormous importance, becoming a weapon brandished in power games between princes and then states, eventually becoming the key ideological mechanism of international confrontation as the doctrine gradually morphed into 'interest of state', 'security of state' and, finally, 'national security'.[24] The doctrine identifies security – simultaneously of the people *and* the state (since these are always ideologically conflated) – as the definitive aspect of state power. Security becomes the overriding political interest, the principle above all other principles, and underpins interventions across the social realm in the name of reason of state. As such, the doctrine would therefore appear to be antithetical to liberalism if liberalism is identified as a doctrine which aims to tip the balance of power towards a principled defence of liberty rather than a demand for security at whatever cost. The doctrine would also appear to be antithetical to an argument which purports to root sovereignty in the people rather than the state, as Locke's philosophy is often said to do. But in fact Locke's argument is not an account of sovereignty at all. 'Sovereignty', in Locke's work, is subsumed in typical liberal fashion under an alternative concept, prerogative, as exercised by the 'supreme power',[25] albeit 'incroach'd upon . . . by positive Laws'. In this context prerogative becomes a liberal synonym for reason of state, justified by the security function that resides ultimately with the state. Under-pinning Locke's account of prerogative, then, is nothing less than a liberal argument for reason of state, and Locke adopts a range of strategies from the reason of state tradition, albeit without the claims about the irrelevance of good conscience. (It might be relevant to note that at the time of writing parts of the *Two Treatises* Locke was taking notes from Gabriel Naudé's defence of reason of state in *Considerations Politiques sur les Coups d'Estat*, 1667,[26] and that between 1681 and 1683 had shown a real interest in political conspiracies.[27]) And out of this we can begin to trace what turns out to be nothing less than a liberal *prioritising of security*.

Writing of Locke's account of prerogative, Geraint Parry comments that 'no constitutional writer of the seventeenth century could deny a legitimate place for the royal prerogative, however much, like Locke, he may have sought to insist upon the rule of law'.[28] While true, this overlooks the way in which insisting upon the rule of law might actually be a way of incorporating prerogative into the rule of law and the wider constitutional framework. But constitutionalising pre-rogative hardly overcomes the potential problems inherent within it. Locke's 'solution', such as it is, is to simply assume that prerogative more or less will be used for the public good. In his view, prerogative was sometimes used by rulers for private ends and not the public good 'in the Infancy of Governments', but now the people have somehow managed to '*incroach upon the Prerogative*' and so declare certain limitations on its use. Because such limitations remain un-specified by Locke, we are left to believe that prerogative could now never be used for anything other than the all-encompassing 'for the public good': prerogative simply *is* the 'Power to do good'. He 'that will look into the *History of England*' will find that the people were increasingly satisfied with their rulers whenever the latter 'acted without or contrary to the Letter of the Law', to the extent that the people have now accepted that '*Prerogative is nothing but the Power of doing publick good without a Rule*'. So long as it is used 'for the good of the People' the power of prerogative remains '*undoubted Prerogative, and never is questioned*', which has increasingly meant that 'the people are very seldom, or never scrupulous, or nice in the point: they are far from examining *Prerogative*, whist it is in any tolerable degree imploy'd for the use it was meant'. Thus the People let the rulers 'inlarge their Prerogative as they pleased', even when exercised 'without Law'.[29] Indeed, even the potentially questionable practice of *'cutting off those Parts* . . . which are so corrupt, that they threaten the sound and healthy' is legitimised.[30]

Sensing that such arguments might raise a few eyebrows, not least given both the wider context of Locke's claims about the people's right to resistance should the rulers fail to protect the people's liberties and the more general liberal tenor of his work, Locke is forced to ask aloud the obvious question: *'who shall Judge* when this Power is made right use of?' Surely there must be occasions when the exercise of prerogative might be questioned and judged? And who will then be the judge: the people, a public tribunal, the courts, the Legislature?

> I Answer: Between an Executive Power in being, with such a Prerogative, and a legislative that depends upon his will for their convening, there can be no *Judge on Earth*: As there can be none, between the Legislative, and the People, should either the Executive, or the Legislative, when they have got the Power in their hands, design, or go about to enslave, or destroy them.

There can be no judge on earth means, literally, that 'the people have no other remedy . . . but to *appeal to Heaven'*.[31] In the face of overwhelming and arbitrary use of state power, Locke's advice appears weaker even than that of Hobbes: start praying.[32]

Now, it is perhaps symptomatic that in developing the argument through Chapters 12 to 14 of the *Second Treatise* Locke slips from the question of the Legislative, Executive and Federative Power to talking of power in terms taken from a tradition deeply unconcerned with the separation and balance of powers and much more closely associated with reason of state: the *Prince*. When speaking of the Federative power, Locke describes the prudence of 'those whose hands it is in' as though speaking of a collective entity. But more often than not he speaks of 'his Prudence' when describing the Executive's, of trusting power 'to the prudence of one', of leaving 'discretion [to] him that has the Executive Power', and adds that the executive and federative power can hardly be 'in the hands of distinct Persons'.[33] Thus it is the 'good Prince' who 'cannot have too much *Prerogative'*, and this is the reason prerogative has always been 'in the hands of our wisest and best Princes', the 'God-like Princes [with] Title to Arbitrary Power' and the ability to use this power 'to secure protection'.[34] One might also note that Locke's use of the word 'prudence' in the *Two Treatises* clearly refers to a form of political discretion transposed from the conduct of personal affairs and the management of an estate.[35] And the 'good', 'wise', 'best' and 'God-like' Prince is simultaneously the *strongest*: it is only the Prerogative of 'weak Princes' that is ever really questioned by the people.[36] That the good Prince cannot have too much prerogative is precisely because prerogative has been defined as the 'Power to do good'. Mansfield has suggested that one should avoid trying to identify Machiavellians merely by counting references to the name of Machiavelli in their work, and this certainly holds true for Locke's *Two Treatises*. For as the extent of the executive's prerogative is gradually unveiled in the *Second Treatise*, the thinker who did so much to put the concept of 'liberty' on the political map begins to sound more than a little Machiavellian. As Leo Strauss puts it, 'Locke is closer to Machiavelli than he is generally said or thought to be'.[37] Locke does however add something new to the idea of the good Prince: where previously it was thought the Prince might well have to exercise dishonesty in order to maintain power, albeit exercised for the good of the people, Locke introduces the novel idea of *sincerity*. For Locke, *Salus Populi Suprema Lex* is so fundamental a rule that 'he, who *sincerely* follows it, cannot dangerously err'.[38] The kind of dishonesty openly proposed by Machiavelli is to be replaced by the claim to sincerity, on which basis the trust of the people – 'entrusting' being central to Locke's vision of government – and thus the very foundation stone of the political community will be based.

Despite all the claims about natural liberty, the Lockean Prince is granted the powers usually subsumed under reason of state, with the sole proviso that these are sincerely exercised for the good of the people. During the very century when absolutists were treating security as the foundation of absolute power, Locke's arguments were crucial to what we might call the liberalisation and thus legitimisation of what is to all intents and purposes an absolutist doctrine. In his moves surrounding prerogative Locke essentially identifies the function of the sovereign as the production of security, for which the main criterion is necessity rather than the rule of law. Indeed, in what will become a crucial move in liberal order-building, and thus central to the argument in the rest of this book, the priority of/for security gets built in to the rule of law. Far from being in opposition, the project of liberty supposedly announced with the onset of modern liberalism has been inextricably bound up in the project of security.

Locke's *Two Treatises* thus performs a subtle but important ideological twist. In contrast to the rooting of the security of good order in actions deemed 'necessary' by the tyrannical Prince (Machiavelli) or the authoritarian state (Hobbes), Locke works such actions into the constitution, actions which he believes will not and should not be challenged so long as they are conducted in the name of security. Liberty is natural; security requires political authority. In positing the key function of the state as the protection of property rights, Locke's recodification of the relationship between politics and economics could hardly fail to point to security rather than liberty as the main liberal thematic.[39] And this political production of security rests largely with the executive power, which maintains security through the criterion of necessity rather than the rule of law. Indeed, the necessity of/for security allows the executive to act in ways that appear to be beyond the law. Far from being in opposition, the project of liberty supposedly announced with the onset of modern liberalism has been inextricably bound up – one might even say wrapped up – in the project of security.

Locke's argument here is far from an isolated case. In fact, the need for prerogative powers exercised in the name of security is found in virtually all liberal conceptions of law and political order thereafter. On the one side, it is given legal expression and ratification in William Blackstone's *Commentaries on the Laws of England* (1865): 'prerogative consisting (as Mr Locke has well defined it) in the discretionary power of acting for the public good, where the positive laws are silent'. It is simultaneously based on the *arcana imperii* and on the assumption that the sovereign knows what is best for the people. In seeking to define the legal parameters of prerogative, Blackstone merely ends up spelling out the imperative towards security: prerogative is designed 'for the security and preservation of the real happiness and liberty of his [the king's] subjects'.[40] On the other side, it is given philosophical expression and ratification by a range of writers. In *The Spirit of the Laws*, for example, Montesquieu famously notes that 'there are cases where a veil has to be drawn, over liberty, as one hides the statues of the gods'. These are cases where 'if the legislative power believed itself

endangered . . . it could, for a brief and limited time, permit the executive power to arrest suspected citizens who would lose their liberty'.
As with Locke, we are led to assume that their liberty would be lost
'for a time only so that it would be preserved forever'.[41]

The argument that prerogative powers allow liberty to be lost 'for a
time' and power to be exercised through some kind of authoritarian or
dictatorial order in order that security might be preserved is indicative
of the extent to which security had by the middle of the eighteenth
century become *the* overriding theme for all writers working at the
interface of politics, philosophy and law.[42] *Salus populi suprema Lex*
becomes the key.[43] In an essay on obedience Hume suggests that:

> it is evident, that, when the execution of justice would be
> attended with very pernicious consequences, that virtue must be
> suspended, and give place to public utility, in such extraordinary
> and such pressing emergencies . . . What governor of a town
> makes any scruple of burning the suburbs, when they facilitate
> the approaches of the enemy? Or what general abstains from
> plundering a neutral country, when the necessities of war require
> it, and he cannot otherwise subsist his army? The case is the
> same with the duty of allegiance; and common sense teaches us
> that . . . duty must always, in extraordinary cases, when public
> ruin would evidently attend obedience, yield to the primary and
> original obligation. *Salus populi suprema Lex.*[44]

Rousseau comments that public order requires that 'provision is made
for the public security by a particular act entrusting it to him who is
most worthy'. This provision allows a 'supreme ruler' to 'silence all the
laws and suspend for a moment the sovereign authority', and is
justified on the grounds that 'the people's first intention is that the
State shall not perish'.[45] Similarly, Adam Smith argues on the one
hand against reason of state, on explicit liberal grounds: 'to hinder . . .
the farmer from sending his goods at all times to the best market,
is evidently to sacrifice the ordinary laws of justice . . . to a sort of
reasons of state'. Yet he immediately comments that such a sacrifice
is acceptable 'in cases of the most urgent necessity'.[46] Likewise *The
Federalist Papers* suggests that the most powerful director of national
conduct is safety: 'even the ardent love of liberty will, after a time, give
way to its dictates'.[47]

What we find, then, is that the overlap between security and reason of state that animates the search for absolute sovereignty, and which comes to the fore in supposed 'emergency situations' or 'states of exception', is supported and legitimised rather than challenged by liberalism.[48] Far from disputing the priority of security, classical liberalism gave it a fundamental place in regimes supposedly founded on consent. Prerogative, and thus executive power seemingly outside morality and law, is not something to be dispensed with. Why? Because security is always paramount. Far from being confined to absolutism or authoritarian politics, the prioritising of security gained just as much ground within liberalism. This is not to suggest that liberalism's commitment to liberty is some kind of ruse. Rather, it is to suggest that maybe liberalism's central category is not liberty, but security. Let's push this idea a little further.

LIBERTY IN SECURITY AND LIBERAL INSECURITY

In exploring the nature of sovereignty in the *Wealth of Nations* Adam Smith links sovereignty to security via military power and the martial spirit of a people. Sovereignty, he says, 'is secured by a well-regulated standing army', while 'the security of every society must always depend, more or less, upon the martial spirit of the great body of the people'.[49] But also running through Smith's argument is what appears to be a very different conception of security and liberty. Smith comments on the establishment of 'liberty and security' at the same time as 'order and good government', a point he enjoys repeating. More-over, Smith defines 'the liberty of every individual' as in part founded on 'the sense which he has of his own security', adding that it is on this security that 'the administration of justice depends'. Time and again he refers to the liberty and security of individuals in the same breath.[50] And describing as 'justice' the taxation paid to the British state by Ireland and America, Smith comments that this is payment for the security rather than the liberty provided by the British state – the 'security which they possess for their liberty'.[51]

Note Smith's ordering of priorities here. He is not suggesting that a certain liberty has to be foregone in order to achieve security. Rather, liberty and security are either rolled together or security is something possessed for liberty – ontologically and politically prior to the com-mitment to liberty. In this context a careful reading reveals that when

Smith discusses questions of military power and technology he is in fact really talking about the link between military power, security and liberty. Noting that republicans have often been wary of a standing army due to their fears that such an army threatens liberty, Smith notes that this is so where the interests of the key officers are not identical to those of the state. But where the sovereign himself is the general and where military power is placed in the hands of those who have an interest and share in the civil authority, 'a standing army can never be dangerous to liberty'. On the contrary, it may in some cases be 'favourable to liberty' on the grounds of 'the security it gives to the sovereign'. Thus 'that degree of liberty which approaches to licentious-ness can be tolerated only in countries where the sovereign is secured by a well-regulated standing army'.[52] Likewise the importance of the martial spirit is that in establishing security it 'would necessarily diminish very much the dangers to liberty'.[53] And people will only accept restrictions on their liberty (for example, in the form of a new tax) if it is introduced for security reasons: 'nothing but either the animosity of national vengeance, or the anxiety for national security, can induce the people to submit . . . to a new tax'.[54]

What we find with Smith, then, is a subsumption of liberty under the idea of security similar to that found in Locke. And we can find this move replicated in the work of a whole range of liberal thinkers in this period. Bentham, for example, suggests that '*political liberty* is another branch of security', namely, 'security against injustice from the ministers of government'. It is security rather than liberty that is 'the pre-eminent object' of civil law, for 'a clear idea of liberty will lead us to regard it as a branch of security'. Perhaps even more significantly, when Bentham comments on the issue that was to become perhaps a key political dilemma – the extent to which equality 'might require a redistribution of property' – his comment is that this is a threat not to liberty but to security.[55] For Montesquieu, liberty 'consists in security or in one's opinion of one's security'. Liberty is thus a question of how we understand our security: 'political liberty consists in security or, at least, in the opinion one has of one's security'; 'political liberty in a citizen is that tranquillity of spirit which comes from the opinion each one has of his security'.[56] David Hume comments on the centrality of 'security and protection, which we enjoy in political society' and suggests that the role of the magistrate in ensuring security is more important than allowing a fall back into that 'state of liberty which preceded the institution of government'.[57] And we find among the major writers of the liberal Enlightenment a whole range of similar comments. 'If population be connected with national wealth, liberty and personal security is the great foundation of both' (Ferguson, in 1767); 'the people, having no political liberty, would have no *security* for the continuance of the same laws' (Priestly, in 1771); 'the design and end of government, viz. freedom and security' (Paine, 1776); 'the loss of security' is 'the loss of liberty' (Paley, in 1785); executive energy is exercised for the 'security of liberty' (*Federalist Papers*, 1787–8); 'I would call security, if the expression does not seem too abrupt to be clear, the assurance of legal freedom' (Humboldt, 1792); 'a Government of as much vigour as is consistent with the perfect security of Liberty' (Washington, 1796).[58] The same idea is also found in less significant writings of the period. Benjamin Newton, for example, comments that 'civil liberty implies Security'.[59] Henry Care's *English Liberties* of 1691 was a dull text on the Magna Carta, the role of juries and various Acts of Parliament. By the time he updated it to *British Liberties* in 1766 he had had a chance to absorb Montesquieu's arguments, including the idea that liberty must sometimes be veiled, such that security becomes the main thematic. Repeating the key chapters of *The Spirit of the Laws*, Care notes that liberty 'consists in security, or at least in the opinion that we enjoy security'.[60]

It is clear that by the end of the eighteenth century security was a common theme for all writers on politics and law. And it was this conception of the priority of security that shaped the concept of liberty, for liberty and security were by no means in opposition or in need of balance. 'Liberty' was in fact so bound up with security in the liberal mind that, if anything, they were synonyms rather than antonyms. Liberty is subsumed under security.[61] Security becomes the cornerstone of the liberal mind, which identifies security with the freedom and liberty to pursue one's individual self-interest. In being framed in terms of the mechanisms of security in this way liberty becomes part of the deployment of security rather than a political end in itself.[62] Hence the development of liberal constitutionalism in the nineteenth and early twentieth centuries would be accompanied by the establishment, extension or professionalisation of a whole range of 'security institutions' – police and armed forces, security services, welfare mechanisms ('social security') – that would rival anything found in the police science of the cameralists.[63] Thus when in

Utilitarianism (1861) John Stuart Mill describes security rather than liberty as 'the most vital of all interests' he is merely restating what had by then become a liberal commonplace. Our interests, he comments, vary enormously from person to person depending on our characters and desires; that is why we must respect liberty.

> But security no human being can possibly do without; on it we depend for all our immunity from evil, and for the whole value of all and every good . . . since nothing but the gratification of the instant could be of any worth to us, if we could be deprived of anything the next instant by whoever was momentarily stronger than ourselves.[64]

Such a claim is reiterated in *Considerations on Representative Government*, published in the same year, where the great defender of liberty comments that 'security of person and property, and equal justice between individuals, are the first needs of society, and the primary ends of government'.[65] It is thus security rather than liberty that is Mill's absolute. Liberty is not without its limits, and must be controlled in some ways: 'liberty is often granted where it should be withheld, as well as withheld where it should be granted'.[66] Security, however, is the very foundation of society and progress: it 'release[s] . . . the individual from the cares and anxieties of a state of imperfect protection, sets his faculties free . . . attach[es] him to social existence . . . fosters all those feelings of kindness and fellowship towards others, and interest in the general well-being of the community'.[67]

It is now well established that the historical emergence of liberalism marked an important development in political discourse. But I am arguing that to understand this development as some kind of shift in balance *away* from security and towards liberty would be misleading. As Foucault points out, liberalism historically became identified with the idea that there might be an excess of government, one which opens the way for the state to trample on civil society in general and liberty in particular. But the suspicion that there is always a risk of too much government is always tied to the question: why is it necessary to govern at all?[68] And this quickly puts liberalism into one of its central tensions. For liberalism's various formulations concerning, for example, 'individual liberty', 'freedom of expression', the 'free market', 'freedom of contract', and so on, all seem to articulate a vision of society with a large degree of *insecurity*. 'Security', Bentham says, is 'always tottering, always threatened, never at rest, lives in the midst of snares'.[69] There is of course no discourse of security that is not simultaneously a discourse of insecurity; no discourse of security that is not also a discourse of fears, anxieties and dangers. Nowhere is this truer than in the fear and anxiety that animates liberalism.[70]

'The chief, if not only, spur to human industry and action is uneasiness', says Locke.[71] This 'uneasiness' is for liberalism multi-faceted. On the one hand it arises from an insecurity surrounding nature.

> Nature impales men, breaks them as if on the wheel, casts them to be devoured by wild beasts, burns them to death, crushes them with stones like the first Christian martyr, starves them with hunger, freezes them with cold, poisons them by the quick or slow venom of her exaltations and has hundreds of other hideous deaths in reserve.

Thus, Mill suggests, 'nearly all the things which men are hanged or imprisoned for doing to one another are nature's every-day perform-ances'.[72] On the other hand the uneasiness is also very much to do with the psychological anxieties that are fundamental to the liberal conception of man: 'fear and anxiety', says Smith, are 'the great tormentors of the human breast', a torment which only ever really ends with death – the ultimate security: 'the happiness of the dead' lies in 'the profound security of their repose'.[73] The real driver behind the search for security, however, is neither protection against nature nor the general anxiety, but the uncertainty of property.

The kind of order envisaged by liberals is one of constant change and uncertainty, rooted in the market mechanism on which it is founded. As Marx and Engels put it:

> The bourgeoisie cannot exist without constantly revolutionising the instruments of production, and thereby the relations of production, and with them the whole relations of society . . . Constant revolutionising of production, uninterrupted disturb-ance of all social conditions, everlasting uncertainty and agitation distinguish the bourgeois epoch from all earlier ones.[74]

But this merely posits the necessity of a political apparatus to maintain order amidst the constant change, to secure the insecure.[75] This is because the future has to be predictable and thus made secure. Bentham saw this clearly. 'Of these objects of the law', he says, referring to subsistence, abundance, equality, and security, 'security is the only one which necessarily embraces the future'.

> In order to form a clear idea of the whole extent which ought to be given to the principle of security, it is necessary to consider, that man is not like the brutes, limited to the present time, either in enjoyment or suffering, but that he is susceptible of pleasure and pain by anticipation . . . The idea of his security must be prolonged to him throughout the whole vista that his imagination can measure.

Security is designed 'to guarantee to him, as much as possible, his possessions against future losses'.[76]

As the decisive criterion of liberty, then, 'security' came to imply a set of expectations concerning the undisturbed development of the life process of society – to be achieved, if necessary and in the final instance, through the exercise of prerogative powers. But since 'society' here is an order founded on property, 'security' comes to imply nothing other than the liberty of secure possession; that is, the liberty of private property. As I have shown elsewhere, the identification of liberty with security should thus be understood as part of the articulation of a certain vision of security, a vision grounded in the assumption that private property be the foundation of society. What Locke sees done for 'the public good' under the prerogative of the Prince, is, in effect, what is done in the protection of private property. The reason for men 'putting themselves under Government', Locke insists, '*is the Preservation of their Property*'.[77] Government exists 'for the security of property', Smith tells us.[78] For liberalism, the link was clear: liberty is dependent on property and vice versa, but both can flourish only in conditions of security. 'Commerce and manufactures can seldom flourish long in any state . . . in which the people do not feel themselves secure in the possession of their property', says Smith.[79] Thus the main function of the sovereign authority is to provide for the industrious the 'most perfect security that they shall enjoy the full recompence of their own industry'.[80] Here and elsewhere Smith links the question of industry and the importance of the industrious to the demand for security, praising certain nations on the grounds that 'industry is perfectly secure . . . though it is far from being perfectly free'.[81] For Bentham, 'security is the seed of opulence. For the work of opulence, what men want principally of government is . . . security, which is the work of protection afforded by government in respect of the different possessions'.[82] And where Mill discusses commerce and property as the foundation of civilisation, it is always in terms of its connection with security rather than liberty: 'the greater security of property is one of the main conditions and causes of greater pro- duction, which is Progress in its most familiar and vulgarest aspect'.[83] The fundamental fear that runs through liberalism, then, is deeply connected to the insecurity of property: a fear that the right to private property might be undermined or challenged; a fear of the pain that comes with the loss of private property. It is this that distinguishes the fear that Hobbes believes drives the atomised individuals in the state of nature into the security of the sovereign from the fear of the loss of liberty-property which Locke believes is the driving force behind the creation of a more secure body politic.

We are often and rightly told that security is intimately associated with the rise of the modern state. But we also need to note that it is equally intimately bound up with the rise of bourgeois property rights and a liberal order-building, and in later chapters we will see the extent of this intimacy. In this way liberalism's conception of security was intimately connected to its vision of political subjectivity centred on the self-contained and property-owning individual. The reason liberty is wrapped in the concept of security, then, is because security is simultaneously wrapped in the question of property, giving us a triad of concepts which are usually run so close together that they are almost conflated ('liberty, security, property'), a triad found in Smith, Blackstone, Paine, the French Declaration of the Rights of Man, and in various other formulations elsewhere.[84] Thus as liberalism generated a new conception of 'the economy' as its founding political act, a conception which integrated the wealth of nations, the world market and the labour of the population, its notion of liberty necessitated a particular vision of security: the ideological guarantee of the egoism of the independent and self-interested pursuit of property. It is for this reason Marx calls security *'the supreme concept of bourgeois society'*.[85]

Marx spotted that as the concept of bourgeois society, security plays a double role. Here is Marx on Henri Storch's *Cours d'économie politique* (1815):

> 'The progress of social wealth,' says Storch, 'begets this useful class of society . . . which performs the most wearisome, the vilest, the most disgusting functions, which, in a word, takes on its shoulders all that is disagreeable and servile in life, and procures thus for other classes leisure, serenity of mind and conventional' (*c'est bon, ça*) 'dignity of character'. Storch then asks himself what the actual advantage is of this capitalist civilization, with its misery and its degradation of the masses, as compared with barbarism. He can find only one answer: security![86]

One side of this double role, then, is that security is the ideological justification for 'civilisation' (that is, capitalism) as opposed to 'barbarism' (that is, non-capitalist modes of production); hence Locke's need to move from the 'state of nature' to the state of civil society. The other side is that security is what the bourgeois class demand once it has exploited, demoralised and degraded the bulk of humanity. For all the talk of 'laissez faire', the 'natural' phenomena of labour, wages and profit have to be policed and secured. Thus security entails the concept of police, guaranteeing as well as presupposing that society exists to secure the conservation of a particular kind of subjectivity (known as 'persons') and the rights and property associated with this subjectivity.[87] The non-liberal and non-capitalist may be 'tolerated' – that other classically liberal concept which also functions as a regulatory power – but they will also be heavily policed . . . for 'security reasons'.[88] The new form of economic reason to which liberalism gave birth also gave new content to the idea of reason of state and thus a new rationale for state action: the 'free economy'.

In other words, if security is the supreme concept of bourgeois society it is equally the *supreme concept of liberal ideology*. On this view, we should read liberalism less as a philosophy of liberty and more as a *technique of security*, as Mitchell Dean puts it,[89] a strategy of governance in which security is deployed as liberty. This technique will eventually underpin the exercises of liberal power carried out in the name of security in the twentieth and twenty-first centuries, and so will become central to the argument in this book, because as a technique it becomes central to a liberal vision of state power. The origins of this lie in liberalism's fraught relationship to absolutism and police science (cameralism), but they also bring us forward to liberalism's fraught relationship to fascism and, in a sense, to its fraught relationship to its own vision of the rule of law. The fraught nature of this relationship lies in the way that seventeenth century liberal accounts of prerogative would morph into twentieth century accounts of emergency.

PREROGATIVE AND NECESSITY: TOWARDS EMERGENCY

Although liberalism set itself against the theorists of absolutism who invoked security as part of the justification of authoritarian state power, and those police scientists which sought the complete regulation of all spheres of social life ('police' as 'policy'), liberalism continued to share with cameralists and absolutists a key commitment to security. While this commitment may have led to the identification of different threats to security and to different political projects for the shaping of the modern state, the *value* of security remained the same.[90] The difference between absolutism and cameralism on the one hand and liberalism on the other is not that where one stresses security the other stresses liberty; the difference does not lie in the tipping of a mythical 'balance' between liberty and security in one direction rather than another. Rather, the difference lies in the fact that absolutists and cameralists saw no need to *identify* security with liberty. But this identification of liberty with security also has a problematic flip side, one which takes us into the argument in the chapters to follow. Holmes points out that no theory with security as its central concern can be dogmatically anti-statist. But then most liberals would in reply point out that they have never set themselves up as dogmatically anti-statist anyway. The real problem is that the commitment to security leaves liberalism with virtually no defence against authoritarian or absolutist encroachments on liberty, *so long as these are conducted in the name of security*. At the very minimal level, this becomes the basis for distinctly non-liberal and authoritarian interventions into the lives and liberties of citizens, as Dean notes.[91] But 'non-liberal intervention' does not go far enough to capture the authoritarian and brutal ways in which liberalism is happy to allow liberties and lives to be destroyed in the name of security; the way, that is, that the most illiberal actions of state can be carried out by means of one of liberalism's most fundamental terms. This has been most starkly illustrated in the liberal defence of torture during the 'war on terror'. The best-known example of this is Alan Dershowitz's demand that judges should be allowed to issue 'torture warrants' in the 'ticking bomb' case on the grounds that security must never be compromised.[92] Michael Ignatieff's 'lesser evil' position also allows for 'justifiable exceptions' to any ban on torture.[93] 'Torture', it should be noted, does not for Ignatieff include simple forms of 'coercion' such as sleep deprivation, permanent light or darkness, disorienting noise, isolation. (It surely says a lot about a person's politics and moral assumptions that sleep deprivation or isolating a human being from all human contact counts as merely 'coercive' rather than a form of torture.)

When not defending such practices, liberals have been lining up to throw out of the window other 'liberties'. Ignatieff's position allows the withholding of information from voters, the suspension of civil liberties, and the surreptitious killing of terrorists in targeted assassinations.[94] He adds that the suspension of liberties can be temporary and information can be made public later, even though it is abundantly clear that suspensions of liberties have the habit of becoming the norm and 'secret' information is notoriously subject to political manipulation. He doesn't say what happens if the surreptitiously killed 'terrorists' turn out not to be terrorists, and the more general problems with the political construction of 'terrorism' and recent ideological expansion of the term to include a whole range of acts of civil and political disobedience are really too obvious to need spelling out.[95] Similar moves are made in all the recent liberal sacrifices of liberty to the value of security, including Bruce Ackerman's proposal of an 'emergency constitution' authorising the detention of suspects without the criminal law's usual protections, Michael Walzer's suggestion that the 'supreme emergency' allows the deliberate killing of the innocent as well as the suspension of fundamental liberties, and Waldron's concession that 'it is not hard to think of scenarios where detention without trial is justified' (adding that classic liberal proviso that what is hard is to make sure that this power is not abused).[96]

The key problem with all such claims is that by presenting such measures to us as the 'lesser evil' they become increasingly normalised and legitimised, an issue we shall take up at much greater length in Chapter 2. The point here, however, is that running through such arguments is the belief that although such practices may not be desirable, they are necessary: 'necessity may require the commission of bad acts', says Ignatieff.[97] This is a modern version of an idea that has underpinned 'cruel and unusual' punishments through the centuries: where historically it was said that 'necessary' cruelty is not really cruelty, now it is said that 'necessary' interrogation is not really torture.[98] Here liberalism once again merely reiterates rather than rebuffs a central principle of reason of state, for which 'necessity' was frequently used to overcome concerns about the justness of a particular action – if something is absolutely 'necessary' then the question of whether it is just or not is merely a philosophical dispute. As Hannah Arendt puts it:

> Necessity, since the time of Livy and through the centuries, has meant many things that we today would find quite sufficient to dub a war unjust rather than just. Conquest, expansion, defense of vested interests, conservation of power in view of the rise of new and threatening powers, or support of a given power equilibrium – all these well-known realities of power politics were not only actually the causes of the outbreaks of most wars in history, they were also recognized as 'necessities'.[99]

Not only does this circumvent philosophical disputes about the just war (for Livy 'the war that is necessary is just'), but it also circumvents philosophical debate about the justness of a whole range of other actions taken by the state: the action that is 'necessary' is thought either to be just or to be so necessary that questions of justice are irrelevant. It is not difficult to see that 'necessity' easily becomes little more than window-dressing for reason of state.[100] In so doing it becomes the justification for prerogative actions of virtually any kind, and contains its own justification: the notion implies that something *has* to be done and *will* be done; necessity is an 'irresistible action' that 'doubles the parts of *indispensable* and *inevitable*'.[101] Hence the implication that acts of necessity *must* be carried out regardless of the legal or moral restrictions or implications.

It was because of the value placed on security that virtually all political and legal theorists of the eighteenth century accepted that fundamental rights and liberties might be 'temporarily' ignored on the grounds of necessity ('temporariness' being another rhetorical device to which we return in the chapter to follow). The widespread accept- ance meant that the central issue was not the acceptability of necessity or arbitrariness, but *who* was to determine when 'necessary' or 'arbitrary' measures were required – the King, Parliament, the executive – and what those measures might be. In England 'necessity' lay at the heart of the disputes between parliament and the crown, in Spain 'necessity' was used to trump the privileges of the Cortes, in France the declaration of war on Spain in 1635 was made in accordance with 'the necessity of state'.[102] What followed from this politically was the question of *when* necessity might be invoked and *what* might be entailed by this invocation. Liberalism used the principle of necessity as part of its own technology of security. In particular, 'necessity' came to play a crucial role in mediating the tension within liberalism between the idea of the rule of law and reason of state.

Prerogative exists, we have seen Locke argue, because the legislature is not always in being and is usually too large and too slow. But he also suggests prerogative exists 'because it is impossible to foresee, and so by laws to provide for, all Accidents and Necessities'.[103] Necessity is here placed on the same level as the legislature being in recess or being slow in generating law. Again, Locke casual is Locke furtive, for it is necessity rather than Parliamentary recess that creates the space for the key feature of prerogative: the latitude it provides to the executive 'to do many things . . . which the laws do not prescribe'. As with Smith's suggestion that the ordinary laws of justice might be sacrificed 'in cases of the most urgent necessity', it is necessity that provides the ground for actions of state which appear to be outside or beyond the law – 'necessity hath no law', as Cromwell put it.[104] Necessity, conflated with the public good and actions taken for the 'welfare of the people', becomes a key constitutive moment of the exercise of prerogative and thus declarations of 'exception'.

The key assumption now is that in a liberal polity prerogative is exercised within the rule of law – this is said to be what distinguishes it from absolutism or totalitarianism. This applies even when prerogative is transferred from the personalised power of the prince to the depersonalised power of the state. For Dicey, for example, the rule of law 'means, in the first place, the absolute supremacy or predominance of regular law as opposed to the influence of arbitrary power', and so exclude[s] the existence of arbitrariness, of prerogative, or even of wide discretionary authority on the part of the government'.[105] This position is often traced back to Locke himself. In one major case Lord Roskill argued that:

Much of the modern thinking on the prerogative power of the executive stems from John Locke's treatise, True End of Civil Government, which I have read again with much profit, especially chapter 14, 'Of Prerogative' . . . The prerogative is a discretionary power exercisable by the executive government for the public good, in certain spheres of governmental activity for which the law has made no provision . . . The law does not interfere with the proper exercise of the discretion by the executive in those situations; but it can set limits by defining the bounds of the activity; and it can intervene if the discretion is exercised improperly or mistakenly. That is a fundamental principle of our constitution. It derives from two of the most respected of our authorities . . . Seeing that the prerogative is a discretionary power to be exercise for the public good, it follows that its exercise can be examined by the courts just as any other discretionary power which is vested in the executive . . . Likewise, it seems to me that, when discretionary powers are entrusted to the executive by the prerogative . . . the courts can examine the exercise of them so as to see that they are not used improperly or mistakenly.[106]

Thus it appears that prerogative is not a problem for liberalism so long as it is exercised within agreed constitutional limits and as part of the rule of law – the legitimacy lies in its legality. The view does not preclude the use of prerogative, but suggests that prerogative can only function in the context of the wider rule of law. And yet liberal regimes have just as commonly worked on the basis that in some sense prerogative is *not* subject to law, especially when the 'security of state' is at stake:

Prerogative powers . . . are not, I think, susceptible to judicial review because their nature and subject matter are such as not to be amenable to the judicial process. The Courts are not the place wherein to determine whether a treaty should be concluded or the armed forces disposed in a particular manner or Parliament dissolved on one date rather than another.[107]

Leaving aside the danger that prerogative gets reduced to little more than the personal whim of the sovereign ('When the President does it that means that it is not illegal'[108]), the reason the law struggles with the concept of prerogative in these ways lies in part in the concept of necessity, generating a fundamental tension within liberalism concerning the relationship between the rule of law and prerogative powers carried out in the name of necessity.

Now, what we are dealing with here is in some sense a version of what Ernst Fraenkel has called the 'dual state'. Fraenkel distinguishes between the Normative State in which the state is endowed with powers for safeguarding the legal order, expressed in statutes and exercised by courts (that is, the 'rule of law') and the Prerogative State in which executive arbitrariness and violence are exercised more or less unchecked by any legal guarantees. The main function of the Prerogative State is dictatorship, in the sense that it grants to the executive untrammelled and arbitrary powers. For this reason it is easy to read National Socialism through the logic of prerogative (embodied in the will of the leader). Yet while it is often assumed that the complete abolition of the rule of law under the exercise of prerogative is the chief characteristic of National Socialism, the Normative State in fact continued to exist. And it continued to exist because it remained the best way to regulate capital: the courts strove to maintain the supremacy of the law in the context of the sanctity of contracts, patents and trademarks, private property as a whole, and the right of the entrepreneur to control labour. In other words, the *legal* foundations of the *capitalist* order were maintained and the rule of law continued to function as the legal framework for private property. Capital will happily cast its vote for the irrationality of arbitrary prerogative so long as it is granted the rationality of functional regulation, thereby accommodating itself to the irrationality of an arbitrary power which maintains the conditions of rationality and the rule of law. Hence the *dual* state consists in the parallel existence of the Normative State and the Prerogative State. Indeed, the Normative State works well in conjunction the Prerogative State in that the latter functions as an indirectly supporting power for capitalist order.

We might argue that the argument applies equally to liberal democracy. For as Fraenkel notes, 'one reservation always lurks in the background of the Normative State: considerations of political expediency'. And so the state run according to the rule of law can never be treated in isolation; there is always a precarious tension between prerogative and the rule of law, to the extent that 'the Prerogative State and the Normative State constitute an interdependent whole'. The prerogative power will never be given up, even by those purporting to live and govern according to the rule of law.[109]

This captures the fundamental tension at the heart of the modern state between the rule of law and prerogative, 'normal' and 'exceptional' politics, the state of regular order and the state of emergency. The second dimension in each of these dualisms has tended to be associated with fascism, in the sense that one might read fascism as a form of dictatorship founded on prerogative powers in a state of exception and driven by the logic of emergency. As an ideology generated by and within modern capitalism, fascism tends to reveal its presence as a will to power through which liberties thought to be fundamental are in fact suspended by the exercise of prerogative power concentrated in the will of the leader. By insisting on the rule of law, liberalism seeks to distance itself from such practices and thus from fascism per se. And yet just as early liberalism sought to distance itself from some of the main planks of reason of state and the police idea but was constantly drawn back to them, so it has also found itself in constant recourse to the main planks of political dictatorship: prerogative, exception, emergency powers. This is most apparent in those 'zones of exception' such as the colonies and in those moments during which liberalism pushes at the limits of its own constitutional constraints: the 'emergency situations' in which liberalism seeks to restore order by any means necessary, when liberty and fundamental rights are 'suspended' and acts of violence carried out as of necessity; moments when prerogative is most easily justified. But to understand why, and to identify how this is part of liberalism's fraught relationship to fascism, we have to understand emergency powers and their connection to security. For in the twentieth century the use of prerogative powers of violence and coercion came to be explained as an outcome of 'states of emergency' rather than 'normal' situations. The prerogative state, as the state of necessity, becomes the state of emergency, enacted on the grounds of and in the name of security: national security becomes the last prerogative.[110] What we are getting at, then, is the liberal use of emergency powers within a broader ideology of the 'state of emergency', a state which, in the liberal view, is an order of security entirely consistent with its principle of liberty.

Chapter 2

EMERGENCY? WHAT EMERGENCY?

... Right now he's trying the War Emergency Power to see how it
works, even though there seems to be no War, no Emergency ...
Thomas Pynchon, *Gravity's Rainbow* (1973)

Since the event that has quickly passed into the English language as
'9/11', countless individuals have been imprisoned without charge
or trial at Guantánamo Bay, at the detention centre at Bagram in
Afghanistan and at Abu Ghraib in Iraq. It is clear that while in
detainment some have been tortured and all have been subject to
inhumane treatment. Others have been shipped to prisons, peniten-
tiaries and police stations in countries known for their human rights
abuses. At the same time, liberal democracies have also devised new
and unusual methods to discipline and punish, such as the 'control
orders' recently introduced in the UK. Less startling but equally
significant have been the systematic ways in which international laws
seem to have been overridden by a new imperial power and the way
most western liberal democracies have generated new policies that
appear to undermine the basic tenets of liberal jurisprudence and
constitutional democracy. In response to the shock and outrage
expressed by many against these developments, we have been told
that we are living in exceptional times, and such times require
exceptional powers: it's a state of emergency. Perhaps, then, the key
date for our times is 9/14 rather than the actual attack three days
earlier, for this was the day the US President declared a state of
emergency.

For those working in the cottage industry based on the work of Carl
Schmitt, such a declaration proved to be more than a little fortuitous.
Most of the workers in this industry considered themselves as radical
or critical theorists on the political Left, and much of their interest

centred on Schmitt's concept of sovereignty: sovereign is he who decides on the exception.[1] So what could offer better proof of the cogency of Schmitt's central problematic than the world's most powerful state asserting its sovereignty by declaring a state of emergency? The period since September 2001 has therefore been a field day for those interested in the concept of the state of emergency.

But this story has a little twist. For many have suggested that since the 'war on terror' will probably never end – at least not until 'every terrorist group of global reach has been found, stopped, and defeated', as Bush put it just nine days after the attacks – or will last 'at least . . . the lifetime of most of us' (Cheney) and thus may 'take a generation to defeat' (Blair), the emergency in question appears to have quickly become a permanent feature of the political landscape.[2] In this 'long war' or 'lengthy campaign' of 'unknown duration' the emergency seems to have become the 'new normalcy'.[3] With *this* state of emergency, it is said, normal times are gone. Central to the Left's response to this war, then, has been the claim that the emergency itself appears to be becoming permanent. The standard device for many is to then throw in a well-known quote from Walter Benjamin: 'the "state of emergency" in which we live is not the exception but the rule'.[4]

The influential figure here has been Giorgio Agamben, who has built on Schmitt's concept of exception in developing his argument concerning the camp as the nomos of the modern and related themes such as the refugee and 'bare life'. As the space that opens up when the state of exception starts to become the rule, the camp is both *a* space of exception – a piece of territory placed outside the normal juridical order – and at the same time the *ultimate* expression of the logic of the exception. As such, the state of exception has now become the norm. Agamben was pushing this argument prior to the attack on the 'war on terror', but he has pursued the argument even more thoroughly since.[5] The same observation might be made about Michael Hardt and Anonio Negri. In *Empire*, Hardt and Negri had already suggested that what stands behind the intervention now so prevalent in international politics is 'a permanent state of emergency and exception justified by *the appeal to essential values of justice*' and that the justification for deployment of military forces in this new 'Empire' rests on a state of permanent exception.[6] Pushing this further in their follow-up work since 9/11, they suggest that '*the state of exception has become permanent and general*; the exception has become the rule, pervading both foreign relations and the homeland'.[7]

Similar claims can be found in all sorts of other places, and so a few examples will have to suffice. For Leo Panitch the new anti-terrorism and emergency legislation in Canada mean that 'we have stepped outside the rule of law' towards 'the permanence of the temporary, an attempt to normalize the exception'.[8] Tony Bunyan of *Statewatch* suggests that the exceptional has along with the draconian become the norm,[9] while for Jean-Claude Paye the new anti-terrorist measures are so significant that they 'overturn the norm' – 'deviations become the rule' and 'emergency procedures replace the Constitution and the law',[10] a point repeated by Savas Michael-Matsas[11] and Vivienne Jabri.[12] Alex Callinicos cites Agamben's work to explore the way 'the terrifying military apparatus deployed on the banks of the Tigris commands the world to accept a permanent state of emergency'.[13] The same idea that emergency is the new paradigm now permeates political and intellectual debate: from collections of essays by leading critical theorists[14] to various civil liberties pressure groups[15] and human rights lawyers;[16] from the first book-length sociology of the camp[17] to analysis of urban panic;[18] from writings on postcolonial melancholia[19] to black groups campaigning in the US;[20] from arguments about the demise of utopianism[21] to debates on the Schengen Agreement.[22]

The idea that emergency is now permanent or that the exception is now the rule is, it seems, the standard position on the Left. The libertarian Right has also used the idea.[23] And this position has at its heart one basic proposition: that the emergency involves a suspension of the law. The state of necessity is not a 'state of law', but a space without law, suggests Agamben, and others have duly followed suit.[24] The general feeling is that the declared state of emergency has so transformed the legal landscape that we are in a 'lawless world', with detainees residing in a legal 'black hole', in 'legal limbo', in 'anomalous zones', in the 'legal equivalent of outer space', all of which are said to be inconsistent with the rule of law and what had been generally assumed to be fundamental liberties and inalienable rights. International law appears to have been abandoned in the name of reason of state and national security, while key states which once carried the flag for liberal democracy appear to have abandoned a commitment to the rule of law and basic rights. The emergence of categories such as 'enemy combatants', 'battlefield detainees', or 'extraordinary rendition', all of which are said to have a legal status which is less than clear, only serves to reinforce the notion that 'ordinary' or 'normal' law has been abandoned.

In this chapter I want to challenge some of these ideas about contemporary politics by tracing a wider historical thread connecting the politics of emergency to the question of security.[25] We saw in the previous chapter how the language and assumption of prerogative gave rise to a set of ideas centred on the notions of necessity and emergency. In the twentieth century it is the latter which comes to the political foreground. In so doing it becomes a mechanism for liberal democratic states to manage the logic of prerogative and thereby sets the scene for a recasting of security. In that sense, the concept of emergency becomes integral to a continuation of the authoritarianism found in classical liberalism in the very different political context of liberal democracy, and paves the way for security to be articulated as a means of liberal order-building.[26] This chapter therefore aims to connect the discussion of security and prerogative in classical liberal-ism in the previous chapter with the discussion of social and national security in the chapters to follow by identifying the logic of emergency as central to the politics of security. It has been claimed that render-ing an issue a 'security issue' – that is, 'securitizing' it – relies on the declaration of an existential threat such that emergency action and exceptional measures are said to be necessary.[27] My intention here is to identify the way certain techniques of power in the twentieth century found their strategic primacy in an ideological circuit between security and emergency, and to explore the way this circuit operates not on the site of the battlefield, and not even at the level of the state or city, but across the entire world. We begin, however, with a key technology for the exercise of prerogative: martial law.

MARTIAL LAW TO EMERGENCY POWERS

Until around the 1830s martial law was equated with military law – the rules for governing armed forces in the field. In its original meaning the term thus referred to jurisdiction over soldiers of the crown and jurisdiction over alien enemies. The Petition of Right of 1628, for example, sought to limit the abuse of monarchical powers by making martial law applicable only to soldiers, and thus held that the Crown had no authority to administer military law within the realm during a time of peace. Likewise, the Mutiny Act of 1689 permitted the trial and punishment of soldiers by courts martial and allowed the King to 'proclaim martial law' for the government of the army during peace and war. Although there was some debate about the nature and extent of martial law powers – martial law had on occasion been used to prosecute poachers, vagabonds and rioters, for example, while the Petition of Right applied in England but not Ireland[28] – Sir Matthew Hale's position in 1713 was the widely accepted one:

> Touching the Business of Martial Law, these Things are to be observed, viz.
>
> *First*, That in Truth and Reality it is not a Law, but something indulged rather than allowed as a Law; the Necessity of Government, Order and Discipline in an Army is that only which can give those Laws a Countenance . . .
>
> *Secondly*, This indulged Law was only to extend to Members of the Army, or to those of the opposite Army, and never was so much indulged as intended to be (executed or) exercised upon others . . .
>
> *Thirdly*, That the Exercise of Martial Law, whereby any Person should lose his Life or Member, or Liberty, may not be permitted in Time of Peace, when the King's Courts are open for all Persons to receive Justice, according to the Laws of the Land. This is in Substance declared by the Petition of Right.

In other words, martial law applied only to the members of the armed forces and its jurisdiction ended at the battleground. Civilians within the area of battle might be temporarily subject to the martial law in question, but martial law could not be exercised in times of peace, which many took to be illustrated by the fact that the courts were open.[29] In other words, the position in the late-eighteenth century was that martial law did not apply to citizens.

In the first half of the nineteenth century, however, the concept gradually took on a new meaning. The use of the military during the Gordon riots of 1780 had led many to claim that this was an imposition of martial law. But in response the Lord Chief Justice claimed that since the constitution had not been suspended and the trials had taken place in the ordinary courts, martial law had not in fact been declared. The major factor behind the new meaning was an increasing use of martial law in governing occupied territories in the early-nineteenth century. Where on the mainland the British state could muddle through well enough with sporadic use of the Riot Act to maintain order and, as in the case of the Gordon riots, fudge the issue of whether the use of the military internally was a form of martial law, it was quite clear that martial law most definitely *was* being used in that standard locale of political experimentation, the colonies: in Barbados in 1805 and 1816; Demerara in 1823; Jamaica in 1831–2 and 1865; Canada in 1837–8; Ceylon in 1817 and 1848; Cephalonia in 1848–9; Cape of Good Hope in 1834–5, 1849–51 and 1852; the Island of St Vincent in 1863; and on several occasions in Ireland.[30] As such declarations increased it became apparent that martial law seemed to involve a kind of suspension of law; that certain 'liberties' were being taken with the 'indulgence' in question. In this context some constitutional authorities began to argue that in times of crisis constitutional norms might indeed have to be abandoned. Henry Hallam, in his widely read *Constitutional History of England* (1827) commented that

> there may indeed be times of pressing danger, when the con-
> servation of all demands the sacrifice of the legal rights of a few;
> there may be circumstances that not only justify, but compel the
> temporary abandonment of constitutional forms. It has been
> usual for all governments, during an actual rebellion, to proclaim
> martial law, or the suspension of civil jurisdiction.[31]

In other words, what was emerging was an understanding that martial law might be applicable not simply to the military, but also to the use of the military to maintain 'order' and 'security' in general. Within this was the belief that such a form of governance had two dimensions. First, that martial law involved the suspension of some fundamental liberties and thus the law *per se*; something 'indulged in' rather than actual law, as Hale put it. In a heated debate in the House of Commons in April 1851 concerning the repression of rebellion in Ceylon, for example, the Duke of Wellington and Earl Grey agreed that because martial law is neither more nor less than the will of the general who commands the army, martial law means no law at all.[32] For this reason some have suggested that we should better speak of 'martial rule' than 'martial law'.[33] The second dimension was that such exercises of martial law powers could be justified on the grounds of necessity: that public order and the security of the state *necessitated* the suspension of basic liberties – 'martial law is a rule of necessity', the Judge Advocate General put it in a Commons committee debate in 1849.[34] Many writers therefore saw the roots of the argument for the use of martial law as lying in the concept of prerogative and the arbitrary powers it appeared to allow. And once this was established for the colonies it took little effort for the practices of colonial violence to be exercised on the mainland, in the kind of boomerang effect that colonial practice often had on the juridico-political structures of the colonising state.[35]

A parallel to this development in Britain can also be traced in the US context. The key shift came following the attempt by militant Rhode Islanders to adopt a written constitution for the state in 1841. Their desire for popular sovereignty led them to assemble a popularly elected convention, drafting a constitution, submitting it for ratification and then declaring it ratified, following which they elected officials to a People's government under Thomas Wilson Dorr and scheduled for inauguration in May 1842. The response to 'Dorr's rebellion' by the authorities was the mobilisation of the state militia across the entire state; in other words, to declare martial law against the insurgent radicalism of a popular democratic movement. Hundreds were arrested without warrant and detained without a clear statement of charges. Many Rhode Islanders believed that since the military was being used in a way never before seen in American history – even General Jackson's declaration of martial law for New Orleans in 1814 was based on the threat of an 'enemy' invasion – this clearly would not stand the test of being subject to real law, and so they instituted two suits in late 1843 and early 1844, one of which focused specifically on the legitimacy of the substitution of military for civilian authority and the deliberate suspension of due process. The Circuit Court dismissed the cases after cursory hearings, with Justice Story arguing that the situation in 1842 had been so urgent that the Rhode Island legislature resorted to the use of martial law as a matter of necessity. But the issue at stake was deemed so important that it made it to the Supreme Court in 1849.

In the intervening years, a debate took place concerning the definition of martial law. Two books published in 1846, William C. De Hart's *Observations on Military Law* and John Paul Jones O'Brien's *Treatise on American Military Laws*, sought to distinguish martial from military law and argue that the Constitution in fact sanctioned martial law as a means of defence when the civil institutions were closed or suppressed by emergency conditions. In the meantime the war in 1846 substantially increased the size of the Union, which now contained a considerable 'alien' population supposedly unfamiliar with American institutions and apparently incapable of self-government. The obvious question arose: surely martial law might be appropriate for such a situation and such people? By the time the Rhode Island case came to the Supreme Court in 1849, the political implications of the debate about martial law were clear for all to see. The decision which emerged came, ironically, in the context of an attempt by Chief Justice Taney to separate 'political' questions from 'justiciable' ones, and to argue that declarations of martial law are government actions which should not be questioned in a court of law.[36] In the process Taney argued that the declaration of martial law to subdue the Rhode Island insurrection was acceptable, not least because the insurrection con-stituted 'a state of war'. This decision – the *Luther* decision, following *Luther v. Borden* in which Luther originally challenged the search on his house and being placed under arrest – altered the understanding of martial law in America, ratifying a process that had been taking place since the early 1830s: martial law now appeared to refer to the necessity for the use of prerogative powers for dealing with situations thought to constitute some kind of crisis or emergency. Taney had specifically argued that the plaintiffs had been wrong to refer to ancient meanings of martial law in trying to show the wrongness of the government's actions. Ancient usage could not be compared 'in any respect to the declaration of martial law by the legislative authority of the State, made for the purposes of self-defense'. And since such 'self-defence' must of necessity include defence from insur-rection, itself a form of war, martial law is an appropriate measure. Fundamental liberties can rightfully and *necessarily* be suspended on the grounds of security and order. It did not take much to see that Taney's reasoning was easily applicable at federal level. After all, the Constitution itself provided for the suspension of habeas corpus and allowed for Congress to call forth the militia in cases of rebellion or invasion. It was thus easy for Taney ruling in *Luther* to be invoked throughout the nineteenth century.

What we find, then, is an enormous historical shift taking place in the nineteenth century concerning the logic and focus of martial law, a shift which allowed the state to avail itself of the right to use special, constitutionally prescribed powers in 'emergency situations' or 'states of exception' in which 'public security and order' was thought to be in danger. This shift had its parallel in a shift in the understanding of the state of siege in civil-law countries. The state of siege took as its precedent the Roman dictatorship on the one hand and the history of conferring plenary powers upon the commander of a besieged fortress on the other, but during the nineteenth century the concept slipped from the military to the political sphere and became applicable to civilians in periods of crisis or emergency. The French constitution of 1800, for example, allowed for the suspension of civil liberties and rights in the places and for the time determined by law 'when the security of the state required', while the *Acte additionnel* of 1815 adopted the terminology of 'state of siege' to describe the general regime of exception. But the key shift came in the imposition of a state of siege in Paris between June and October 1848, and a new Law on the State of Siege of 9 August 1849. The logic inherent in the law was that a state of siege entailed the same processes and justifications as those of martial law. As with the development of martial law, the 'state of siege' shifted gradually from a military to a political register, referring less and less to military encounters with enemy forces and more and more to questions of internal disorder.[37]

Thus the history of both martial law and the state of siege is the history of a shift from regulation *of* the military within the state to regulation *by* the military of the whole social order on behalf of the state. The emerging political and juridical logic was that these powers involved an increase in executive power *vis-à-vis* the legislature and judiciary ('a trial by martial "law" is a purely executive act'),[38] a shift of power to military authority, and the suspension of basic liberties and rights. 'Martial law' shifted gradually from a military to a political register, referring less and less to military encounters with enemy forces and more and more to questions of internal security and public order: from being a code for the internal governance of military power to being a rationalisation for the use of military power across the face of society in which basic liberties and rights and possibly even the law *tout court* appear to be suspended. This was comfortably in place by the late-nineteenth century. Dicey, for example, in his *Introduction to the Study of the Law of the Constitution* (1885) held that martial law as government through military tribunals is not known to English law, but that if by 'martial law' we mean the common-law right of the Crown and its servants to maintain public order by repelling invasion and insurrection then martial law certainly is part of the law of England. A more or less identical position was held by Sir James Fitzjames Stephen in his *History of the Criminal Law* (1883) and by F. W. Maitland in his *Constitutional History of England* (1888).[39]

The extent to which this view was in place by the twentieth century can also be seen in a number of landmark cases. In 1902, in *Ex parte Marais*, the applicant sought release from detention without trial under martial law, claiming that not only had he committed no crime but that even if he had he should have been tried before the civil courts. The Judicial Committee of the Privy Council found that because war had become so extended and the conditions of emergency so diverse, the rule that martial law only applied when the ordinary courts could no longer physically convene was no longer operative. Moreover, the fact that for some purposes the courts were still in operation did not mean that war was not taking place. In addition, the Committee held that the Petition of Right is applicable only to conditions of peace. For Frederick Pollock writing in the *Law Quarterly Review*, the judgment tried to 'keep alive the fallacious notion that martial law is identical or logically connected with military law', when in point of fact it was that 'martial law' is now simply the name for 'acts done by necessity for the defence of the Commonwealth when there is war within the realm'.[40] Similarly, in the US Governor Peabody declared martial law in Colorado in 1903 and 1904, suspending *habeas corpus*, imposing a curfew, and detaining without trial the president of the miners union Charles Moyer. Moyer bought a suit for damages for being detained without trial, alleging that he had been deprived of liberty. The Supreme Court in *Moyer v. Peabody* (1909) affirmed the dismissal of the action, suggesting that the Governor is rightly the final judge and that, in the words of Justice Holmes, 'when it comes to a decision by the head of the state upon a matter involving its life, the ordinary rights of the individual must yield to what he deems the necessities of the moment'. In so doing the Court transformed much of the 1849 Taney judgment into binding law.[41]

To reiterate: what was at stake in these judgments was the possibility of using martial law during times of 'peace' or, rather, reconceptualising 'war' so that broader moments of crisis, rebellion or insurrection could be easily brought under its remit – if these constituted 'wars' of sorts then surely there could be no objection to the use of martial-law powers? In both martial law and the state of siege we find the principle that the modern state had the right to avail itself of special, constitutionally prescribed emergency powers in situations in which 'public security' or 'the security of the state' were thought to be in danger. But what is also important to note is that these ideas were coming to the fore in states which were developing into liberal democracies. Now, on the one hand this means that through martial rule liberal democracies were handed a political manoeuvre which provided a means of simultaneously liberating executive power from constitutional restraints and suspending basic liberties. Martial law was thus a solution to the increasing number of rebellions and insurrections that seemed to be taking place. On the other hand, however, the ruling class recognised that within the broader context of an increasingly democratised polity, declarations of martial law were becoming increasingly inflammatory to the new citizenship. Martial law was a solution, then, but also a problem.

The initial way this problem was dealt with was to consider its modern employment a 'qualified' form of martial law. In the case of *Commonwealth* v. *Shortall* (1903) the Pennsylvania Supreme Court argued that calling out the militia to maintain order even though the courts were still open was 'a declaration of qualified martial law'.

> Qualified, in that it was put in force only as to the preservation of the public peace and order, not for the ascertainment or vindication of private rights, or the other ordinary functions of government. For these the courts and other agencies of the law were still open . . . But within its necessary field and for the accomplishment of its intended purpose it was martial law with all its powers.[42]

In other words, the ordinary Courts remained open and so liberty in general appeared untouched – in *Milligan*, 1866, the Supreme Court had held that 'martial rule can never exist where the courts are open' – but it was, in effect, martial law: a form of rule declared *necessary* even though the state *was not formally at war* with another state; indeed, the court held that it was an error to think that a state must be either at peace or war.

As the twentieth century progressed however, as western states became more democratic and incorporated more and more of the working class into the system, even a 'qualified martial law' sounded a little too harsh, a little too violent, a little too undemocratic; a little too, well, martial. So new forms of policing 'disorder' seemed to be required which used some of the key practices of martial law but eschewed the label. What was needed was a new form of language, less obviously violent and without the military overtones; that allowed the exercise of martial-law powers, in other words, but in times of peace. The initial move was found in the logic of emergency.

At the end of May 1922 it was suggested at a meeting of the British Cabinet that martial law should be introduced in Northern Ireland to deal with the emergency in the province following partition. The suggestion was rejected on the grounds that martial-law powers were, in effect, already being exercised.[43] But how? How could martial law be exercised without being declared? The Cabinet was revisiting a problem it had faced for the whole of Ireland for several years prior to partition. In 1916 martial law had been declared for Ireland, and yet even then Prime Minister Asquith insisted in the Commons that despite the formal declaration, 'martial law has never been put in force for any practical or effective purpose in Ireland'. Rather, he suggested, 'there is no proceeding which has been taken [in Ireland] which could not be justified by the Defence of the Realm Act'.[44] His reference was to the sweeping regulatory powers granted by the Defence of the Realm Act 1914 (DORA), including the use of detention and courts-martial for anyone contravening the new regulations. These powers meant that many thought of DORA as establishing 'martial law and something more'[45] or 'a kind of statutory martial law',[46] or 'a hurriedly devised translation of martial rule and prerogative concepts into statutory provisions'.[47] But of course the powers were not *called* martial law, but simply 'regulations' for the 'defence of the realm'. Something important was happening to the legal and political language.

For the following years the powers granted by DORA were integral to the running of the UK. At the same time, the aura and ideology surrounding martial law began to be transformed; hence Asquith's claim that martial law had not really been put in force in Ireland. This explains the rather bizarre situation, pointed out by the military governor at the time, General Sir John Maxwell, that martial law had been proclaimed and extended in Ireland even though virtually all the public bodies were at the time passing resolutions condemning martial law.[48] In a range of memos, Maxwell pointed out that martial law *sensu stricto* had not been put into operation anywhere, even in Dublin, and put his finger on the key issue: that discussion of martial law merely encouraged public grievances and so fanned the flames of the struggles taking place. Or as General Sir Neville Macready put it in a meeting between the Cabinet and the Irish Executive in May 1920, 'the difficulty behind martial law is that you would put certain persons in prison and they would hunger-strike. What would the people in England say?'[49] More to the point, a decision as inflammatory as declaring martial law was unnecessary given that the practices of martial law could be conducted under DORA, as they were in Ireland; hence the rebels were eventually tried and executed under DORA, not by military tribunals under martial law. In other words, the *effect* of martial law could be achieved without its declaration and possibly even without using the term. As Asquith commented in a Cabinet meeting, 'all the trials and sentences have been carried out under the statutory powers of the Defence of the Realm Act. There is no single case in which it has been or is likely to be necessary to resort to what is called "Martial law" and there is no adequate ground for its continuance'.[50] And so when the Judge Advocate General prepared a memorandum on martial law for the Chief Secretary for Ireland in July 1920 he could simply remind the Secretary that 'a form of Statutory Martial Law already exists in Ireland under the Defence of the Realm Acts and Regulations'.[51]

What this convoluted and sometimes confused way of thinking about and using martial-law powers tells us is that this was a crucial period in the development of the powers in question, not just in Ireland but across the whole of the UK. DORA needs to be read as a bridging moment between martial law and emergency powers doctrine in Britain, introduced in the wider context of a ten-year crisis of the British state. Following this, measures that *seemed* like martial law could be introduced under the new logic of 'emergency powers', which would come to offer the *substance* of martial law but without the legal and politically controversial form. The really fundamental move therefore came with the first Emergency Powers Act (EPA), passed in October 1920. The EPA granted to the executive extensive use of the military to preserve security and order and, within this, the suspension of basic rights and liberties. They were, formally, emergency powers, but the use of martial law was still recent enough for most people to recognise them for what they were: when they were being exercised during the General Strike, the former Solicitor General for the Labour government commented that the government had introduced 'what is really martial law'.[52] The language of 'emergency', in other words, was increasingly supplanting the language of 'martial law'.[53] Symptomatically, the sister legislation for Northern Ireland conferring on the police and security services powers to impose curfews, proscribe organisations, censor literature, restrict individual movement, stop, search and seize any vehicle and detention without trial – in other words, the usual mishmash of martial-law powers – was understood as introducing 'special powers', in the form of the Civil Authorities (Special Powers) Act (Northern Ireland) 1922 (SPA). So while the language of martial law was being supplanted, the powers in question were being re-presented in a new guise. Martial-law powers were being subsumed under the logic of emergency in what can only be described as the *liberalisation* of martial law, a political shift which would become central to the development of liberal authoritarianism through the twentieth century and to the politics of security.

One noticeable change was, however, occurring. For all the talk about the need for such powers in times of 'war', the focus of the legislation was very clearly industrial disputes and labour revolts. The real story of emergency powers is much less a story of wartime responses, and much more a story of two interrelated processes. First, a broadening of the *definition* of emergency, taking the notion well beyond military conflict and problems of 'terrorism'. And, second, a drastic increase in the *scope* of emergency powers.[54] As William Scheuerman has suggested, although there is no question that wartime experiences played a major part in the proliferation of emergency powers, from a broader historical perspective such a focus risks both overstating the novelty of wartime emergency powers and understating the manner in which emergency powers have been used for other purposes. In particular, it underplays the way emergency powers have been used in controlling labour and dealing with industrial unrest. On the one hand, the use of emergency power to crush labour unrest and socialist agitation built, albeit tenuously, on the limited understanding of an emergency situation as one involving violent conflict. But on the other hand, such use of emergency authority as a political instrument against the labouring classes 'foreshadowed the open employment of emergency power *during peacetime*'.[55] Thus emergency powers are politically more revealing when considered in terms of periods of 'peace' and the everyday functioning of civil society, for they are then exposed as nothing less than a persistent attempt at the fabrication of order by imposing discipline on an oppositional labour movement and obedience on radical political organisations – for 'securing' a particular social order generally rather than merely 'securing' it from external enemies. For example, the extensive powers granted by the EPA were immediately exercised during a miners' strike of 1921, and then again in 1924 during a London Transport strike, for eight months during 1926 to manage the General Strike (even though the strike lasted only a few days), 1948 and 1949 during dock workers' strikes, 1955 during a railway strike, 1966 during a seamen's strike, 1970 during strikes by refuse collectors, dock workers and electricity workers, 1972 during the miners' strike and a dock workers' strike, 1973 during the strike by miners and Glasgow fireworkers, 1975 during a refuse collectors' strike in Glasgow, and 1977–8 during a fireworkers' strike.[56] Parallel to this use, the first prosecutions to follow on from a perceived 'emergency' in 1921 were of Communists.

Far from military conflict, then, it was war of a rather different kind – the class war – within the more general regulation of capitalist modernity for which the emergency powers were exercised. If we briefly take just three further examples from the inter-war period – the Weimar Republic, Nazi Germany and New Deal America – we also find that emergency powers were more commonly used for the political management of economic regulation and labour relations.

'From a juridical standpoint the entire Third Reich can be considered a state of exception that lasted twelve years'.[57] Many commentators have followed Agamben in describing Nazi Germany in this way. This helps stress, either implicitly or explicitly, some of Schmitt's arguments concerning Article 48 of the Weimar constitution, in particular the possibility of using the Article to defend the constitution from the political 'extremes'. But the key principle behind Article 48 was not so much the political 'extremes' and more the possibility of security and order in the most general sense. It became clear from a very early moment in the history of Weimar that Article 48 had much broader uses, on the grounds that 'public order' and 'security' could be economic in character. Reich Chancellor Luther noted this in 1928 when he commented that Article 48 'proved to be very useful in cases of extreme urgency when economic measures . . . had to be carried out'.[58] It has been estimated that from the autumn of 1922, when currency difficulties became acute, it was emergency ordinances and decrees of a social and economic nature that pre-dominated. During the first few weeks of the Stresemann regime of 1923 a dozen or so decrees were issued to deal with ongoing problems of the mark and the financial sector, culminating in an Enabling Act authorising the federal government to take whatever financial, econ-omic and social measures it considered necessary and disregarding fundamental rights in the process. During the three weeks following its promulgation on 13 October 1923 – the crucial weeks leading up to the Beer Hall putsch – it was then used as the basis for no less than forty emergency decrees, including those for the overhaul of the tax structure and relief for distressed areas. The Marx Cabinet continued this practice, introducing its own Enabling Act and broadening the scope of powers beyond that of the Stresemann regime including, for example, the opportunity to dictate hours of labour. On the basis of this followed what one commentator describes as 'the most spectacular period of emergency legislation in the history of the Republic',[59] a period in which 70 legislative decrees were issued. Again, it was economic issues that were most obvious: of the total of sixty-seven decrees issued between October 1922 and 1925, forty-four were devoted to economic, fiscal and social problems. This pattern continued after a lull in the use of emergency powers from 1925 to 1930. Bruning's tax programme of July 1930 was enacted in the form of two executive decrees issued on the basis of Article 48, justified by him on the grounds that public safety and order were endangered by the failure of Parliament to supply adequate financial resources. The progressive deterioration of the economic situation from 1930 to 1932 facilitated an even greater use of emergency measures, to the extent that virtually all of the approximately sixty emergency decrees passed during the progressive deterioration of the economic situation in the early 1930s were for economic purposes.[60] Depending on how one measures them, emergency powers of one sort or another were operational for about one-half of the Weimar period and, crucially, were used largely for the purpose of securing capitalist order.

It is precisely this logic of 'emergency' for the security of economic order that fed into the use of emergency powers by the Nazis. On this score as with so many others, Hitler was hardly revolutionary, merely adopting and adapting ideas that were central to bourgeois state formation at the time. Following Hitler's appointment as Chancellor at the end of January 1933 a flurry of initial decrees utilised either Article 48 or Article 25, such as the 'Decree for Establishing Ordered Government in Prussia' and a 'Decree to Protect the German People' (both 6 February 1933). But the key date was 28 February 1933, the day on which Hitler used Article 48 to introduce an Emergency Decree for 'The Protection of the People and the State' (the 'Reichstag Fire Decree'). Described by Ernst Fraenkel as a form of martial law providing for the constitution of the Third Reich,[61] the Decree established a new state of emergency and suspended some of the fundamental constitutional rights. The Decree was then invoked for virtually all the measures of the Third Reich, nearly all of which were carried out 'for the restoration of public security'.[62] So while the Third Reich may well have been a state of emergency that lasted twelve years, in this it was little different to the Weimar period in Germany. It was also little different to similar measures being taken elsewhere.

'This Nation asks for action, and action now', said the new leader on 4 March 1933. 'I assume unhesitatingly the leadership of this great army of our people dedicated to a disciplined attack upon our common problems', he went on.

> Our greatest primary task is to put people to work. This is no unsolvable problem if we face it wisely and courageously. It can be accomplished in part by . . . treating the task as we would treat the emergency of a war . . . I shall [use] the one remaining instrument to meet the crisis – broad Executive power to wage a war against the emergency, as great as the power that would be given to me if we were in fact invaded by a foreign foe.

Thus spoke Franklin D. Roosevelt in his inaugural address. In speaking this way he was inaugurating nothing less than a period of emergency rule – to 'meet the emergency with emergency action' he was to describe it later.[63]

Like Hitler, Roosevelt lead a country in which national income had dropped to half the level it had been four years earlier, unemployment stood at approximately 14 million, and class struggles were intensifying. The years 1933 to 1934 were one of those few periods in American history of intense class conflict, with almost 2,000 work stoppages involving around 1.5 million workers, many of which saw military intervention and which led many, including Roosevelt, to believe that a communist revolution was possible.[64] Also like Hitler, the 'analogue of war' was the key to overcoming these problems.[65] 'Fifteen years ago my public duty called me to an active part in a great national emergency, the World War', commented Roosevelt in 1932, adding that 'the Nation faces today a more grave emergency than in 1917'.[66] Organisations such as the Civilian Conservation Corps (CCC), established under emergency legislation in the spring of 1933, were consciously designed to mobilise people for the war in question, while the New Dealers consciously spoke of the 'infantry of our economic army'.[67] In formulating policy Roosevelt and his 'lieutenants' drew heavily on war precedents to establish the basic principles of the New Deal programme. And since war is an emergency, then by definition emergency powers must be required.

Two days after his inaugural speech, and without Congressional approval, Roosevelt referred to a state of national emergency and proclaimed a 'bank holiday' forbidding the export of gold and silver and prohibiting transactions in foreign exchange. His purported authority was the Trading with the Enemy Act 1917 (TWEA), but his real authority was the combined ideology of 'emergency' and 'security'. Roosevelt was explicit about its use:

> The full meaning of that word 'emergency' related to far more than banks: it covered the whole economic and therefore the whole social structure of the country. It was an emergency that went to the roots of our agriculture, our commerce, and our industry; it was an emergency that had existed for a whole generation . . . It could be cured only by a complete reorganization and a measured control of the economic structure. It could not be cured in a week, in a month, or a year.[68]

To this end the TWEA was tweaked in an important way. The TWEA was 'an Act to define, regulate, and punish trading with the enemy' by regulating certain financial and banking practices. In the context of the World War I it was recognised that there might be enemies of the US living within its borders, but in passing the TWEA Congress had been careful to ensure that the provisions of the Act applied to those who were 'other than citizens of the United States'. The assumption was that citizens couldn't be enemies. In March 1933, however, as part of the exercise of emergency powers, the government amended Section 5(b) of the TWEA so that it now covered 'any person within the United States'. In terms of the area covered by Section 5(b), US citizens were no longer to be distinguished from enemies of the US. More generally, the whole nation could now be governed according to the war emergency power.

This mode of governing underpinned a series of proclamations, promulgations and institutional developments throughout the 1930s, mirroring the use of emergency powers in the UK and Germany as a means of economic regulation in general and for class management in particular. The Emergency Relief Act of May 1933 established the Federal Emergency Relief Administration, while other Acts followed the same logic: the Agricultural Adjustment Act 1933 began with a 'Declaration of Emergency' and held that the emergency was undermining the public interest through adverse effects on key agricultural commodities, and the Agricultural Adjustment Administration was charged with pre-empting any future crises as well as dealing with the current one, while the National Recovery Act of the same year gave the President a more or less unlimited right to issue regulations concerning industry. Key Acts the following year, such as the Municipal Bankruptcy Act and the Gold Reserve Act, also made reference to 'the existing emergency', and the language of emergency continued to permeate political and legislative developments into the 1940s. And as we will see in Chapter 3, it was central to the new politics of security being developed. The New Deal, in other words, was emergency rule writ large.[69]

Once we start looking, then, we find the use of emergency powers has been a regular feature of economic regulation in both liberal democracies as well as fascist states in the last century, and liberal democracies with very different sorts of polities.[70] Nasser Hussain has also shown the extent to which the concept of emergency was deeply inscribed in the colonial mode of rule.[71] A range of illustrations could be found, from the twelve-year state of emergency in Malaya from 1948 to the eight-year state of emergency in Kenya from 1952. Writing in 1960, Denys Holland noted that from 1946 to 1960, states of emergency had been proclaimed on no less than twenty-nine separate occasions in British dependent territories alone, ranging from

Aden to Zanzibar. These were proclaimed either under the Emergency Laws Orders in Council, 1939 and 1956, or under local emergency legislation of either a temporary or permanent character and allowed for the control of people and movement, curfews, the confiscation of property and land, pass laws, the banning of publications, the disbanding of political organisations, suspension of due process, detention without trial.[72] Again, these often had little to do with war and everything to do with economic regulation and class power: the emergency law in Kenya, for example, not only imprisoned the best part of 1.5 million people (nearly the entire Kikuyu population) and employed 'screening' techniques (that is, torture), but it also involved forced labour on settler estates, with the Kikuyu required to work unpaid for ninety days a year on 'communal projects'. The emergence of new nations from colonialism to independence did little to change the operational logic under which they had been previously governed, with their 'underdeveloped' economies and polities being used to justify the imposition of emergency measures as their main form of rule and the writing of these measures into their constitutions.

It is thus safe to say that in the twentieth century the 'state of emergency' became perhaps the most common prescription in the pharmacopoeia of statecraft. This is as true of the liberal as the fascist state: indeed, it was liberalism which perfected the practice. Nothing could be further from the truth, and no greater disservice has been rendered to our understanding of either liberalism or the state, than Schmitt's suggestion that liberalism ignores the emergency and that the liberal state is somehow a 'weak' state, intent on merely discussing issues and unable to make 'decisions' about 'exceptions'.[73] Indeed, one might say that the legitimisation and constitutionalisation of emergency powers is liberalism's gift to the modern state. And the extent to which states of all varieties have accepted this gift can be seen in official report after official report. In 1963 the Inter-American Commission of Human Rights found that more than a hundred states of emergency had been declared in the member states of the Organization of American States during the preceding decade, while one study in 1978 estimated that at least 30 of the 150 countries then in existence were in a state of emergency.[74] The 1986 Interim Report to the International Law Association found that approximately seventy states were at the time undergoing some type of emergency.[75] The Despouy Report for the UN found that between January 1985 and

May 1997 some 100 states or territories – that is, *over half the member states of the United Nations* – had at some point been under a state of emergency. The Report points out that 'if the list of countries which have proclaimed, extended or terminated a state of emergency [in this period] were to be projected onto a map of the world . . . the resulting area would cover nearly three-quarters of the Earth's surface'.[76] As the International Commission of Jurists put it in 1983: 'It is probably no exaggeration to say that at any given time in recent history a considerable part of humanity has been living under a state of emergency'.[77] At the same time, however, we find that crisis, exception, emergency, are no longer sporadic episodes in the lives of many states but have been a constant resort for the ruling class: under Roosevelt's emergency measures, the US by 1939 appeared to be in its thirty-ninth emergency in six years.

WALTER BENJAMIN GOES TO SENATE

The thirty-ninth emergency in six years? That's a lot. It sounds like something odd has happened in the form of political rule. 'Plain bad management', as Congressman Barton put it.[78] But in fact what we are dealing with is much more than bad management, and not even crisis management, but just plain, everyday, political management – the normal state of affairs for modern capitalist states. But *why* it is the norm is the important question. For this question takes us to the heart of emergency powers, the rule of law, and the exercise of violence; it takes us, in other words, to the political administration of capitalist modernity. It also sheds some light on current debates about the war on terror. Most important, it tells us something important about the logic of security in modern politics. Let us get at this in a roundabout way.

In the early 1970s an increasing concern about emergency powers prompted Senate to establish a Special Committee on the Termination of the National Emergency. The aim was to examine the use of emergency powers in the US and to propose how to bring them to an end. The report which eventually emerged from the Committee opens by noting that the American conception of emergency government is derived from Locke's concept of prerogative, and points out that 'since March 9, 1933, the United States has been in a state of declared national emergency'. It goes on:

In addition to the national emergency declared by President Roosevelt in 1933, there are also the national emergency proclaimed by President Truman on December 16, 1950 during the Korean conflict, and the states of emergency declared by President Nixon on March 23, 1970, and August 15, 1971. These proclamations give force to 470 provisions of Federal law. These hundreds of statutes delegate to the President extraordinary powers . . . [to] seize property; organize and control the means of production; seize commodities; assign military forces abroad; institute martial law; seize and control all transportation and communication; regulate the operation of private enterprise; restrict travel; and, in a plethora of particular ways, control the lives of all American citizens.[79]

In other words, the Report found that not only was the Vietnam War being conducted under forty-year-old emergency legislation, but the whole of America seemed to be governed under the same powers. As the Committee notes, a forty-year state of emergency can in no way be defined as 'temporary'. Emergency government had become the norm.

That this was so can be seen, ironically, by the Act which followed. What emerged from the Senate Report was the National Emergencies Act 1976 (NEA) and the International Emergency Economic Powers Act 1977 (IEEPA), designed ostensibly to constrain the authority granted to the executive via emergency powers. The four existing states of emergency and the majority of the emergency statutes were to be terminated as of 1978, and new procedures created for delegating legislative power to the President. But the new legislation *kept in place* the key provisions which had underwritten emergency law through the twentieth century, namely Section 5(b) of the TWEA and the key sections of the United States Code dealing with emergencies. The NEA held that anything determined by the Act would not apply to Section 5(b) of the TWEA and its subsequent amendments. In retaining this as part of the Federal Code, the US state effectively consolidated its permanent war footing in the everyday policing of its own citizens. As if to confirm this, more or less immediately following the final termination of the four states of emergency there was a declaration of a national emergency – in November 1979 in response to the US embassy being seized and hostages taken in Tehran. Since then, over thirty national emergencies have been declared, all the way up to the more recent ones dealing with the post-9/11 'war on terror'. It is worth noting, however, that the vast majority of these have concerned trade and economic relations dressed up in the guise of national security.[80] In this sense, it is no exaggeration to say that the US spent most of the twentieth century and, so far, all of the twenty-first century, in a 'state of emergency'.

Is the US a particular case here? Research suggests that far from being peculiar, the US was following the *normal* route for states. The pattern is that new forms of emergency powers to deal with 'exceptional' events end up becoming permanent and normalised; the liberalisation of martial law morphs into the constitutionalisation of emergency powers.

One standard example is the repressive strategy adopted by the British state in Northern Ireland. The SPA of 1922 conferred on the police and Ministry of Home Affairs wide powers: to impose curfews; proscribe organisations; censor literature; attend or ban meetings; restrict individual movement; stop, search and seize any vehicle; to arrest without warrant on the grounds of suspicion; to question, search and detain; and, most significantly, to use internment without trial. Originally meant to last for one year, it was renewed annually until 1928 when it was then extended for five years, at the end of which it was made permanent. In other words, emergency legislation was entrenched and normalised as a key mechanism for governing Northern Ireland from its inception. The Northern Ireland (Emergency Provisions) Act 1973 was likewise passed as a temporary measure following a declaration of emergency by the then Conservative government (the fifth emergency measure in three years). Though ostensibly designed to replace the SPA, in effect it took the powers of the SPA and added a few more, such as the elimination of juries from the court system. The Secretary of State for Northern Ireland, Merlyn Rees, stated that the Act 'makes emergency provisions and is by its nature temporary, to cover the period of an emergency'.[81] The Act remained in force for twenty-six years, being gradually incorporated into further Northern Ireland (Emergency Provisions) Acts in 1978, 1987, 1991 and 1996. The story of the Prevention of Terrorism (Temporary Provisions) Act 1974 (PTA) is the same. Passed for one year with the Home Secretary Roy Jenkins stating that no one 'would wish these exceptional powers to remain in force a moment longer than is necessary',[82] the Act was amended in 1975 and 1983, re-enacted in 1984 and became permanent in 1989. The cumulative effect has been that emergency powers have *de facto* been exercised as a permanent feature of the political landscape. Thus the permanent crisis in Northern Ireland stands in stark contrast to the notion that a state of emergency is by definition exceptional. Far from being an exception, in Northern Ireland emergency has been the norm: born into a form of martial law it has been policed under emergency powers ever since; any analysis of Northern Ireland's history reveals that it has known nothing other than emergency rule.[83] The extent to which this is the case is witnessed by the complete retention of emergency powers through the period of the ceasefire and beyond.

It is also evident from the fact that emergency legislation in Northern Ireland has almost always become general legislation applicable to the whole of the UK. Many of the principle emergency measures for Northern Ireland in the 1920s eventually made their way into the regular law in the 1930s and thereafter, supporting and extending the range of the EPA by seeping into other legislation such as the Incitement to Disaffection Act 1934, the Public Order Act 1936 and the various police and public order acts which followed. Major provisions of the PTA eventually came to apply to the whole of the UK via the Police and Criminal Evidence Act 1984. What we see with these shifts is a prime example of the normalisation of originally 'special' powers: what was designed yesterday for a specific region applies today to the whole nation; what was exceptional yesterday becomes normal today. More recently the abolition of the right to silence was first tried in Northern Ireland in the Criminal Evidence (Northern Ireland) Order of 1988, but then was very easily extended to the rest of the UK – Articles 34 through to 37 of the Criminal Justice and Public Order Act 1994 repeat almost verbatim the provisions regarding the right to silence in the 1988 Order.[84] This is a perfect example of the ways in which the political technology of emergency powers seeps into the ordinary criminal law, becoming normalised in the process. Countless other examples might be given: the 1998 Criminal Justice (Terrorism and Conspiracy) Act codified into a non-temporary statute various measures previously thought to be temporary and extended practices used in Northern Ireland to deal with 'international terrorism', while section 23 of the Anti-Terrorism, Crime and Security Act (ATCS) 2001, introducing detention without trial for non-UK nationals, is merely an expansion and normalisation of internment as practised in Northern Ireland and during the various 'emergencies' in the colonies.

For the sake of some brevity we can get a strong sense of how common this pattern is by setting this broad historical sketch of the US and UK against a wider backdrop of four formative political transformations in the post-1945 period in world politics. These are meant to be illustrative rather than exhaustive: alongside the examples from the UK and the US, they are intended to show the extent to which emergency powers have been integral to the consolidation of capitalist modernity in different national and political contexts.

First, Israel. The state of Israel has been under continuous emergency since its inception in 1948. In September 1945 the British in Palestine promulgated the Defence (Emergency) Regulations, which the Jewish community in the region originally thought of as a form of police state under martial law. But the creation of the state of Israel maintained the regulations as a feature of the 'new' legal system, albeit as a temporary measure. The temporary status of the emergency was quickly held up to be yet another piece of political mythology, however, as the powers in question came to be used time and again for dealing with labour disputes and economic crises as well as 'the Palestinian question'. Under the legal structure put in place by Article 9(a) of the Law and Administration Ordinance of 1948, once an emergency had been declared the government enjoyed the power to govern by decree, including the power to alter, suspend or modify the application of any piece of primary legislation by way of emergency regulations, to the extent that the emergency regulations could change or suspend provisions of the Basic Law (unless the latter had been entrenched against such encroachment). As Oren Gross has shown, the 'constitutional revolution' of 1992 changed little. There are now some additional legal hoops that the government must jump through to renew the declared state of emergency and periodic calls for making the annual review process more effective and meaningful, or for even lifting the state of emergency, but no real change has taken place: the state of emergency has continued uninterrupted. In this respect, emergency government has been the norm in Israel.[85] What started as a temporary transition mechanism during a 'war of independence' quickly became and remained a permanent feature of the Israeli state.

Second, apartheid South Africa. The Sharpeville Massacre is well

known for signalling the start of armed resistance in South Africa. It
was also the start of a permanent emergency. While the declaration of
emergency was successful in suppressing political opposition, with
over 11,000 people held in detention, from an economic point of view
it was disastrous as foreign investors lost faith in the country's political
stability. As John Dugard has shown, the apartheid state sought a
new method that would permit it to combat radical political opposition effectively without endangering economic security. Initially the
solution took the form of temporary measures, such as the ninety-
day detention law, which required annual renewal by Parliament. As
foreign investors became more convinced of the ability of the security
forces to counter political change the government became bolder
and enacted more severe emergency measures, and these became a
permanent part of the South African legal system.[86] Hence the with-
drawal of the ninety-day detention law in January 1965 was quickly
followed by a 180-day detention law, extended and enhanced by the
Terrorism Act 1967 which permitted the indefinite detention without
trial of suspected 'terrorists', and then the introduction of preventive
detention with the Internal Security Amendment Act 1976. Following
the declaration of a further state of emergency in July 1985, reimposed
in June 1986 and renewed annually thereafter, South Africa began
formally incorporating portions of its emergency provisions into
ordinary legislation, to the extent that the 'normal' law of the land
constituted a massive and widespread derogation from international
human rights agreements. There was therefore never such thing as a
'temporary' emergency in apartheid South Africa.

Third, postcolonialism. In the above example of Kenya, the British
government announced in November 1959 that the eight-year emergency was to end and the Emergency Regulations revoked. But two
Ordinances were immediately passed conferring semi-emergency
powers: first, the Preservation of Public Security Ordinance, 1959,
replaced the Emergency Powers Ordinance, 1948, and was designed
to be used for 'security reasons'; and, second, the Detained and
Restricted Persons (Special Provisions) Ordinance, 1959, empowered
the Governor to make Regulations providing for detention or restric-
tion of a range of persons. The powers given by these two Ordinances
fall very little short of those which may be taken in a full emergency.
Indeed, they had been thought through during the actual emergency
so that any post-emergency laws would legalise the continued use

of detention without trial and forced labour; the British colonial government's main concern seemed to be that without the continued emergency it would not be able to derogate from international human rights conventions. The Ordinances seem to have enabled the government to proclaim the end of the emergency without making a huge difference to the way Kenya was governed. This pattern has been the same for virtually all post-colonial situations, from Malaysia's permanent state of emergency since independence, reinforced by the Emergency Ordinance 1969 which has never been terminated, to Brunei's repeated extension of the state of emergency first declared on 12 December 1962. As the one-time UN Commissioner on Human Rights Kéba M'Baye put it in 1969, 'all these developing States, constantly threatened by disorder and economic difficulties, consider themselves to be permanently in an emergency situation'.[87] It is as though they were constitutionally obliged by the departing colonial powers to live under a continual state of emergency.

Fourth, Latin American regimes. The unsurpassed example here is Alfredo Stroessner's regime in Paraguay. A Report on the Situation of Human Rights in Paraguay by the Inter-American Commission on Human Rights in 1978 found that although the Paraguayan Constitution required that a state of siege must be limited in duration, it did not establish any guidelines as to the extent of that limitation. The Commission therefore suggested that the Paraguayan Constitution had led to a continuous use of the extraordinary institution of state of siege, making 'it possible for such an emergency measure to be extended more or less indefinitely, even to the point of becoming permanent'.[88] The Inter-American Commission found that it was impossible to gather exact information as to the date on which Paraguay first came under the state of siege. According to reliable information an emergency had been in continual effect between 1929 and 1946. After an interruption of six months in 1946, the emergency was again put into effect in 1947 and appears to have been in force until 1987. In other words, the Stroessner regime was ostensibly a parliamentary democracy with entrenched constitutional freedoms and rights, and also in a permanent state of emergency. Well, not quite permanent: for one day every four years the emergency was suspended in order for elections to take place. But Paraguay is not alone among Latin American countries. The Despouy Report noted the similar case of Columbia, 'where a state of emergency, in various forms, has been almost uninterruptedly in force for some 40 years'. The Report added that 'Chile, Argentina, Uruguay and El Salvador, amongst others, have experienced long periods of institutionalized states of emergency under military regimes'.[89]

These four examples are interesting because they show the extent to which emergency powers have been used in very different types of regime: the racial state of Israel, the apartheid state, postcolonial states, and authoritarian Latin American regimes. If we add them to the examples of the UK and the US it becomes very clear that not only have emergency powers been crucial to the consolidation of capitalist modernity, almost always introduced to deal with a form of resistance by the oppressed, but also that these powers have become exercised as a permanent feature of oppression: the tradition of the oppressed that teaches us that the 'state of emergency' is not the exception but the rule. In case after case the state of emergency is either enacted again and again, or simply remains in place by virtue of not being explicitly repealed, or it is eventually placed on the statute books as part of 'ordinary' legislation. Emergency measures, almost always introduced for 'security reasons', more often than not have a way of remaining in place well beyond the life of the situations which supposedly justified their introduction in the first place.

Because of this that one finds *permanent* emergency wherever one looks. Of the 100 states which the UN had found to have at some point been in a state of emergency between January 1985 and May 1997, many of them had presented their emergency to the UN as permanent (either *de facto* or *de jure*): Zambia from 1964 to 1991, Zimbabwe from 1965 to 1990, Peru from 1981 onwards, Pakistan from 1977 to 1985, Malaysia from 1969 onwards, Ireland from 1976 to 1995, Brunei from 1962 onwards; Turkey's public emergency for more than 77 per cent of the period between June 1970 and July 1987, including a continuous stretch of almost 7 years from September 1980 to May 1987; Greece's formal state of war mobilisation from 1974 to May 2002; India's 21 uses of the constitutional emergency clause between 1950 and 1983; Egypt's almost continuous state of emergency since 1967.[90] The list goes on and on. As the Despouy Report commented, the tendency for the exception to become the rule *is in fact a world-wide phenomenon*. The search for security through the permanent exercise of emergency powers has become the primary strategic political operation deployed across the world. In this sense, there appears to be no time which actually *was* normal.

Part of the reason for this is that the concept of 'emergency' evokes images of short-term measures to deal with a specific and temporary problem. The assumption that runs through official documents on emergency powers is that once the 'temporary' problem is dealt with the state can return to normalcy. But states have constantly and systematically failed to fulfil the requirement to treat to 'emergency' as temporary, and so the tendency is for the measures in question to become part and parcel of a new conception of normality. The pattern is almost always the same: an event occurs which leads to the demand for new and more powerful security measures; emergency legislation is enacted; these new emergency powers are then gradually 'stretched' beyond their original scope and/or used to police situations for which they were never intended; this stretching is gradually justified and legitimised, until the powers are exercised way beyond their original context; finally, the legislature normalises those very emergency powers by transforming them into the ordinary criminal law.[91] What appear initially to be *extra*ordinary powers developed under the auspices of something labelled 'emergency' very quickly and easily infiltrate the *ordinary* legal system, becoming regularised as a technique of government and normalised as a technology of power. 'Temporariness' becomes merely a rhetorical device in the deployment of emergency powers and to justify new security measures: temporary security fences become permanent borders; temporary camps become permanent settlements; temporary closures become permanent; temporary revocations of travel permits become permanent; temporary changes in orders of engagement become permanent.[92] The ubiquitous way in which 'temporariness' is invoked belies the fact that it is almost impossible to find a case of a liberal democracy going through a period of 'emergency' without some permanent and purportedly irreversible alteration in its political technique. Either the state of emergency is constantly re-enacted, or it remains in place by virtue of not being explicitly repealed, or it is eventually placed on the statute books as part of 'ordinary' legislation and so carried over into a period of 'normalcy'. The *de facto* becomes *de jure*; emergency becomes the norm.[93]

This tendency has been facilitated by the ever-expanding notion of what constitutes an 'emergency',[94] masking the term's real political origins. Anything – and thus, in effect, *everything* – affecting the 'security of the state' and the 'life of the nation' must by definition be included, and its polymorphous nature suits its integral relation to the politics of security since it elides the differences between, say, 'war' in the conventional sense which is thought to 'obviously' constitute an emergency, and political rebellions which are now easily treated as emergencies. It also elides the differences between these things and everything else that might be thought to be a problem for security and good order: drugs (for example Reagan's use of troops to counteract the drug trade on the grounds that the emergency constituted a threat to national security); football hooliganism (the communications officer of UEFA described a series of crowd troubles in European football in the 2006–7 season as an 'emergency situation');[95] child abuse (in 1990 a panel of government-appointed childcare experts concluded that 'child abuse and neglect in the United States now represents a national emergency');[96] 'natural' emergencies such as floods (for example, during Hurricane Katrina) or even just a bit of unusual weather (in the hot spring weather in Italy in 2007 officials declared that they were moving towards declaring a state of emergency and Macedonia actually did so in July of that year); famines (too numerous to mention); the possible extinction of species (see, for example, the United Nations Environment Programme Report of February 2007 called *Last Stand of the Orang-Utan: State of Emergency*); resistance to globalisation (such as the declaration of a state of emergency by Paul Schell, Mayor of Seattle, in response to the protest against the annual meeting of the World Trade Organization being held in the city);[97] and, of course, the intensification of class struggle (also instances too numerous to mention).[98]

This overwhelming abundance of emergency and the ever increasing diffuseness of the concept is politically important since it helps create and sustain an emergency mentality among the population, eliding the difference between the natural and the national and so making the political decision to declare a national state of emergency appear as on a continuum with the actions taken in the face of earthquakes and hurricanes. This emergency mentality then feeds into and feeds on an overwhelming '(in)security consciousness' in which internal rebellion, enemy forces and 'terrorists' are rolled together with minor forms of disorder and even 'Nature' itself. This continued iteration of even the lowest level of emergency helps condition people to live with *some* notion of emergency, which makes it easier for states to 'upgrade' to a higher-level emergency regime as and when necessary.[99] And as the margins of emergency are broadened, so the possibilities for political action become increasingly circumscribed, to the point where they ultimately disappear.[100]

But if, historically speaking, times are never 'normal', then we really have to abandon the concept of the 'state of emergency' and instead explore the ways emergency powers are used in relation to 'normal law'. Or maybe 'normal times' is the biggest political myth going. And if it is, what does this say about the current fad for describing our situation post-9/11 as a permanent emergency? And what might it tell us about the way 'security' is used as a political tool?

AGAINST NORMALITY

The assumption that the 'state of emergency' is outside or beyond law assumes a distinction between law and politics. The argument is that the state of emergency/exception creates a legal black hole, or introduces 'anomalous zones' and practices of dubious juridical status, in which basic liberties and rights are abandoned and the rule of law thereby suspended. Moreover, many have suggested that the current abandonment of law now appears permanent due to the ongoing war on terrorism. The logic is then that we must reinstate the rule of law and resist the possibility of any further black holes. But this argument is badly misplaced.

For a start, one has to wonder about the idea of legal black holes. To take the current conflict: despite the occasional outburst such as that by Bush on the evening of 11 September 2001, in which he stated boldly that 'I don't care what the international lawyers say, we are going to kick some ass'; despite Bush's response to a reporter who asked about international law – 'International law? I better call my lawyer . . . I don't know what you're talking about'; and despite Rumsfeld's suggestion that whether prisoners at Guantánamo should be covered by the Geneva Convention is a question that should be addressed to those who did not drop out of law school, as he had; despite all this, the Bush administration has in fact been at pains to hold the line that 'we're a nation of law, we adhere to the laws'.[101] Rhetoric as this may be, it is important rhetoric since its implication is that any lawbreaking is down to some wayward individuals who, if identified and caught, will be punished – *within* and *by* the law. This classical and powerful ploy – the 'few bad apples' thesis – is used time and again by political leaders to reiterate their position as upholders of the law: we as guardians of the state follow the law; unfortunately sometimes our underlings don't understand this and go about working outside and against the law; for that they are punished. See: that's how 'lawful' *we* are.

At the same time, states employ countless legal advisors to explain and defend emergency tactics which might *appear* unlawful. A claim made in a House of Commons Report on the law of occupation as it may pertain to the Iraq conflict is interesting in this regard: 'In the case of Iraq, the main purpose of obtaining a mandate in the form of a Security Council resolution was to evade legal difficulties if the occupying powers sought to move beyond the limited rights conferred by the Hague Regulations and Geneva Convention IV to vary existing arrangements'.[102] It was known that some 'evading' of legal difficulties would be necessary; a Security Council resolution would simply have made it easier. The key is the acknowledgement that 'evading legal difficulties' takes place. (This of course gives rise to the suspicion that some laws are made with the understanding that they will be evaded: law as merely a 'legal difficulty' for the state.) While this evading can sometimes take the form of complaints about being 'lawyered to death', as George Tenet put it when Director of the CIA, and often involves some real casuistry – one thinks of the recent debates over the Geneva Conventions concerning 'prisoners of war' or the meaning of 'torture' – it is nonetheless *legal* casuistry: it involves serious attempts to *interpret* the law from within, and that is a practice that, after all, lawyers constantly tell us needs to happen. Hence the official position which insists on the need for 'new thinking in the law'.[103] It's new thinking – *in* the law.

The manipulation of law and the evasion of 'legal difficulties' – internationally by the ruling states, domestically by the ruling class – has a long history. But it does not mean that the law is not operative. If anything, recent events show that the emergency is a work of legal representation and classification, evidence, as Fleur Johns suggests, that 'exceptional' moments of power are always filled to the brim with legal expertise, procedure and analysis.[104] Governments much prefer to work under the cloak of legality rather than have their operations exposed as 'purely' executive powers exercised outside the law. More-over, while we might debate whether this or that practice carried out in the name of emergency is legal or illegal, we must also bear in mind that underpinning the logic of emergency is the logic of necessity. And as we noted in the previous chapter, in the world of political necessity *anything* can be justified. To that end, any cursory examination of the laws of war reveals that 'despite noble rhetoric to the contrary, the laws of war have been formulated to deliberately privilege military necessity at the cost of humanitarian values. As a result, the laws of war have facilitated rather than restricted wartime violence'.[105]

In other words, far from *suspending* the law, violent actions conducted in 'emergency conditions' have been legitimated *through* law on the grounds of necessity and in the name of security. It is because of this that the courts have in general been more than happy to accede to the political excesses carried out under emergency powers, constantly doffing the judicial cap at executive declarations that this or that event constitutes an emergency as part of their wider deference to executive determinations about the interests of national security. But, contra Schmitt, this does not mean that rule of law is not operative or that the sovereign decision is legally uncontrolled, for the doffing of the judicial cap plays a crucial role in what then takes place. Hence virtually every exercise of violence conducted in the name of emergency and under the label national security has been justified and legitimised on legal grounds and accepted by the courts.[106] That this is so should not be a surprise since, as we have seen, emergency powers *per se* are *entirely constitutional.* The ruling class was never going to be so stupid as to produce a liberal-democratic constitution which does *not* allow it to exercise power and violence in the name of emergency, and to defend its vision of order; constitutions, after all, are designed primarily to underscore the security of the state.

To criticise the use of emergency powers in terms of a suspension of the law, then, is to make the mistake of counterpoising normality and emergency, law and violence. In separating 'normal' from 'emergency', with the latter deemed 'exceptional', this approach parrots the conventional liberal wisdom that posits normalcy and emergency as two discrete and separable phenomena. This essentially liberal paradigm assumes that there is such a thing as 'normal' order governed by rules, and that the emergency constitutes an 'exception' to this normality. 'Normal' here equates with the separation of powers, entrenched civil liberties, an ongoing debate about public policy and law, and the rule of law, while 'emergency' is thought to require strong executive rule, little time for discussion, and premised on the supposedly necessary suspension of the law and thus the discretion to suspend key liberties and rights. But this rests on two deeply ideological assumptions: first, the belief that emergency rule is aberrational; and, second, an equation of the emergency/non-emergency dichotomy with a distinction between constitutional and non-constitutional action. Thus liberalism seeks to ideologically separate 'normal' constitutional order from emergency rule, thereby preserving the constitution in its pristine form while providing the executive with the power to act in an emergency.[107] The critique of security involves seeing through this ideological sham and recognising emergency powers not as exceptional but as part and parcel of the political administration of contemporary capitalist states.

Emergency, in this sense, is what emerges from the rule of law when violence needs to be exercised and certain 'limits' of the rule of law overcome. The genealogy of 'emergency' is instructive here. 'Emergency' has its roots in the idea of 'emerge'. The *Oxford English Dictionary* suggests that 'emerge' connotes 'the rising of a submerged body out of the water' and 'the process of coming forth, issuing from concealment, obscurity, or confinement'. Both these meanings of 'emerge' were once part of the meaning of 'emergency', but the first is now rare and the second obsolete. Instead, the modern meaning of 'emergency' has come to the fore, namely a sudden or unexpected occurrence demanding urgent action and, politically speaking, the term used to describe a condition close to war in which the normal constitution might be suspended. But what this genealogy tells us is that in 'emergency' lies the idea of 'emergent': what is emerging, coming out of concealment or issuing from confinement by certain events. This is why 'emergency' is a better category than exception: where 'emergency' has this sense of 'emergent', exception instead implies a sense of *ex capere* (being taken outside). I am suggesting that far from being outside the rule of law, emergency powers emerge from it. They are part and parcel of the political technology of security and thus central to political administration.

But there is a wider argument to be made, one with political implications. The idea that the permanent emergency involves a suspension of the law encourages the idea that resistance must involve a 'return to legality', a return to the 'normal' mode of governing through the rule of law. This involves a serious misjudgement in which it is simply assumed that legal procedures – both international and domestic – are designed to protect human rights from state violence. 'Law' itself comes to appear largely unproblematic and the rule of law 'an unqualified human good'.[108] What this amounts to is what I have elsewhere called a form of legal fetishism, in which Law becomes a mystical answer to the problems posed by power. In the process, the problems inherent in Law are ignored. Law is treated as an 'independent' or 'autonomous' reality, explained according to its own dynamics, a Subject in itself whose very existence requires that individuals and institutions 'objectify' themselves before it. This produces the illusion that Law has a life of its own, abstracting the rule of law from its origins in class domination, ignoring the ways in which the rule of law is deployed as a political strategy, and obscuring the ideological mystification of these processes in the liberal trumpeting of the rule of law. To demand the return to the 'rule of law' is to seriously misread the history of the relation between the rule of law and emergency powers and, consequently, to get sucked into a less-than-radical politics in dealing with state violence. Part of what I am suggesting is that emergency measures are part of the everyday exercise of powers, working *alongside* rather than against the rule of law as part of a unified political strategy in the fabrication of social order.

The question to ask, then, is less 'how can we bring law to bear on violence?' and much more 'what is it that the law permits emergency measures to accomplish?'[109] This question – the question that Schmitt, with his fetish for the decision cannot understand,[110] which is also why contemporary Left Schmittianism is such a dead loss – disposes of any supposed juxtaposition between legality and emergency and allows us to recognise instead the extent to which the concept of emergency is deeply inscribed within the law and the legal condition of the modern state, and a central part of liberalism's authoritarian moment: the iron fist in the velvet glove of liberal constitutionalism. Far from suspending law or bracketing off the juridical, emergency powers lie firmly within the legal domain. How could they not, since they are so obviously central to state power and the political technology of government – part of the deployment of law, rather than its abandonment? Once this is recognised, the supposed problematic of violence disappears completely, for it can then be seen that emergency powers are deployed *for* the exercise of a violence necessary for the permanent refashioning of order – the violence *of* law, not violence contra law. Liberalism struggles with this, and thus presents it as an exceptional moment; fascism recognises it for what it is, and aestheticises the moment. As David Dyzenhaus points out, while the stripping of liberties in the name of emergency, the denial of rights on the grounds of necessity, and the suspension of freedoms through the exercise of prerogative might appear quite minor compared to what happens in fascist regimes, the fact that the stripping, denial and suspension does happen under the guise of emergency and in full view of the courts brings the legal order of liberal democracies far closer to the legal order of fascism than liberals would care to admit.[111] But in a wonderful ideological loop, the rule of law is also *its own ideological obfuscation of that fact.*[112]

The political implications of this are enormous. For if emergency powers are part and parcel of the exercise of law and violence (that is, law *as* violence), and if historically they have been aimed at the oppressed – in advanced capitalist states against the proletariat and its various struggles, in reactionary regimes against genuine politicisation of the people, in colonial systems against popular mobilisation – then they need to be fought not by demanding a return to the 'normal' rule of law, but in what Benjamin calls a *real* state of emergency, on the grounds that only this will improve our position in the struggle against the fascism of our time. And this is a task which requires violence, not the rule of law. As Benjamin saw, the law's claim to a monopoly of violence is explained not by the intention of preserving some mythical 'legal end' such as security or normality but, rather, for 'the intention of preserving the law itself'. But violence *not* in the hands of the law threatens it by its mere existence *outside* the law. A violence exercised not by the state, but used for very different political ends. For 'if the existence of violence outside the law, as pure immediate violence, is assured, [then] this furnishes proof that revolutionary violence . . . is possible'.[113]

That this possibility of and necessity for revolutionary violence is so often omitted when emergency powers are discussed is indicative of the extent to which much of the Left has given up any talk of political violence for the far more comfortable world of the rule of law, regardless of how little the latter has achieved in just the last few years. But if the history of emergency powers tells us anything it is that the *least effective response* to state violence is to simply insist on the rule of law. Rather than aiming to counter state violence with a demand for legality, then, what is needed is a counter-politics: against the permanent emergency, by all means, but also against the 'normality' of everyday class power and the bourgeois world of the rule of law. And since the logic of emergency is so deeply embedded in the rhetorical structure of liberalism's concept of security, this means being against the politics of security. For the very posing of political questions through the trope of emergency is always already on the side of security. To grasp why, we need to now refocus our attention more specifically on security as a political technology.

Chapter 3

FROM SOCIAL TO NATIONAL SECURITY: ON THE FABRICATION OF ECONOMIC ORDER

———

Least Keith's back. Back with his new teeth – Police State took them out, he laughs. Welfare State put them back in.

David Peace, *GB84* (2005)

In the days leading up to the declaration of a new national emergency on 14 September 2001, the Bush administration made it clear that the rationale behind any response to the attacks on the World Trade Center was security: all the talk was of a 'heightened security alert' and the introduction of new emergency measures in the name of 'national security'. But this begs a question: what is 'national security'?

It is well known that following World War II a range of civilian and military heads of different parts of the US state were brought together before a Senate committee to consider the unification of the military services. In his message to Congress in December 1945, Truman had asked for the creation of a unified military establishment along with a 'national defense council', and by May 1946 both Army and Navy were advocating a 'Council of Common Defense'. Yet by 1947 'common defense' had been dropped and replaced with 'national security' – hence the creation of the National Security Council and the National Security Act. The most forceful advocate of the concept, Navy Secretary James Forrestal, commented that 'national security' can only be secured with a broad and comprehensive front, and made a point of adding that 'I am using the word "security" here consistently and continuously rather than "defense"', highlighting just how new and exciting this idea seemed. 'I like your words "national security"', one Senator commented.[1] It was certainly new: 'It has become impossible to read a newspaper, or leaf through a magazine, or go to a dinner party, without being made sharply aware by a story or an article, or a chance remark, of the widespread interest in the future security of the United States', noted one commentator.[2] But it was also exciting: the fact that it was 'national *security*' was part of the excitement, for 'security' was a far more expansive term than 'defence', which was seen as too narrowly military,[3] and far more suggestive than 'national interest', seen by many as either too weak a concept to form the basis of the exercise of state power or, with its selfish connotations, simply too negative.[4]

The combination of novelty and excitement meant that from thereon national security has had a great career. Just a decade earlier the multi-volume *Encyclopaedia of the Social Sciences*, published by Macmillan in 1934, contained no entry for 'national security'. But the next edition of the *Encyclopaedia* in 1968 (by which time it had become the *International Encyclopedia of the Social Sciences*) not only contained an entry for 'national security', but also suggested that the term 'has long been used by politicians as a rhetorical phrase and by military leaders to describe a policy objective'.[5] 'Long been used' may have been an exaggeration: although Arnold Wolfers in 1952 described 'national security' as 'well enough established in the political discourse of international relations',[6] one major text on national security from 1965 containing essays by leading political scientists of the day (including Harold Lasswell, Hans Morgenthau, Gabriel Almond, Charles Beard, and Bernard Brodie) was still happy to describe national security merely as 'a concept emerging' and 'a concept developing' – the titles of Parts One and Four.[7] The editors of the book, Morton Berkowitz and P. G. Bock, were the authors of the encyclopaedia entry, and even they had described 'national security' as only an 'emerging field' in 1966.[8] Nonetheless, this begs the question: from where did it emerge and why, by the late-1960s, did the concept also seem to have so seeped into political discourse that it clearly *felt* like it had been in use for a long time? Or to put it another way: just what was it about this idea that made it so exciting?

'The doctrine of national security', Yergin suggests, 'developed to explain America's relationship to the rest of the world'.[9] Many have accepted that this is indeed what national security is about – international relations. This assumption has been reiterated and reinforced by the birth of a new class of 'national-security managers' (policy wonks, military officers, corporate leaders and scientists) and a new breed of security intellectuals. So the obvious route to take here would be to follow the mainstream tendency of highlighting the centrality of 'national security' to the discourse of foreign policy and the Cold War. But to do this would be to remain within what Robert Latham calls the auto-referential paradigm of national security, where the issues and stakes are exactly what the policymakers say they are.[10] This would be to adopt the language, discursive traditions and key assumptions of the national-security managers and intellectuals, and thus the rationale and rhetoric of Cold War policymakers. Instead, I want to suggest that the impetus and thrust of the idea of national security towards international relations and foreign policy has in fact buried an interesting part of its history, thereby obscuring some interesting links between this and related concepts. What I want to do here, then, is to unearth some of the history of national security, and to do so by exploring one of its hitherto unexplored dimensions – in the emergence of *social* security in the 1930s.

Social security and national security are not often talked about together. The extent to which 'security' has been 'disciplined' over the years has meant that the study of social security and the study of national security are often miles apart – or at least several corridors apart in the modern university – with the one seen simply as a set of social policies concerned with levels of subsistence and well-being and the other seen as pertaining to foreign policy, intelligence-gathering and counter-subversion. This remains the case despite the recent surge of interest in widening the security agenda. For example, even in the hugely influential new 'framework' for analysing and expanding security proposed by those working in the 'Copenhagen School', social security is way down the agenda, if it appears at all. Despite one of the new 'sectors' through which security might be analysed being the 'societal' sector, little is said about the idea, institutions or practices of 'social security' as such, other than that there is perhaps a link through the idea of collective identity.[11] More generally, even though international relations theory has increasingly been interested in the 'inside-outside' relationship,[12] little has been said about the possible relation between the security discourse most obviously associated with 'outside', namely national security, and the security discourse most obviously associated with 'inside', namely social security.

So for all the talk about expanding the concept of security, very few people have sought to draw together social and national security. Simon Dalby has commented that 'income support payments were sometimes considered in terms of the provision of "economic security". The historical dimension of these themes should not be forgotten in all the claims to novel understanding of security'.[13] But the historical dimension clearly *has* been forgotten, not least because the more 'coercive' security agencies and the academics which write about them have tended to exclude key aspects of 'insecurity' from their understanding and treatment of 'security'.[14] The first aim of this chapter, then, is to revisit and recast the concept of national security by arguing for a better grasp of its historical links with social security. In other words, I want to suggest that the national security state which emerged after World War II, and which has been the object of so much academic debate and political discussion, has its roots in the 'social security state' which emerges in the 1930s.

Making this argument will allow me to suggest that if there is any mileage in the idea of 'securitization' as a process, its primary example may lie not in the field of international politics and national security, but in what passes as 'social security'. As part of the broad agenda for widening the field of security studies, 'securitization theory' treats security as the product of social processes and has thereby set out its stall as a critical exploration of the social construction of security issues through an analysis of who or what is said to be being secured. 'Security', on this view, is 'a self-referential practice, because it is in this practice that the issue becomes a security issue – not necessarily because a real existential threat exists but because the issue is presented as such a threat'.[15] It strikes me that securitization theory has missed perhaps the most remarkable historical example of this process, namely in the political fabrication of a set of concerns as 'social security'.

The final aim of the chapter is more conceptual, which is to link social security and national security via the notion of economic security. To do this not only requires moving between conceptual history and social history; it also involves bringing together themes within the study of international political economy (IPE) and security studies. During much of the Cold War, IPE and security studies tended to be worlds apart. The security studies literature was often dominated by a rather naïve distinction between 'high' and 'low' politics, with political economy thought of as a rather lowly affair.[16] This was always more than a little strange, for a number of reasons. First, because given the extent to which the state system is obviously cut through by the dynamics of production, consumption and class, the extent to which the international economy is penetrated by state structures and vice versa, and the budgetary constraints on grand strategy, an obvious connection exists between national security and political economy; second, because for these very reasons the main actors in global politics certainly never divorced security from political economy; and third, because a number of key academics had pointed to the integral relationship between economics and security during the rise of the idea of national security during the 1940s.[17] Yet despite all of these pointers, mainstream 'security studies' came to conceive of security rather narrowly, in terms of the military and intelligence services, while IPE developed an independent path treating economic power separately from 'security questions'. As recently as 1988 the editors of one major journal reporting on a key conference in the field were still suggesting that 'the division between the fields of international political economy and international security is one of the most serious problems within the discipline of political science'.[18] And although this division has become less entrenched as more and more scholars have come to recognise the importance of the complex interrelationships between security and political economy, not least following some institutional shifts,[19] for the most part the work in this field focuses on the state as the referent object; only then does economic security come to figure. '*If* the state is taken as the referent object, *then* economic security becomes part of the national security agenda', says Buzan, adding that 'the idea of economic security becomes awkwardly entangled with a range of highly politicized debates about employment, income distribution and welfare'. For this reason, Buzan suggests, the conflation of social and national security can be electorally persuasive.[20]

I want to suggest that there is much more at stake here than the question of electoral gains. At stake are the far more substantive political gains to be had by the state from the idea of security. If we think of security as a deployment of power, then we can consider security as a key political technology behind the re-ordering of the social world. Focusing on security in America,[21] I will argue that what is at stake in this deployment of security is the fabrication of economic order, at the heart of which has been the idea of 'economic security' and which can be seen in both its internal/domestic dynamics (social security) and external/international dynamics (national security). This was a process of liberal order-building in the name of security. Part of this order-building has already been touched on in the discussion of emergency powers in the previous chapter. Excavating the origins and rationale of national security in this chapter will reveal some real political gains to be had by both liberalism and the state from the idea of security, the *raison d'être* of which is the legitimisation of the re-ordering of the social world. This re-ordering has been underpinned by a particular conception of economic order, on both the inter-national and domestic fronts. In other words, it is through the *combined* effect of 'social' and 'national' security that security *per se* has come to be one of the major mechanisms for the fabrication of the political order of capitalist modernity, a nexus of power conjoining capital and the state.

THE GARDEN OF SECURITY, OR 'SECURITY – THIS IS MORE LIKE IT'

On 8 June 1934, Roosevelt announced that among the objectives of his administration 'I place the security of the men, women and children of the Nation first'. Comparing simpler societies in which security was attained through the interdependence of family members and of the families within communities, Roosevelt suggested that 'the com-plexities of great communities and of organized industry make less real these simple means of security'.

> Therefore, we are compelled to employ the active interest of the Nation as a whole through government in order to encourage a greater security for each individual who composes it . . . If, as our Constitution tells us, our Federal Government was established among other things, 'to promote the general welfare,' it is our plain duty to provide for that security upon which welfare depends . . . Hence I am looking for a sound means which I can recommend to provide at once security against several of the disturbing factors in life.[22]

Later that month he signed Executive Order 6757 creating the Committee on Economic Security (CES) to prepare recommendations for 'A Program of National Social and Economic Security'.[23] Roosevelt's choice of the language of security was important, since it would not only prove to be an important addition to the political discourse of the New Deal, but would also be crucial to the developing centrality of security in political discourse.

In Roosevelt's biographical fragment of 1934, *On Our Way*, he told of the story of his administration up to March 1934. The concept of security is almost entirely absent from the book – he refers to 'securities' as in the Securities Act 1933, dealing with the money supply, and makes an oblique reference to the 'permanent welfare and security' of every class of people in the context of pricing policies.[24] Other than that, the language when discussing such things as worker employment is the language of emergency – hence the proposal to deal with unemployment is dealt with in an Emergency Relief Act 1933. Nowhere does security figure as a major theme. The same is true of his Inaugural Address of 4 March 1933. And yet between June 1934 and 1936 security became *the* concept of New Deal politics. To understand why we need to note that by 1934 Roosevelt was faced with various insurgents who had gained ground through the previous years, including the followers of Huey Long, the organisations of the unemployed, elderly people organised and led by Francis Townsend, and religiously motivated activists around Charles Coughlin.[25] As noted in the previous chapter, it was also a time of intense class conflict which led many to believe that a communist revolution was possible. Less obvious politically but important in terms of the story here, he also faced various left-wing social-insurance experts. The latter in particular had been increasingly using the notion of 'insecurity' as a theme for social criticism and public policy proposals. The economist Abraham Epstein, for example, had published *Insecurity: A Challenge to America* (1933) in which he spoke of 'the specter of insecurity' as the bane of the worker's life under capitalism, while Max Rubinow had been articulating demands for social insurance in terms of 'a complete structure of security' in a book called *The Quest for Security* (1934).[26] At the same time we might also point to the influence of someone like Harold Laski, who spent various month-long visits lecturing in America in the 1930s, becoming one of the intellectuals close to Roosevelt, and writing articles in favour of strong Presidency, the New Deal and, of course, emergency powers.[27] His course of lectures at Brown University in the summer of 1929, published as *Liberty in the Modern State* in 1930 and reissued in 1937, had as a theme the idea that without economic security liberty is meaningless:

> If [a man] is deprived of security . . . he becomes the prey of a mental and physical servitude incompatible with the very essence of liberty. Nevertheless, economic security is not liberty, though it is a condition without which liberty is never effective . . . Without economic security, liberty is not worth having.[28]

Roosevelt's adoption of the rhetoric of security in mid-1934 represented an attempt to outflank critics and build on the suggestions of writers such as Laski. In so doing Roosevelt adopted and pushed the idea of security, helping to drive the concept into the very heart of political discourse. The emerging ideology of security became central to all political debates of the time, permeating the articles of national journals and becoming a major theme for books, newspapers and conferences. For example, *The New Republic* ran a series on 'Security for Americans' in late-1934 and early-1935, with contributions from major figures such as Rubinow, Epstein, Mary Van Kleeck and Paul Douglas,[29] while the *Survey Graphic* ran a series of articles on 'welfare and security' with pieces by social workers, economists and welfare experts.[30]

Many of these were critical of the way the Roosevelt administration was working. Most of the articles in *The New Republic* continued to insist on insecurity as the fundamental problem generated by capitalism: 'For a long time now people have been saying that perhaps the greatest evil of capitalist industrialism is not its unequal distribution of wealth but the insecurity it brings to the majority of the population', noted one commentator.[31] And so, in the words of another, 'mass provision by government and industry to provide for mass insecurity is the new definition of social insurance'.[32] Similarly, *The Nation* challenged the government on the grounds that the 'feebleness' of the proposals would leave the majority still insecure regardless of the 'high-sounding talk of economic security'.[33] Moreover, political scientists such as Harold Lasswell and politicians such as Herbert Hoover had also come to highlight the question of insecurity as a pressing concern. In *World Politics and Personal Insecurity*, published in 1934, Lasswell focused on insecurity caused by shifts in the division of labour, changing patterns of violence and changes in the symbolic environment, and called for an audit of the levels of insecurity and their political effects, having already argued, in his 1933 essay on 'The Psychology of Hitlerism' that Hitler's success was due in part to the feeling of insecurity felt by many Germans. Similarly, ex-President Hoover, in a book also published in 1934, suggested that one of the greatest challenges to liberty is the problem of economic security: of 'finding systematic methods of positive individual security against the misfortunes of unemployment and sickness, and for assurance in old age'.[34] Influential philanthropic organisations such as the Rockefeller Foundation were also highlighting the issue of security: 'existing insecurity . . . constitutes a serious threat to the existing system', commented one proposal for a potential Foundation Program in Fields of International Relations and Economic Security in 1934.[35] Either way, insecurity was the problem and security – of some sort – the solution. Security was now at the heart of political debate.[36]

Throughout 1934 and 1935, while the CES was at work assembling the Economic Security Bill, Roosevelt could barely stop speaking about security. On topics as diverse as banking legislation, industrial relations and the gold standard, security was the major theme. In his 'fireside chat' of 30 September 1934, for example, on the theme of 'Greater Security for the Average Man', Roosevelt suggested that his administration was moving towards a 'broader definition of liberty under which we are moving forward . . . to greater security'.[37] In an address to the Advisory Council of the CES in November 1934, held in Washington and attended by activists from across the country, Roosevelt equated 'greater general security' with economic recovery: 'In developing each component part of the broad program for economic security, we must not lose sight of the fact that there can be no security for the individual in the midst of general insecurity . . . Everything that we do with intent to increase the security of the individual will, I am confident, be a stimulus to recovery'.[38] In his message to Congress in January 1935 he reiterated the theme: 'the main objectives of our American program . . . the security of the men, women, and children of the Nation'.[39] So enormous was the theme that the film *We the People and Social Security*, distributed days before the 1936 election, had by 3 November been seen by approximately 4 million people.[40] 'Security' became the theme of all sorts of new pieces of legislation: the new authority to administer the Bankhead-

Jones Farm Tenant Act of 1937, for example, was called the Farm Security Administration.[41]

Thus by late-1934 the New Dealers had begun to claim the language of security. In trying to outflank critics by adopting their language and by pushing the CES and the Bill for Economic Security, New Deal politics became centred on an ideology of security.[42] 'In the present time "security" is the word that is being bandied about on every tongue', noted the *Spectator* in 1936.[43] This ideology of security became central to the task of national reconstruction. If, as we saw in the previous chapter, the New Deal was a prime example of emergency rule writ large, then security was perhaps its key concept. Symptomatically, this ideology of security built on the declaration of a state of emergency in Roosevelt's inaugural address of March 1933, in the sense that the power to wage a war against the emergency was inextricably bound up with the new need to 'secure the insecure'. The New Deal represents a prime example of the ideological circuit between emergency powers and security. Epitomised by the Federal Emergency Relief Administration of 1933 being taken over by the Social Security Board in 1935 (yet another example of emergency powers becoming normalised), this ideological circuit helped legitimise the forms of political administration and policing which would come to the fore in the twentieth century.

But this was not an ideology of just security; it was also very much an ideology of what became known as *social* security. The idea of social security had been used on occasion before, in a letter of 1908 by Winston Churchill (the first noted reference cited by the *Oxford English Dictionary*), but it was in the context of the political administration of contemporary US capitalism in the mid-1930s that the idea really took off. In July 1933 the American Association for Old Age Security had become the American Association for Social Security and its journal, *Old Age Security Herald*, became *Social Security*. Note that the *Economic* Security Bill eventually became the *Social* Security Act of 1935. As late as spring of that year the leading figures in the US administration, including Roosevelt himself, had still not firmly settled on this as an idea: they were still talking in terms of economic security and the Economic Security Bill. Note also that the original Executive Order 6757 that set in motion the program that would eventually lead to the Social Security Act was designed to develop a scheme for 'national social and economic security'. The security in question is social and economic, but it is also national. The legislation that would eventually emerge would be 'social security', which then became the label used by other states. The idea of 'national security' disappears, but, as I will suggest, then re-emerges in the context of a different set of debates. And as I shall also suggest, the idea of 'economic security' initially behind the Social Security Act is what will link national security to its social forebear. We can get at this through placing the development of 'social security' in the wider context of class tensions and capital accumulation during the period.[44]

At the heart of the Social Security Act was the notion of social insurance. It is now generally accepted that social insurance is a key feature of the 'social' ways of governing which can be traced back to the 1880s and the 'new' and 'social' liberalism that develops out of this in the twentieth century.[45] Between the mid-1880s and the First World War much of Western Europe, Canada and Australasia put some form of social insurance scheme into place. The chief attraction to social liberalism of the practice of social insurance is that because insurance requires regular contributions from the beneficiary, the practice appears as a form of individual thrift and prudence; moreover, it has a contractual form. In contrast to the nineteenth-century poor law and charitable relief, in which it was believed that the recipients made no 'contribution' to their security and were not required to exercise self-reliance, social insurance could be thought of as a legally enforceable right that is also 'earned', rather than the relationship of dependence characteristic of the poor law and charity. That is, social insurance 'carried into the core institutions of social liberalism an underlying concern with independence and prudence, which more than anything else had characterized classical liberalism'.[46] Thus as a 'moral technology of governance, constantly articulating how people should act',[47] the introduction of social insurance involved a shift in the cultural and political understanding of individual 'security' in relation to both the present and future, using state power to reconstitute individual subjectivity around a set of particular practices of citizenship. The Beveridge Report in the UK puts it succinctly: 'social security must be achieved by co-operation between the State and the individual'. In other words, the 'State should *organize* security', but individuals should also show 'incentive, opportunity, responsibility' to cover themselves and their family.[48] But all of this presupposes an objective *in*security in economic life. Via the idea of social insurance this objective insecurity was taken as read, with thrift used to think about and govern the subjective assumptions surrounding it. Far from being the binary opposite of security, insecurity became a tool for the marketing of new security mechanisms. Concomitantly, security becomes a tool for the reshaping of individual behaviour and notions of citizenship, constituting a certain vision of economic order in the process.[49] Roosevelt's New Deal programmes lay clearly within this historical trajectory: the 'social' had become 'securitized'. If social insurance is part of a broader 'will to security',[50] Roosevelt's New Deal programmes conducted under the logic of emergency are a fundamental expression of this historical trajectory and political will.

On the one hand, then, this idea of social security was very much aimed at the working class: it went some way to help reshape notions of responsibility and risk, independence and thrift, among the working class, and so foster new conceptions of citizenship and social solidarity. In so doing it helped cultivate the idea of 'economic security' and popularise the new means by which such security could be achieved: through social, political and cultural reconstruction engineered by the state. This coincided with Roosevelt's attempt to constrain and undermine the more militant tendencies of the organised working class through other means, such as the use of emergency powers to crush industrial action and the introduction of new laws regulating strikes. Through this the industrial working class became increasingly ordered around a regime of insurance contributions administered by the state.[51]

On the other hand, the idea of social security also became important to the way capital reorganised itself during this period. Jennifer Klein has shown that the conjunction of interests around security helped launch a new economy of welfare which in turn helped set in motion a rapid expansion of the insurance, health care, and income maintenance options offered by non-state institutions. Where critics on the Left had used the notion of security as part of a challenge to government, businesses and corporations quickly came to recognise the social and political premium to be gained from the new stress on security. What ensued was a range of political tensions and struggles – between state, capital and labour; and between commercial insurers and non-profit, community- or labour-controlled means of social provision – the outcome of which was that in the years immediately following the Social Security Act major corporations leapt on security as a way of reorganising their corporate interests.[52]

The corporate mentality which had allowed financial and industrial corporations to accommodate themselves to the New Deal more generally meant that insurers and business advisors could very quickly and easily adjust their language and arguments to the new discourse of security – part of their accommodation to the wider idea of uniting 'enlightened industry' and 'enlightened administration' within a National Recovery Administration (NRA).[53] Klein comments that security had become a politically useful term now that the economic times had changed. But it was also an economically useful term now that the political times had changed. William Graham, chief group insurance spokesman of Equitable Life, gave lectures to business groups around the country on the theme of security, while presidents of key corporations preached the new ideology. In the journal *Factory Management and Maintenance* Packard Motor Company President Alvin MacCauley contributed his own views on how 'We Work Toward Worker Security', while in the same journal a few months earlier Standard Oil's President Walter Teagle wrote 'we subscribe to the ideals of worker security'; his essay (February 1936) was called 'Security – This is More Like It'.[54]

Unsurprisingly, insurance companies took the lead in pushing this new idea of security to other companies. 'We in the life insurance business are selling security and preaching security', is how Equitable's Thomas Parkinson put it.[55] Insurance companies became behind-the-scenes promoters of the government programme for security, while government promoted the new corporate 'initiatives' – each legitimised and affirmed the other. Klein writes that by 1940 'life insurers believed that Social Security had been a tremendous boon to the sale of insurance and old-age pensions. Insurance executives instructed their agents to incorporate the new Social Security programme in their sales pitch, emphasizing that federal old-age pensions would meet only the barest subsistence needs'.[56] This quickly led to a set of close institutional connections between 'welfare entrepreneurs' and their main clients, the larger corporations, which increasingly initiated group pension, accident and health plans throughout the mid- to late-1930s. Thus both the commercial purveyors of 'social security' and the immediate consumers of the new policies saw that they could not only survive within this new system, but might actually flourish.

This provided a number of advantages to companies. For a start, the purchase of commercial group insurance became a key mechanism for containing union power, not least through the idea of 'worker security'. More importantly, the plans for security were 'twisted' in ways conducive to business rather than the workers. The key practice was for a company to dovetail its own plans for worker security with those of the government. For example, companies modified their own existing pension plans so that the total retirement annuity including social security benefits ended up being the same as under the former plan. In other words, if the amount of a public pension was likely to equal or exceed the amount owed by the company, the company pension would not be granted. Thus companies directly reduced the benefits by the amount being paid in 'social security' by the state. Moreover, dovetailing benefited upper-income employees and corporate executives most, since companies stared offering supplemental pensions solely for their most well-paid employees: GM created an 'Employees Retirement Plan' for executives and managers earning over $250 per month, while at Kodak anyone earning less than $5,000 was excluded from the company pension plan. Finally, for top corporate executives, pension trusts became a useful tool for avoiding taxes since individual taxes on pension income were deferred. Thus the new insurance schemes functioned as a huge subsidy for large employers who had company plans, and corporations quickly learnt how to use the social security system as a class subsidy for the well-paid, salaried middle class.[57]

It is clear, then, that during these years the concept of security was quickly transformed, tweaked and adjusted as part of a new attempt to restructure social order. The new ideology of security reshaped working-class behaviour and expectations, worked against trade union radicalism, improved the position of the well-paid middle class, preserved the notion of the paternalistic employer, and helped sustain levels of capital accumulation despite the supposedly 'stringent' demands made on business by the state. The radicalised political climate of the 1930s centred on the politics of security compelled corporations to offer a degree of economic security that they had previously failed to do, but corporations did so very much on their own terms, without making old-age or illness support an employee right and by maintaining managerial control. And behind all of this was the implicit idea that those living within capitalism will have to accept the inherent insecurity it produces. In other words, employers sought to use the security plans to demonstrate that the firm was a generous employer. But in shifting emphasis away from state and political arena to private individual economic relationships, employers and insurers redefined the meaning of security, creating a new understanding of security centred on the logic of capital. In this way 'social security' could easily come to reflect liberal ideology and the main assumptions of corporate capital. Thus as well as securing the state, 'social security' became a tool for fabricating a new set of mechanisms around which industrial capital could be re-ordered. As the Chairman of the Board of Directors of Chase National Bank put it, security must imply 'not merely security for certain individuals or groups, however needy or worthy, but *security for the productive system as a whole*'.[58]

The notion of 'economic security', then, was easily applied to corporations and the capitalist system as a whole as much as to the individual worker. 'Worker security' slipped easily into 'corporate security' and turned to the advantage of the capitalist class, thereby strengthening the sinews of capital. And, moreover, the logic of security provided a means for *reshaping* capital and the behaviour of workers around a new regime. Kees Van Der Pijl has shown that while far from being the realisation of a clear-cut programme, Roosevelt's New Deal nonetheless 'consisted of a process of class formation in which various fractions, through intense struggles, successively were integrated into the new hegemonic coalition'.[59] The logic of 'social security', as both theory and practice, was crucial to this new corporate-liberal synthesis, a liberal police power *par excellence* in being used to secure the existing state of corporate capital and fashion around it appropriate behaviour patterns on the part of its subjects and agents. As well as securing the state, 'social security' easily became a mechanism for simultaneously securing capital.

According to Bruce Ackerman, the New Deal was a crucial moment in American constitutional history: in legitimising the activist state via a great act of popular sovereignty, the New Deal consolidated the foundations of activist government and so fundamentally altered America's constitutional politics.[60] We might add that security was central to this activist government, key to the new reformist politics and twentieth-century 'social' liberalism. In *practical* terms 'security' legitimised some limited working-class demands *vis-à-vis* the capitalist economy and could thereby satisfy the demands of large numbers of radicals and socialists. At the same time, however, it also satisfied middle-class desires and was turned to the advantage of corporations, legitimating the latter's place in the modern polity. In *theoretical* terms, 'security' had become central to the dominant ideology, if not *the* dominant idea itself; the modern capitalist social formation had gone some way to becoming 'securitized'.

'Security! The modern world is in constant search for security'; so said Thomas Parkinson, President of Equitable Life Assurance Society.[61] He was speaking at the opening ceremony for the company's exhibit at the New York World's Fair in 1939, at which the company's exhibit was called 'The Equitable Garden of Security'. The *Garden* of Security? It's an interesting thought. Gardens are very much pieces of territory, fenced off from cattle, neighbours and, of course, enemies: a garden without a fence, wall or border is no longer a proper garden. And this fencing is meant to secure the garden: the garden is expected to be a secure space – albeit not as secure as the house. But gardens do not exist 'naturally', despite the rhetoric of the 'natural' which surrounds them. Rather, they are cultivated through human intervention. The garden is an ordered environment: a space fabricated and managed politically. Zygmunt Bauman has commented that 'throughout the modern era, the legislative reason of philosophers chimed well with the all-too-material practices of the states . . . Rationally designed society was the declared *causa finalis* of the modern state. The modern state was a gardening state.'[62] Security was now central to this notion of cultivation, to the gardening state in general. If order has to be fabricated, then security was to become a key technology for the purpose, a key part of the political administration of capitalist modernity: a new form of liberal order conducted in the name of security. From here on in, 'security reasons' could be cited for any and every attempt at a political reordering of society, part and parcel of political action and at the heart of political discourse. Gaining its cardinal political legitimacy in the form of 'social security', the especially important legitimacy attached to this idea would then create an important opening for the idea of *national* security when it eventually emerged in the late-1940s. This would then help legitimise and sustain the new national security state and its march into world history. For more than anything, the garden operates as a metaphor of control: order and surveillance on the one hand, cultivation and progress on the other.[63] Internally it needs to be ordered; externally it needs to be protected. The garden is an image of containment.

CONTAINMENT I: NATIONAL SECURITY, INTERNATIONAL ORDER AND SIX MILLION CORPSES

Despite the commonplace assumption that social security refers merely to a set of social policies concerned with welfare, Roosevelt in fact had a much greater vision for his social security reforms, which were to be introduced as a means of strengthening and defending the nation. At the same time, his emerging idea of national security was not to be restricted to military defence but would have major social consequences. This is the logic of 'national security' originally behind the CES and the Economic Security Bill. 'Our nation's program of social and economic reform is therefore a part of defense, as basic as armaments themselves', he commented in 1939.[64] This was a hint as to how much Roosevelt equated the New Deal with national defence. On the one hand, 'national security' was far from reducible to a question of military hardware; rather, his idea was that American security rested on all constituents of national power, especially on the unity of the American people. On the other hand, 'social security' was a means of strengthening the nation – hence the metaphor of war which so permeated the New Deal. Thus the security policies of the New Deal wove together the domestic and international such that they were almost indistinguishable. Roosevelt's famous 'Four Freedoms' speech of 6 January 1941 rested heavily on a notion of security which oscillated between the security of individual liberties and the security of nations. Writers interested in developing the international dimensions of security in this period were also picking up on the same connection. In an attempt to define security in terms of national strength *vis-à-vis* the strength of allies and other international powers in his 1941 article on 'American Security', for example, Edward Mead Earle initially distinguishes this kind of security from 'domestic' security: 'this definition does not deal, of course, with security in the domestic sense, important as that is'. But he then adds that 'social security, especially manifest in the phenomenon of unemployment, has important repercussions in foreign affairs'.[65] In this light, social security programmes were seen as the first line of national defence by many liberals.[66]

It was this broad vision of security at the heart of the New Deal that helped shape and develop the idea of national security. In his State of the Union Address in January 1944, Roosevelt outlined his discussions with other leaders concerning the conduct of the war and the prospects for the postwar world.

> The one supreme objective for the future, which we discussed for each Nation individually, and for all the United Nations, can be summed up in word: Security. And that means not only physical security which provides safety from attacks by aggressors. It means also economic security, social security, moral security – in a family of Nations.

The project of security at home had in Roosevelt's view achieved a new set of rights to decent housing, education, good health, protection from economic fears: 'all of these rights spell security'. But this security was to be the basis for peace in the world. Just as the New Deal brought 'social security' to the US, so 'one world' of a family of nations would bring 'political security' to the entire world. Aid to other nations would have the same effect as social welfare programmes within the United States – it would achieve 'security' for 'all individual men and women and children in all Nations'.[67] As Schurman has argued:

> Roosevelt's vision of the postwar world was an extension of his New Deal to the world as a whole . . . The essence of the New Deal was the notion that big government must spend liberally in order to achieve security and progress. Thus, postwar security would require liberal outlays by the United States in order to overcome the chaos created by the war . . . Aid to Russia and other poor nations would have the same effect as social welfare programs within the United States – it would give them security to overcome chaos and prevent them from turning into violent revolutionaries.[68]

This 'one world' would quickly become the 'free world' and be founded on a particular concept of economic order and pitched against an enemy the existence of which would justify the permanent use of emergency powers and a perpetual war. 'Dr. New Deal' of the 1930s may have handed the scalpel and drugs to 'Dr. Win-the-War' in the

1940s, but they were always working on the same body politic and dealing with different symptoms of the same disease. Security was the cure.[69]

But 'social security' was clearly an inadequate term for this, associated as it now was with 'soft' domestic policy issues such as old-age insurance. 'Collective security' would not do, associated as it was with the dull internationalism of Wilson on the one hand and still very much connected to the institutions of social security on the other.[70] Only one term would do: national security.

This not to imply that 'national security' was simply adopted and adapted from 'social security'. Rather, what we are dealing with here is another ideological circuit, this time between 'national security' and 'social security', in which the policies 'insuring' the security of the population are a means of securing the body politic, and vice versa;[71] a circuit in which, to paraphrase David Peace in the epigraph to this chapter, one can have one's teeth kicked out in the name of national security and put back in through social security. Social security and national security were woven together: the social and the national were the warp and the weft of the security fabric. The warp and the weft, that is, of a broader vision of economic security.

Robert Pollard has suggested that 'the concept of "economic security" – the idea that American interests would be best served by an open and integrated economic system, as opposed to a large peacetime military establishment – was firmly established during the wartime period'.[72] In fact, the concept of 'economic security' became a concept of *international* politics in this period, but the concept itself had a longer history as the underlying idea behind social security in the 1930s, as we have seen. *Economic* security, in this sense, provides the important link between social and national security, becoming liberalism's strategic weapon of choice and *the* main policy instrument from 1945.[73] As one State Department memo of February 1944 put it, 'the development of sound international economic relations is closely related to the problem of security'.[74] But it would also continue to be used to think about the political administration of *internal* order. Hence Roosevelt's comment that 'we must plan for, and help to bring about, an expanded economy which will result in more security [and] so that the conditions of 1932 and the beginning of 1933 won't come back again'.[75] On security grounds, inside and outside were constantly folding into one another, the domestic and the foreign never quite properly distinguishable. The reason why lay in the kind of economic order to be secured: both domestically and internationally, 'economic security' is coda for capitalist order.

Giving a lecture at Harvard University on 5 June 1947, Secretary of State George C. Marshall recalled the disruption to the European economy during the war and Europe's continuing inability to feed itself, and suggested that if the US did not help there would be serious economic, social and political deterioration which would in turn have a knock-on effect on US capital. The outcome was a joint plan submitted to the US from European states at the end of August, after much wrangling with the Soviet Union, requesting $28 billion over a four-year period (the figure was reduced when finally agreed by Congress). The European Recovery Program (ERP, known as the Marshall Plan) which emerged has gone down as an economic panacea, 'saving' Europe from economic disaster. But as the first of many such 'Plans', all the way down to the recent 'reconstruction' of Iraq, it does not take much to read the original Marshall Plan through the lens of security and liberal order-building.

Alan Milward has suggested that the conventional reading of the Marshall Plan and US aid tends to accept the picture of post-war Europe on the verge of collapse and with serious social and economic discontent, such that it needed to be rescued by US aid. In fact, excluding Germany, no country was actually on the verge of collapse. There were no bank crashes, very few bankruptcies and the evidence of a slow down in industrial production is unconvincing. There is also little evidence of grave distress or a general deterioration in the standard of living. By late-1946 production had roughly equalled pre-war levels in all countries except Germany. And yet Marshall Aid came about. Milward argues that the Marshall Plan was designed not to increase the rate of recovery in European countries or to prevent European economies from deteriorating, but to sustain ambitious, new, expansionary economic and social policies in Western European countries which were in fact already in full-bloom conditions. In other words, the Marshall Plan was predominantly designed for political objectives – hence conceived and rushed through by the Department of State itself.[76]

Milward's figures are compelling, and complicate the conventional picture of the Marshall Plan as simply a form of economic aid. But to distinguish reasons that are 'economic' reasons from reasons that are 'political' misses the extent to which, in terms of security, the economic and the political are entwined. This is why the Marshall Plan is so inextricably linked to the Truman Doctrine's offer of military aid and intervention beyond US borders, a new global commitment at the heart of which was the possibility of intervention in the affairs of other countries. As Joyce and Gabriel Kolko have argued, the important dimension of the Truman Doctrine is revealed in the various drafts of Truman's speech before it was finally delivered on 12 March, and the private memos of the period. Members of the cabinet and other top officials understood very clearly that the United States was now defining a strategy and budget appropriate to its new global commitments, and that a far greater involvement in other countries was now pending, especially on the economic level.[77] Hence the plethora of references to 'a world-wide trend away from the system of free enterprise', which the State Department's speech-writers thought a 'grave threat' to American interests. Truman's actual speech to Congress is therefore more interesting for what it implied than what it stated explicitly. And what it implied was the politics behind the Marshall Plan: economic security as a means of maintaining political order against the threat of communism.

The point, then, is not just that the Marshall Plan was 'political' – how could any attempt to reshape global capital be anything *but* political? It is fairly clear that the Marshall Plan was multi-dimensional, and to distinguish reasons that are 'economic' reasons from reasons that are 'political' misses the extent to which the economic, political and military are entwined. The point is that it was very much a project driven by the ideology of security.[78] The referent object of 'security' here is 'economic order'. The government and the emerging national security bureaucracy saw the communist threat as economic rather than military. As Latham notes, at first glance the idea of military security within a broad context of economic containment merely appears to be one more dimension of strength within the liberal order. But in another respect the project of economic security might itself be viewed as the very force that made military security appear to be necessary. In this sense, the priority given to *economic* security was the driving force behind the US commitment to underwrite military security for Western Europe.[79] The protection and expansion of capital came to be seen as the path to security, and vice versa.

This created the grounds for a *re-ordering of global capital* involving a constellation of class and corporate forces as well as state power, undertaken in the guise of national security. NSC-68, the most significant national security document to emerge in this period, stated that the 'overall policy at the present time may be described as one designed to foster a world environment in which the American system can survive and flourish'.[80] In this sense we can also read the International Monetary Fund (IMF) and General Agreement on Tariffs and Trade (GATT) of 1947, the Brussels Pact of March 1948 and the nascent movement towards 'European Union' as part and parcel of the security project being mapped out.[81] The key institutions of 'international order' in this period invoked a particular vision of order with a view to reshaping global capital as a means of bringing 'security' – political, social and economic – from the communist threat.

'Communist', that is, as opposed to 'Soviet'. Communism, of course, predates and exceeds the Soviet Union. But the nature of the military threat ascribed to the latter is related to the character of the former as a more general threat to the system of private property. The implication drawn from this by David Campbell is that 'the well-developed antipathy towards communism within the United States stems from the way in which the danger to the private ownership of property it embodies is a code for distinguishing the "civilized" from the "barbaric" (or the normal from the pathological)'. This, Campbell suggests, 'is the basis for the interpretive framework which constitutes the Soviet Union as a danger independent of any military capacity'.[82] Thus the rise of the national security state was not dependent on any real military threat posed by the Soviet Union, which even the US national security managers correctly identified at the time as both limited and weak. 'The Soviet Union does not want war with the United States', wrote Allen Dulles in 1948.[83] George Kennan confessed in 1956 that 'the image of Stalinist Russia poised and yearning to attack the West . . . was largely a creation of the Western imagination', and even the much later US *National Security Strategy* released in September 2002 admits that 'in the Cold War . . . we faced a generally status quo, risk-averse adversary'.[84] This view is confirmed by some of the official documents of the time. The 'Resume of the World Situation', 6 November 1947, put out by the Policy Planning Staff (PPS), notes that 'the danger of war is vastly exaggerated in many quarters' and that 'the Soviet Government neither wants nor expects war'.[85] Hence when comparing the US and USSR, NSC-68 makes not one single empirical claim about actual Soviet deployments. Choosing instead to compare production levels in key industries, the document has the US way out in front on almost all measures: 80 million tons of ingot steel produced in the US compared to 21 in the Soviet Union; 617 thousand tons of aluminium compared to 135 thousand; 276 million tons of crude oil compared to 33 million; 582 million tons of coal compared to 250 million tons; 35 million tons of cement compared to 10; 5,273,000 motor vehicles compared to 500,000, and so on.[86] And for as long as the Cold War lasted the US was always superior in military terms and well ahead in the nuclear arms race. It is also necessary to point out that by this historical point it should have been clear that the Soviet Union was a decidedly *anti*-revolutionary force, turning against genuinely revolutionary movements elsewhere, of which the US was well aware.[87] In that sense the Soviet Union was a side issue. As NSC-68 put it, the overall security policy was one which the US 'would probably pursue even if there were no Soviet threat'. Again: 'Even if there were no Soviet Union we would face the problem of the free society, accentuated many fold in this industrial age, of reconciling order, security, the need for participation, with the requirements of freedom'.[88] In other words, the same policies would have been followed *even if there were no Soviet threat*. The issue was communism as a threat to private property and thus to the vision of an 'economic order' of the 'civilised West'; that is, communism as an alternative socio-economic order, not the Soviet Union as a military threat. And the real danger of this communism was that it might reside inside the civilised West rather than 'over there' in the East. The inability to articulate this clearly, however, meant that the Soviet Union remained centre stage of the project being mapped out in the name of security.

This problem of the internal threat will result in the generation of a huge security–identity–loyalty complex, to which I turn in the chapter to follow. The point here is that the response to the real possibility of a socio-economic order distinct from capitalism was couched in the form of 'economic security'. Symptomatically, three other events of note occurred between Marshall's Harvard lecture in early June and the eventual request from the European states in August 1947. First, in July Congress passed the National Security Act, the 'Magna Charta' of the national security state.[89] Second, in the same month George

Kennan's article 'The Sources of Soviet Conduct' appeared (under the authorship 'X') in the journal *Foreign Affairs*, a distillation and development of his 8,000-word 'Long Telegram' from February 1946, which had already been widely circulated and read (Navy Secretary James Forrestal had distributed hundreds of copies throughout the administration).[90] And third, on 10 June the Senate Appropriations Committee wrote to Marshall warning him that in the State Department 'there is a deliberate, calculated program being carried out not only to protect Communist personnel in high places, but to reduce security and intelligence protection to a nullity',[91] a letter which played a pivotal role in the rise of the Loyalty Program announced by Truman in Executive Order 9835 earlier that year; I shall leave aside discussion of this third event until the following chapter.

Kennan's article is now famous for introducing the idea of 'containment' as a military doctrine, but it is worth noting that Kennan's stress was not a Soviet military power as the biggest threat, but Soviet political power: 'what I was talking about when I mentioned the containment of Soviet power was not the containment by military means of a military threat, but the political containment of a political threat'.[92] Kennan thus looked to economic aid to produce the necessary resistance to communism.[93] In such a context it was relatively easy for the Truman government to overcome Congressional recalcitrance to the Marshall Plan by promoting it as *the* security measure – as the key to containment. In a memo to Truman in December 1947 outlining a reply to critics of foreign aid Forrestal suggested that:

> My answer . . . is that you have to look at our own security not merely in terms of great military power or of wealth . . . but rather in terms of these objectives: High domestic production, a balanced budget, a sound currency, and adequate and expendable defense organization resting upon diversified domestic industry.[94]

Similarly, US observers returning to Europe noted that the likely success of the Plan lay in its security implications. The Herter Committee, for example, having travelled to Europe, came to the view that 'any Marshall Plan can have assured returns in security values only'.[95] This view was perhaps put most explicitly by the Herter Committee's legal consultant, Allen Dulles. Later to become Director of the CIA (from 1953 to 1961), Dulles was co-founder of the Committee for the Marshall Plan, consultant to the House Select Committee on Foreign Aid, and President of the Council on Foreign Relations. As part of the concerted effort to sell the Marshall Plan, Dulles wrote a book on the subject, in which he made clear that as the outcome of the trends in foreign policy, the Marshall Plan was 'based on our view of the requirements of American security'. The Plan, in his view, was 'the only peaceful course now open to us which may answer the communist challenge to our way of life and our national security'.[96] The major National Security Council documents from 1948 through to 1950 all highlight this economic dimension of the security project. NSC-20/1, for example, an overview of 'US objectives with respect to Russia' supervised by Kennan and released in August 1948, noted approvingly the role of the Marshall Plan in securing the US in its objectives. NSC-68 noted that 'foreign economic policy is . . . an instrument which can powerfully influence the world environment in ways favourable to the security and welfare of this country', again citing the Marshall Plan as a principle feature of the policy.[97] By conjoining security and political economy in efforts such as the Marshall Plan, the US was able to gain support for both the politico-strategic and economic dimensions of liberal order-building, with 'containment' acting as a policy unifying economic statecraft and security objectives.

Even in programmes which seem obviously focused on military issues, it was in fact economic security that was the driving force. The 'Military Aid Program' (MAP) to help rearm Western Europe in the light of an emerging NATO was administered by the State Department rather than the Defense Department because MAP's main purpose was to continue the Marshall Plan's policy of organising economic stability and thus political order in Western Europe. The Mutual Defense Assistance Act of 1949 explicitly stated this: 'Congress recognizes that economic recovery is essential to international peace and security and must be given clear priority'.[98] Moreover, although the Marshall Plan formally ended in December 1951, US aid to Europe continued throughout the 1950s, albeit ostensibly focused on military support, under its new title: 'The Mutual Security Program'. This laid the foundation for 'economic modernisation' as the central paradigm of US strategy thereafter, and for the ideology of security to appropriate the mantle of 'development', about which I say more in Chapter 5.

In other words, the new international order moved very quickly to reassert the connection between economic and national security: the commitment to the former was simultaneously a commitment to the latter, and vice versa. As the doctrine of national security was being born, the major player on the international stage would aim to use perhaps its most important power of all – its economic strength – in order to re-order the world. And this re-ordering was conducted through the idea of 'economic security'.[99] Despite the fact that 'economic security' would never be formally defined beyond 'economic order' or 'economic well-being',[100] the significant conceptual consistency between economic security and liberal order-building also had a strategic ideological role. By playing on notions of 'economic well-being', economic security seemed to emphasise economic and thus 'human' needs over military ones. The reshaping of global capital, international order and the exercise of state power could thus look decidedly liberal and 'humanitarian'. This appearance helped co-opt the liberal Left into the process and, of course, played on individual desire for personal security by using notions such as 'personal freedom' and 'social equality'.[101]

Marx and Engels once highlighted the historical role of the bourgeoisie in shaping the world according to its own interests.

> The need of a constantly expanding market for its products chases the bourgeoisie over the whole surface of the globe. It must nestle everywhere, settle everywhere, establish connections everywhere . . . It compels all nations, on pain of extinction, to adopt the bourgeois mode of production; it compels them . . . to become bourgeois in themselves. In one word, it creates a world after its own image.[102]

In the second half of the twentieth century this ability to 'batter down all Chinese walls' would still rest heavily on the logic of capital, but would also come about in part under the guise of security. The *whole world* became a garden to be cultivated – to be recast according to the logic of security. In the space of fifteen years the concept 'economic security' had moved from connoting insurance policies for working people to the desire to shape the world in a capitalist fashion – and back again. In fact, it has constantly shifted between these registers ever since, being used for the constant reshaping of world order and resulting in a comprehensive level of intervention and policing all over the globe. Global order has come to be fabricated and administered according to a security doctrine underpinned by the logic of capital-accumulation and a bourgeois conception of order. By incorporating within it a particular vision of economic order, the concept of national security implies the interrelatedness of so many different social, economic, political and military factors that more or less any development anywhere can be said to impact on liberal order in general and America's core interests in particular. Not only could bourgeois Europe be recast around the regime of capital, but so too could the whole international order as capital not only nestled, settled and established connections, but also 'secured' everywhere.

Security politics thereby became the basis of a distinctly liberal philosophy of global 'intervention', fusing global issues of economic management with domestic policy formations in an ambitious and frequently violent strategy. Here lies the Janus-faced character of American foreign policy.[103] One face is the 'good liberal cop': friendly, prosperous and democratic, sending money and help around the globe when problems emerge, so that the world's nations are shown how they can alleviate their misery and perhaps even enjoy some prosperity. The other face is the 'bad liberal cop': should one of these nations decide, either through parliamentary procedure, demands for self-determination or violent revolution to address its own social problems in ways that conflict with the interests of capital and the bourgeois concept of liberty, then the authoritarian dimension of liberalism shows its face; the 'liberal moment' becomes the moment of violence. This Janus-faced character has meant that through the mandate of security the US, as the national security state *par excellence*, has seen fit to either overtly or covertly re-order the affairs of myriads of nations – those 'rogue' or 'outlaw' states on the 'wrong side of history'.[104]

'Extrapolating the figures as best we can', one CIA agent commented in 1991, 'there have been about 3,000 major covert operations and over 10,000 minor operations – all illegal, and all designed to disrupt, destabilize, or modify the activities of other countries', adding that 'every covert operation has been rationalized in terms of U.S. national security'.[105] These would include 'interventions' in Greece, Italy, France, Turkey, Macedonia, the Ukraine, Cambodia, Indonesia, China, Korea, Burma, Vietnam, Thailand, Ecuador, Chile, Argentina,

Brazil, Guatemala, Costa Rica, Cuba, the Dominican Republic, Uruguay, Bolivia, Grenada, Paraguay, Nicaragua, El Salvador, the Philippines, Honduras, Haiti, Venezuela, Panama, Angola, Ghana, Congo, South Africa, Albania, Lebanon, Grenada, Libya, Somalia, Ethiopia, Afghanistan, Iran, Iraq, and many more, and many of these more than once. Next up are the '60 or more' countries identified as the bases of 'terror cells' by Bush in a speech on 1 June 2002.[106] The methods used have varied: most popular has been the favoured technique of liberal security – 'making the economy scream' via controls, interventions and the imposition of neo-liberal regulations. But a wide range of other techniques have been used: terror bombing; subversion; rigging elections; the use of the CIA's 'Health Alteration Committee' whose mandate was to 'incapacitate' foreign officials; drug-trafficking;[107] and the sponsorship of terror groups, counter-insurgency agencies, death squads. Unsurprisingly, some plain old fascist groups and parties have been co-opted into the project, from the attempt at reviving the remnants of the Nazi collaborationist Vlasov Army for use against the USSR to the use of fascist forces to undermine democratically elected governments, such as in Chile; indeed, one of the reasons fascism flowed into Latin America was because of the ideology of national security.[108] Concomitantly, 'national security' has meant a policy of non-intervention where satisfactory 'security partnerships' could be established with certain authoritarian and military regimes: Spain under Franco, the Greek junta, Chile, Iraq, Iran, Korea, Indonesia, Cambodia, Taiwan, South Vietnam, the Philippines, Turkey, the five Central Asian republics that emerged with the break-up of the USSR, and China. Either way, the whole world was to be included in the new 'secure' global liberal order.

The result has been the slaughter of untold numbers. John Stockwell, who was part of a CIA project in Angola which led to the deaths of over 20,000 people, puts it like this:

> Coming to grips with these U.S./CIA activities in broad numbers and figuring out how many people have been killed in the jungles of Laos or the hills of Nicaragua is very difficult. But, adding them up as best we can, we come up with a figure of six million people killed – and this is a minimum figure. Included are: one million killed in the Korean War, two million killed in the Vietnam War, 800,000 killed in Indonesia, one million in

Cambodia, 20,000 killed in Angola – the operation I was part of – and 22,000 killed in Nicaragua.[109]

Note that the six million is a minimum figure, that he omits to mention rather a lot of other interventions, and that he was writing in 1991. This is security as the slaughter bench of history.

All of this has been more than confirmed by events in the twenty-first century: in a speech on 1 June 2002, which became the basis of the official *National Security Strategy of the United States* in September of that year, President Bush reiterated that the US has a unilateral right to overthrow any government in the world, and launched a new round of slaughtering to prove it.

While much has been made about the supposedly 'new' doctrine of preemption in the early twenty-first century, the policy of preemption has a long history as part of national security doctrine.

The United States has long maintained the option of pre-emptive actions to counter a sufficient threat to our national security. The greater the threat, the greater is the risk of inaction – and the more compelling the case for taking anticipatory action to defend ourselves . . . To forestall or prevent such hostile acts by our adversaries, the United States will, if necessary, act pre-emptively.[110]

In other words, the security policy of the world's only superpower in its current 'war on terror' is still underpinned by a notion of liberal order-building based on a certain vision of 'economic order'. The *National Security Strategy* concerns itself with a 'single sustainable model for national success' based on 'political and economic liberty', with whole sections devoted to the security benefits of 'economic liberty', and the benefits to liberty of the security strategy proposed.[111] Economic security (that is, 'capitalist accumulation') in the guise of 'national security' is now used as the justification for all kinds of 'intervention', still conducted where necessary in alliance with fascists, gangsters and drug cartels, and the proliferation of 'national security'-type regimes has been the result. So while the national security state was in one sense a structural bi-product of the US's place in global capitalism, it was also vital to the fabrication of an international order founded on the power of capital. National security, in effect, became the perfect strategic tool for landscaping the human garden.[112] This was to also have huge domestic consequences, as the idea of containment would also come to reshape the American social order, helping fabricate a security apparatus intimately bound up with national identity and thus the politics of loyalty.

Chapter 4

SECURITY, IDENTITY, LOYALTY

_____

The standards of patriotism for my profession are about to be set by three policemen from the FBI . . . Who should be employed on radio and who shouldn't be employed will be determined by three guys whose favored source of information is the House Un-American Activities Committee. You'll see how courageous the bosses are in the face of this shit. Watch how the profit system holds out against the pressure. Freedom of thought, of speech, of due process – screw all that. People are going to be destroyed, buddy. It's not livelihoods that are going to be lost, it's *lives*. People are going to die. They're going to get sick and die, they're going to jump off buildings and die. By the time this is over, the people with names on that list are going to wind up in concentration camps.

Philip Roth, *I Married a Communist* (1998)

On 26 October 2001, President Bush signed into law a rather substantial bill, running to over 340 pages, specifying roles for some 40 federal agencies and carrying 21 legal amendments, called the Uniting and Strengthening America by Providing Appropriate Tools Required to Intercept and Obstruct Terrorism Act. The Act changed criminal law and immigration procedures to allow people to be held indefinitely once charged, altered intelligence-gathering procedures to allow for the monitoring of people's reading habits through surveillance of library and bookshop records, and introduced other new measures to allow for greater access to property, e-mail, computers, and financial and educational records; all for the purpose of defeating the new terrorist enemy. The Act, in other words, was about national security: how to get it, how to maintain it, how to defend it. But it was also immediately notable for the somewhat wordy title, clearly designed for the acronym it would produce: USA PATRIOT. The implication was clear: this was an Act for American patriotism; to oppose it would be unpatriotic. In other words, it was not just about national security, but also very much about national identity. If we set the Act alongside the wider outburst of patriotism within the US since 11 September 2001, it becomes clear that the attacks on that date were seen as a crisis in national identity as well as national security. And one of the most notable features of the subsequent 'war on terror' has been its grounding in 'identity' – in the construction of both the 'evil' 'alien' enemy and the 'good' American.[1]

In this chapter I aim to explore this connection between security and identity. I do so by shifting the focus to the ways in which security is both cultivated and mobilised internally. Benedict Anderson's insight that the nation is an imagined community[2] has generated a whole range of important work on national identity: its origins, construction, myths and practices. What interests me here is that if national identity is integrally linked with the imagination and, as we also know, one of the things about the imagination is that it plays around with fears, dangers and insecurities,[3] then what if the nation is imagined as insecure? And if it is imagined as insecure, then what does this tell us about the links between security and identity – between an imagined national identity and an imagined national (in)security?

To deal with these questions this chapter explores the ways that domestic order has been cultivated through the logic of national security by examining the shaping of identity during and through the rise of the national security state. The central argument is that security and identity are inextricably linked, not in the obvious existential or ontological ways discussed by sociologists and psychoanalysts,[4] but in a far more political way: that the fabrication of national security goes hand in hand with the fabrication of national identity, and vice versa. Thus as well as being a form of political discourse centred on the state, as we have seen in previous chapters, the ideology of security also serves as a form of identity-construction, a construction which in turn reinforces the security measures enacted in its name. To develop this argument, and build on some of the insights from work in this field,[5] I return to some of the formative texts and practices during the rise of the national security state to tease out the mutually constitutive relationship between a particular national identity and the claims of national security. To capture this mutual constitution I draw on the idea of loyalty as a key political technology for simultaneously gauging identity and reaffirming security. The hope – which I will keep at arms length – is that tracing the historical emergence of this security–identity–loyalty complex might shed some light on current political practices in the 'war on terror'.

CONTAINMENT II: NATIONAL SECURITY, DOMESTIC ORDER AND THE FEAR OF DISINTEGRATION

A number of scholars have shown that the ideology of national security depended – and continues to depend – on a system of symbolic representation defining national identity by reference to an 'Other'. At the end of the Second World War in America this 'Other' lacked specificity. Truman's references to 'two ways of life' in the speech to Congress which launched the Truman Doctrine were to totalitarianism and democracy, not communism and capitalism, and 'totalitarian' referred to many different things: 'Nazi, Communist or Fascist, or Franco, or anything else – they are all alike', as Truman put it; hence the use of 'Red Fascism' to try and describe the Stalin regime.[6] This was no doubt due to the conceptual indeterminacy of 'totalitarianism', the fact that the war against fascism was still recent and, perhaps, an intellectual and political unwillingness to try and make sense of some of the distinctions. But a range of changes in international power meant that communism in general and the Soviet regime in particular soon became the focus of US policy: the refusal or unwillingness of the Soviets to participate in the Marshall Plan, having fallen into the trap set for them by Marshall;[7] the emergence of rifts within communism, such as Tito's defiance of Soviet power and the possibility that Mao might follow in Tito's footsteps, with the US aiming to exploit any rifts in the international communist movement;[8] and the militancy of the communist movement world-wide, in both its Stalinist and non-Stalinist versions. This focus on the Soviet Union was encouraged by a thoroughly reactionary Congress and the influence of Kennan's essay on the sources of Soviet conduct.

In this context the logic of 'totalitarianism' underwent a major political shift, coming to refer almost entirely to 'Soviet communism'. This made it a lot easier to justify the increasing use of former Nazis by a security elite happy to use 'any bastard as long as he's anti-

Communist', even those known to be guilty of serious war crimes.[9] It also helped circumvent any suggestion of hypocrisy concerning, for example, the increasingly obvious fact that there were quite a few regimes which might have qualified for the title 'totalitarian' but with which the US state appeared perfectly happy. But the major gain was that all that had once been intended with the term 'totalitarianism' could now be captured with the term 'communism', which could now stand alone as the radical Other.[10] As such, communism became *the* security threat, and in the broadest possible sense of the term: national, social, and economic.

As we noted in Chapter 2, it quickly became clear that this un-American Other was potentially inside as well as outside, an enemy within as much as an enemy without. George Kennan believed that it was 'human impulses which give rise to the nightmares of totalitarianism' which, until now, 'Providence had allocated only to other peoples'.[11] But if the impulse to totalitarianism – that is, to communism – lay inside human beings, then America could easily go in that very direction. This lent weight to the 'Trojan Horse theory', in which it was thought that the Soviet Union could undermine American society by having communists within unions and other mass organisations, and establishing 'front' organisations of their own.[12] NSC-68 suggested that one of the Kremlin's 'preferred techniques' was to 'subvert by infiltration and intimidation'. As a consequence:

> Every institution of our society is an instrument which it is sought to stultify and turn against our purposes. Those that touch most closely our material and moral strength are obviously all the prime targets, labor unions, civic enterprises, schools, churches, and all media for influencing opinion. The effort is not so much to make them serve obvious Soviet ends as to prevent them from serving our ends, and thus to make them sources of confusion in our economy, our culture and our body politic.[13]

We need to therefore understand the ideology of national security not only as an expression of US global reach, but also in the context of the state's everyday policing of its own citizens noted in Chapter 2. This policing would come to act as a crucial expression of domestic transformation in the name of security.

Typical here is the Internal Security Act (the McCarran Act). Passed in 1950 after a difficult legislative process (Truman of all people initially sought to veto the bill on the grounds that it was too authoritarian), the Act saw a newly formed Senate Internal Security Subcommittee working closely with the FBI, required 'Communist organizations' to register with the Attorney General, strengthened the espionage laws, and tightened the immigration and naturalisation laws for anyone who had been connected with advocating any form of totalitarianism (to stop too many from 'outside' getting 'inside') unless they had since demonstrated a positive rejection of it. Title II of the Act, known as 'The Emergency Detention Act', embodied the ideological circuit between security and emergency by allowing for the declaration of an 'internal security emergency' under which individuals thought likely to be spies or saboteurs could be interned. The Justice Department had since 1946 secretly authorised a 'Security Index' empowering the FBI to maintain a list of persons, known as 'the Portfolio', for internment during states of emergency and arrested under a single 'master warrant'. By 1950 the Index held the names of just under 12,000 persons, of which 11,539 were American citizens, and at its peak in 1954 contained the names of 26,174 persons; by 1952 Congress authorised and funded six detention centres for an even wider use of internment for such persons.[14]

Like much 'security legislation' the Internal Security Act reiterated and repeated other laws already in existence, but in the wider context of the other security documentation of the period it has a profound significance. Taken alongside the documents put out by the National Security Council, the Internal Security Act helped enact a strategy of Otherness which re-drew the boundaries of national identity by simultaneously aiming to exclude the external threat and to police and suppress internal dissent, a tactic performed by eliding any differences between the two. The discourse of national security thus generated a mode of thought which simultaneously posited a distinction between inside and outside and then just as quickly obliterated it. The binary system of symbolic representation in which this discourse was and is conducted implies an un-American other and operates a language of ideological opposites (communism v. capitalism, terrorism v. democracy, totalitarianism v. free world). Yet because the external dangers have internal ramifications, and the internal dangers are generated by external connections, the internal and external, domestic and foreign, national and international, are ultimately indistinguishable. By the twenty-first century this had been clarified by the security state itself: 'We have taken a broad view of national security. In the new era, sharp distinctions between the "foreign" and the "domestic" no longer apply'.[15]

National security, then, does not just facilitate the reordering of international society, but postulates the interrelatedness of so many different *internal* political, economic and social factors that virtually nothing is beyond its concern. Characterised by expansiveness concerning domestic issues and a tendency to colonise more and more areas of social being, security comes to obscure any distinction between the civil and military, the internal and external, to the extent that the whole of civil society ends up being administered according to the doctrine. This political administration of civil society by the state, the police project *par excellence*, concerns not just the modes of economic life, as discussed in Chapter 3, but also operates on the psychological and cultural level. In this regard the NSC documents of the early national security state are instructive. NSC-20/4, the definitive statement of US policy toward the Soviet Union until NSC-68, stressed that to 'maximise our economic potential' and assure 'the internal security of the United States' against the Soviet Union, the state should 'keep the U.S. public fully informed and cognizant of the threats to our national security so that it will be prepared to support the measures we must accordingly adopt'.[16] Reasserting this insight, a January 1951 study by the Joint Chiefs of Staff suggested that as 'the basic menace to the United States and its allies from within is as great as the menace from without, the mobilisation of the non-physical assets, the minds and hearts of men of the free world, is as important as the mobilisation of the physical resources'.[17]

This mobilisation of hearts and minds again worked in a number of directions, all of which remain pertinent to current security practices. The most obvious is of course the constant exaggeration of the enemy threat and capabilities, aided by the possibility of annihilation through nuclear war or 'weapons of mass destruction' and made all the more easy by the cult of secrecy surrounding the information in question. Moreover, since security is heavily dependent on 'intelligence', *all* information becomes potentially useful for security reasons. On this basis 'the State Department monitored editorials in 125 newspapers, assessed the articles of leading columnists, reviewed the statements of political leaders, and studied the resolutions of private religious, philanthropic, and economic organizations.'[18] As well as gathering information, however, the Truman administration also aimed to *shape* opinion and attitudes, a form of surveillance and intelligence-gathering designed to decide on the outcome of public debates. The US national security documents of the time, and more or less every national security document ever since, are interesting for their stress on psychological operations targeted *internally* towards the American people as much as externally towards the enemy and suggesting that the security project is as much an ideological and cultural offensive as it is military or economic; conversely, it also suggests the extent to which culture has been used as one of the disciplinary techniques of liberal power.[19] To this end, the political warfare carried out under the guise of national security involved a huge cultural, psychological and ideological propaganda operation – a security-driven *Kulturkampf* and a culture-driven security struggle.

The NSC ordered the State Department to 'develop a vigorous and effective ideological campaign' to protect American values, virtues and interests on a global scale.[20] The Information and Educational Exchange Act 1948 (the 'Smith-Mundt Act') aimed at deploying all forms of media 'to promote the better understanding of the United States among the peoples of the world'. This was followed by the creation of the Psychological Strategy Board in 1951 with much the same remit. Through developments such as these much of news about the early Cold War could be scripted, and often produced, by the defence establishment, such as through the CIA-run Radio Free Europe and Radio Liberty. These were broadcast to countries behind the Iron Curtain with the air of a private spontaneous anti-communist organisation (a common feature of security strategy – Kennan played up the supposed 'voluntarism' of traditional American life in generating 'organized public support of resistance to tyranny': 'throughout our history, private American citizens have banded together to champion the cause of freedom for people suffering under oppression . . . Our proposal is that this tradition be revived to further American national interests').[21] The Campaign for Truth, launched two months before NSC-68, aimed at encouraging newspaper editors to back the Cold War and support the strategic content of NSC-68. Described at the time as a 'Marshall Plan in the field of ideas', none of the newspaper editors questioned their enlistment in the Campaign, and most went so far as to falsify their reports to the public of the security service's role in these programmes.

The most elaborate part of this ideological attempt to create a public sense of the 'American heritage' came with the red-white-and-blue Freedom Train sponsored by Attorney General Tom Clark and an organisation formed to carry through the plan, the American Heritage Foundation, and launched in May 1947 between the Marshall Plan and the National Security Act. Christened 'The Spirit of 1776' and touring 322 cities across 37,000 miles and through 48 states from September 1947 to the end of 1948, some 3.5 million visitors came to see the Train's documents, including the Declaration of Independence, the Bill of Rights, one of the 13 original copies of the Constitution, the Gettysburg Address, and the German and Japanese surrender documents that ended World War II as a contrast to the sacred texts of American history. Visitors were also encouraged to sing a 'Freedom Pledge' and sign a 'Freedom Scroll' before boarding the Train. While it is true to say that 'the train became the focus of disputed meanings', including 'the liberal aim of curbing right wing bigotry, the conservative goal of combating left wing ideologies, and rather neutral targets like juvenile delinquency',[22] the key intention of the Train is not disputed: it was to reaffirm for the American people a faith in the nation's heritage and in their own identity as Americans, to construct a specifically 'American' ideology, and to thereby spread a certain message of freedom, democratic consumption and consensual capitalism by wiping out from the image of America any hint of class and race conflict. A press release from Clark's Department of Justice in December 1947 suggested that 'indoctrination in democracy is the essential catalytic agent needed to blend our various groups into one American family'; 'preaching Americanism is an affirmative declaration of our faith in ourselves'.[23] In this it was aided by the same message carried in alternate cultural forms: a song written for the same project by Irving Berlin, called 'The Freedom Train' – 'not the Chattanooga Choo-Choo . . . This song is a train song where the engineer is Uncle Sam' – recorded by Bing Crosby and the Andrews Sisters; books such as *Our American Heritage*, compiled by the editors of *Life* magazine and relating the American past to a contemporary society full of white middle-class themes and images, and *Good Citizen*, prescribing the duties of good Americans; a film called *Our American Heritage*, shown in over 15,000 theatres and in schools which had been given free prints of the film; and a *Reader's Digest* reprint of an article on the Bill of Rights that was given to visitors of the Train. At the same time, the Junior Museum of the Metropolitan Museum of Art opened an exhibition in autumn 1947 called 'The New Nation: 1783–1800', the press release of which called attention to 'a parallel between the free world's present struggle to unite and the American colonies' attempts at unity'.[24] The point here is not that the Freedom Train was a politically constructed and managed cultural artefact – that much is obvious – but that it was designed to help fabricate an American identity as part of the security project being developed at the time. Clark told a Congressional meeting that he saw in it the 'means of aiding the country in its internal war against subversive elements and as an effort to improve citizenship by reawakening in our people their profound faith in the American historical heritage'.[25] Symptomatically, critics of and protestors against this crude articulation of the American way of life were placed under surveillance by the security services and described as a Communist front by the media.

Events such as these are indicative of the extent to which institutions such as the CIA seemed to operate as much as a cultural as a security service, not least in their cultivation of an intellectual consensus around 'security'. For example, the CIA established the Congress for Cultural Freedom (CCF) in November 1950 as part of a wider campaign to shape American and world opinion, with book-publishing (most significantly, both the ideology of 'the end of ideology' and the ruminations on 'the God that failed' were sponsored by the CCF), sponsoring of academic research in general and 'political culture' in particular (about which I say more in Chapter 5), and the funding of journals such as *Encounter* in Britain, *Der Monat* in Germany and *Preuves* in France. The CIA helped support and develop abstract expressionism as a Cold-War weapon, encouraging its presentation as representative of a big, vibrant US cultural life, as far from socialist realism as possible, and helped shape the development of a 'national security cinema' as an extension of the national security strategy.[26] It has been said that national security needed the greatest selling job in US history.[27] We might also say that as a war of ideas and a psychological battle for the minds of people, national security also generated one of the greatest works of cultural reproduction in history.

Of course, keeping tabs on public debates and in turn trying to shape those debates is hardly a novel strategy on the part of governing elites and ruling classes. What is of real interest is the way in which the US state in this period aimed to shape public opinion about national security in ways which iterate a profound *in*security in the American polity. And for this manufacturing, a permanent (mis)information strategy would be necessary to maintain what NSC-20/2 describes as 'a state of unvacillating mental preparedness'.[28] Here we once again hit on the importance of fear to the ideology of security. For the need for security to become 'obvious' and 'natural', for it to work as ideology, fear must be mobilised. And so people must be constantly told how dangerous the world is and of how many huge threats they face – a 'realism' put to work to 'frighten men in need of security', as Carl Schmitt puts it.[29] Witness, for example, the opening policy statement by the Committee on the Present Danger, a group founded in 1976 by such luminaries as Paul Nitze, George Marshall, Jeanne Kirkpatrick, and Seymour Martin Lipset, which states that it will draw the attention of the American people to the fact that 'our country is in a period of danger, and the danger is increasing'. Or witness again Oliver North's insistence during the 1987 Iran–Contra Hearings that 'it is very important for the American people to understand that this is a dangerous world; that we live at risk and that this nation is at risk in a dangerous world'.[30] Such ideas can be traced back to the very launch of the national security state: reflecting back on his 'Long Telegram', Kennan notes in his *Memoirs* that it can now only be read 'with a horrified amusement': 'Much of it reads exactly like one of those primers put out by alarmed congressional committees or by the daughters of the American revolution, designed to arouse the citizenry to the dangers of the Communist conspiracy'.[31]

One of the ways this fear was put to work and the citizenry 'aroused' was through the elision of the differences between war and peace. The movers and shakers in the US state claimed that, in theory at least, democracies generally separate peace from war as distinct periods and processes, and that this distinction tends to be obliterated by 'totalitarian' regimes. And yet they also claimed that since we live in an age of 'permanent antagonism and conflict' (with 'no lasting abatement of the crisis'), as the NSC-68 put it – 'the smaller the gap between peacetime and wartime purposes, the greater [is] the likelihood that a successful military effort will be politically successful as well'. NSC-20/1 noted that 'a democracy cannot effect, as the totalitarian state sometimes does, a complete identification of its peacetime

and wartime objectives', but nonetheless suggested that the US
needed to 'reduce as far as possible the gap between them'. Indeed,
one Policy Planning Staff Memo of May 1948 suggested that liberal
democracies had been 'handicapped' by 'attachment to the concept of
a basic difference between peace and war' and claimed that what was
needed was the idea of 'political warfare' as 'the logical application of
Clausewitz in time of peace'. NSC-20/1 thus cited Clausewitz's claim
that 'war is a continuation of policy, intermingled with other means'.
The intent was clear: 'the basic objective outlined . . . is one which
would be valid for peace as well as for war'. Or as NSC-68 put it: the
'objectives of a free society are equally valid and necessary in peace
and war', and they are so because the challenge of security is one
'which encompasses both peace and war'. Hence it is 'essential that
this government formulate general objectives which are capable of
sustained pursuit *both in time of peace and in the event of war*'. In other
words, since the enemy is as much within as without, and since the
objectives, fears and insecurities running through the body politic are
present in times of both peace and war, the distinction between the
two is, in essence, obliterated. War and politics become a unity, and
'political warfare' is set in place mobilising 'all the means at a nation's
command'.[32] In this sense, the national security state sought to
legitimise the exercise of war powers during periods of peace by
transforming the concept of 'peace' as applied to liberal democracy.
'Such a peace as the United States is experiencing is not a peace; it is,
in fact, a war'.[33] This transformation was effected through the notion of
security, especially in its ideological circuit with emergency. Herein lies
a further reason to explain the emergence of 'national security' rather
than 'national defence' beyond that discussed at the beginning of
Chapter 3. As Eyal Weizman has noted, the logic of 'defence' deals
with wars and seeks to constitute with borders and barriers a clear
distinction between 'inside' and 'outside', between the territory within
the state and that which is exterior to it.

> The logic of 'security', on the other hand, presupposes that the
> danger is already inside, presented by a population in which the
> subversive elements exist . . . If defence engages directly with the
> concept of war, security engages with the temporarily ill-defined
> and spatially amorphous 'conflict' not only between societies, but
> within them as well.[34]

Eliding the distinction between military practice and the everyday political administration of civil society thereby helps in 'securing' a general willingness among the citizenry to submit to wartime discipline and emergency powers on a permanent basis.

It is this project of total war, total security and permanent emergency that requires the constant reiteration of the existence of fear and danger. Key figures in the national security state such as Nitze and Acheson came to use the various drafts of NSC documents, and especially NSC-68, to simultaneously promote more aggressive foreign policies and to frighten Americans into supporting those policies.[35] By 1949 one Cold Warrior could openly employ a Kierke-gaardian frame and state that the 'reign of insecurity' means that 'anxiety is the official emotion of our time'.[36] This anxiety permeated all the way through the national security state in the early Cold War and after. From panic over the Soviet Union to concern over the 'loss' of China all the way down to 'the posture of the world's most powerful state in the 1980s, a sumo wrestler, as it were, perched on a chair at the sight of a socialist Nicaraguan mouse appearing "on its doorstep" (which is to say, approximately the distance which separates London from Albania)',[37] the national security state has constantly exhibited one insecurity, fear or anxiety after another, turning the entire social symbolic system surrounding national security into the alter image of a collectively anticipated spectacle of disaster.[38] In peddling the fear of disintegration and crisis, the ideology of security is the paranoid style in politics writ large.

Writing about this paranoid style, both Richard Hofstadter and E. H. Gombrich have noted that unlike the clinically paranoid person who sees the hostile and conspiratorial world in which he is living as directed *against him*, the spokespersons of the paranoid style find it directed against a nation, a culture, a way of life. In its most abstract mode this style involves the constant scanning of the social and political environment for signs confirming the wicked threat, and involves imaginative leaps conjuring up a vast and sinister conspiracy, a huge and hidden machinery of influence set in motion to undermine and destroy a way of life. The style also tends to be convinced that the nation is infused with a terror network of enemy agents taking over the institutions of civil society in a concerted effort to paralyse the resistance of loyal citizens.[39] If we see in paranoia a type of investment of a social formation, as Gilles Deleuze and Félix Guattari suggest, then one can read a politics structured around security as deeply paranoid.[40] I have shown elsewhere how this style also operates with the metaphor of disease, with the health of the body politic supposedly being ruined by the 'disease' of communism: 'world communism is like a malignant parasite', says Kennan, 'which feeds only on diseased tissue' while the Soviet Union 'bear[s] within itself germs of creeping disease'.[41] We might add here that such disease is also a form of dis-ease – a profound insecurity about the state, its mode of accumulation, and its place in world order. The ideology of national security is in this sense both hypochondriac and paranoid.

In both hypochondria and paranoia, perception is as important as reality. John Lewis Gaddis notes that by around 1950 key figures in the US were coming to the view that because insecurity could manifest itself in psychological as well as physical terms it could have a wide and indeterminate range of sources, and the implications of this were startling: 'world order, and with it American security, had come to depend as much on *perceptions* of the balance of power as on what that balance actually was'. This was not just a question of the perceptions of statesmen and generals: 'they reflected as well mass opinion, foreign as well as domestic, informed as well as uninformed, rational as well as irrational.'[42] The Cold War, as an 'imaginary war'[43] was to therefore be a war of the imagination. To win this war meant disciplining (and, as we shall shortly see, punishing) the imagination, a process which centred on the constant reiteration of national (in)security. Indeed, one might say that if we are talking about the human imagination and its fears, then there is nothing that might not be transformed into a 'clear and present danger', and thus nothing that might escape becoming a security issue. The national security state would simultaneously be the national insecurity state – permanently.

At first sight such a reading might appear to suggest a problem for states: after all, surely anxiety, fear and insecurity are bad? But for the party of order and security, disorder and insecurity always have their uses. If, as Kennan once put it, 'complete security . . . will never be achieved',[44] and if insecurity is driven by myriad fears, myths and purported dangers, then what better way to develop and embellish the national security state, and to justify the constant re-ordering of domestic civil society and international order, than to *encourage* those very fears and insecurities in the first place? As one of the major supporters and prime movers behind the Marshall Plan, Senator Vandenberg, put it, the administration really had to 'scare hell out of the American people'.[45] The manipulation of insecurity thus becomes a primary stake in the struggle for power and the exercise of domination. This is foreign policy as a discourse of danger and an evangelism of fear.[46] The real danger is then less the feeling of insecurity and much more that the people *might not be sufficiently afraid*. This is perhaps partly what the authors of NSC-68 meant when they stated that even if there were no Soviet threat, the same policy would probably be pursued. In this sense the Cold War might be read as a mutually agreeable explanation for the constant reiteration of the need for security and the permanent 'improvement' of the security apparatus – on both sides. As Diana Johnstone and Ben Cramer put it writing about the more than 1,200 US bases in Europe throughout the Cold War, 'if the danger [of Soviet invasion] never really existed, then it can be argued that a primary mission of U.S. forces in Europe in reality has been to *maintain* the Soviet threat . . . The Soviet and U.S "threats" maintained each other, and thus their double military hegemony over the European continent'.[47] This might also explain why the US spent a large proportion of the Cold War literally feeding its enemy, being one of the largest suppliers of wheat and coarse grains and other imports, as well as various loans and credits to Eastern European satellites. It would almost seem as if it the US needed the Soviet Union's continued existence as tangible explanation for the anxiety it claimed to experience and as justification for the national security state and the proliferation of one 'security measure' after another.[48] And if it were to disappear then a replacement would have to be found: one must never allow the system to 'run out of demons'.[49]

Writing in 1953, after having lived through some of these key political developments in the US and having been engaged in debating with fascist political and legal theorists in Germany, Franz Neumann commented that the integrating element of liberal democracy purports to be a moral one, whether it be freedom or justice. 'But there is opposed to this a second integrating principle of a political system: fear of an enemy'. Such fear, he notes, is a key feature of fascist political thought, which 'asserts that the creation of a national community is conditioned by the existence of an enemy whom one must be willing to exterminate physically'. His reference here is to Carl Schmitt's *Concept of the Political*, in which Schmitt asserts that 'the specific political distinction to which political actions and motives can be reduced is that between friend and enemy', a distinction which 'denotes the utmost intensity of a union or separation, of an association or dissociation' and which receives its real meaning by opening up the possibility of war and death.[50] Neumann comments that when the concepts of 'enemy' and 'fear' come to constitute the energetic principles of politics, democracy becomes impossible and the system is ripe for dictatorship. We might add that this strategic deployment of fear is fundamental to the ideology of security.

To help shape this fear and its deployment, the security state employed a rhetorical strategy focused on the moral fibre and identity of the American people.[51] NSC-68 presented a more or less standard version of American exceptionalism rooted in the unquestioned virtues of the American way of life. The opening sections of the top-secret national security memorandum in particular go to some lengths to outline and elaborate the key differences between 'the fundamental purpose of the US', namely freedom, and 'the fundamental design of the Kremlin', namely slavery. The idea of 'freedom' was reiterated via one of the standard tropes in nationalist discourse, namely by invoking the bonds of community between the living and the dead embodied in the authority of the Constitution, thereby situating the national security state in the context of a long American tradition.[52] The assertion of this identity was consciously linked to the authoritative texts that were/are invoked in US political discourse to silence dissent and to continually reaffirm the benevolence of the American idea of freedom. NSC-68 and related national security documents from the period are replete with references to the Declaration of Independence, the Constitution, *The Federalist*, God-given rights,[53] and the historical duties of America. Just as Roosevelt in the mid-1930s had argued that the freedoms Americans so cherished required the kind of social security he was planning to offer, so now national security was to be thought of in the same terms. This (re-)imagined community of America was then used to distinguish 'American identity' from the 'other' – between 'us' and 'them'; 'good' versus 'evil'; the US as a 'country' compared to the USSR as a 'fortress'; the 'marvelous diversity, deep tolerance and lawfulness of the free society' compared to the 'slave state'; and so on – in a prime expression of the ways in which the politics of security is inextricably bound up with the technologies of cultural difference and an exemplary case of identity as a strategy of containment. This American identity was seen as an outcome of the exceptional and consensual nature of American history, which had to be re-imagined in such a way that obfuscated its former reliance on the slave trade, its relationship with Nazi Germany, its early positive relationship with the Soviet regime and its willingness to happily agree with the Soviet leadership at Yalta in 1945 about how to divide Europe and share the spoils in East Asia. In an exemplary instance of history as ideology, American political and cultural 'tradition' would thereby be placed in a different moral universe from the 'slavery' of the Communist system.[54]

The concept of 'history' here was underpinned by the notion of Providence. In Kennan's view, rather than objecting to the Kremlin's challenge, Americans should 'experience a certain gratitude to Providence which, by providing the American people with this implacable challenge, has made their entire security as a nation dependent upon their pulling themselves together and accepting the responsibilities of moral and political leadership that history plainly intended them to bear'.[55] Kennan was of the view that American security was being weakened in part by the moral laxity of its citizens, a laxity brought about by urbanisation, industrialisation and the decline of simpler modes of life with their 'stronger' moral codes and thus traditional forms of 'security'. (In his diary of his journey on land from Washington to Latin America in 1950 he notes that he woke up on a train going though some industrial city – 'what city I did not know, nor did it matter' – and realised just how 'sinister' cities are, with their dirt, unhealthy conditions and corresponding decadence, compared to the cleanliness, good health and better security provided by the farm.)[56] So Providence is in fact to be thanked for providing the American people with the challenge of saving themselves. But the idea of Providence is also illustrative here because it further peddles the myth of American exceptionalism and panders to the idea of America as the chosen nation.

NSC-68 and related documents were not just about national security, then, but also very much about national culture and national identity. Measures enacted in the name of security could be legitimised through reference to their role in defending a particular identity, while simultaneously constituting that very identity in the first place. This was part and parcel of the overall way in which the Western alliance drew upon security strategy to articulate a common cultural as well as political agenda; conversely, it was also part and parcel of the overall way in which the Western alliance drew upon a cultural agenda to articulate a security strategy, as can be seen in the cases of both NATO[57] and Canada.[58] 'In this sense', David Campbell comments, 'the texts which guided national security policy did more than simply offer strategic analyses of the "reality" they confronted: they actively concerned themselves with the scripting of a particular American identity'. Security and its discourse of danger become central to the production and reproduction of the very identity in whose name it operates.[59]

In other words, the ideology of (national) security served and continues to serve as a means of delineating, framing and asserting identity. Security functions as a means not just for identifying and dealing with potential military threats, but also as a mechanism for the political constitution and cultural production of identity and, as such, for the unity of political community. Thus the struggle for security against the enemy – be it the communist menace or global terrorism – becomes a reaffirmation of the historical burden of a distinctive identity around which the nation must unite. And yet we might equally say that the ideology of national identity serves to delineate, frame and assert national security: identity becomes a mechanism for the constitution of security. This is a double-edged process. On the one hand, it involves simultaneously distancing this identity from the Other, often through distinguishing the values central to this identity from the values of the enemy (or, more usually, the 'lack' of values of the enemy).[60] In Michael Shapiro's terms, as a key dimension of foreign policy, national security involves the *making* of the 'foreign' and the *constitution* of 'Otherness'. The making of the Other as something foreign is not simply an exercise in differentiation, but is integrally linked to how the self is understood. A self constructed with a security-related identity leads to the constitution of Otherness in terms of the level of threat the Other is said to offer to that security.[61] On the other hand, this reasserts and reinforces the acceptability of only certain forms of behaviour, modes of being, and political subjectivities. In so doing it steers us away from other alliances – those which might encourage us to contemplate a possible society not organised around security, private property and bourgeois order – and impresses on us the importance of loyalty.

THE GARDEN OF PANSIES, OR 'NO COMMUNISTS OR COCKSUCKERS IN THE LIBRARY'

The political importance of loyalty has been clear since Socrates offered philosophical and political reasons for sacrificing himself for the sake of order and the maintenance of the state. But it was Hobbes who first articulated the importance of the relationship between loyalty and security for the modern state, albeit in its most abstract terms. Since then the connection between the two has been stressed time and again by the ruling class, for which three things have been clear. First, that loyalty is best founded on what Burke called 'pleasing illusions': a 'decent drapery' simultaneously covering the ruder elements of power and authority, engaging the affections and sentiments of the people and thereby creating both a 'generous loyalty' and 'dignified obedience'.[62] Second, that the 'sentiment' of loyalty is made to appear as a natural phenomenon, the spontaneous response of human beings to a national tradition – the national order of things is reinforced as the natural order of things, thereby prioritising loyalty to the state as the most fundamental of all loyalties. And third, that political radicalism tended to be associated with forms of disloyalty: treason and sedition in particular, a critical mind in general, revolutionary politics especially. The crowning achievement of the national security state was to connect these themes to a particular national identity and target a particular political Other.

In the context of the rise of the national security state, the stress on loyalty was by no means new. The House Un-American Activities Committee (HUAC) had already been in place since 1938 to investigate internal subversion; the Hatch Act (1939) had made membership of the Communist party grounds for refusal of federal employment; the Smith Act (1940) had made it a crime to advocate the violent overthrow of the US government or to belong to any organisation advocating such an overthrow; and Roosevelt had issued Executive Order 9300 (February 1943) establishing an 'Interdepartmental Committee on Employee Investigations'. But the development of the national security state significantly ratcheted up its significance. In November 1946 Truman established a Temporary Commission on Employee Loyalty charged with establishing whether existing security procedures were adequate to prevent the employment of subversive persons, what procedures were necessary to deal with them, how to judge loyalty, and whether new legislation was necessary. The Commission questioned major agencies, including the FBI, and the intelligence services of both Army and Navy, all of which intimated that a danger to national security existed but seemed not to know the extent of the threat arising from the presence of 'disloyal' employees, with talk of some 70,000 actual communists, 500,000 fellow travellers and 150,000 underground workers. Attorney General Tom Clark cut the Gordian knot in his testimony to the Commission by stating that he 'did not believe the gravity of the situation should be weighed in the light of numbers, but rather from the view of the serious threat which *even one* disloyal person constitutes to the security of the Government'.[63] As J. Edgar Hoover put it two years later, just '*one person* whose loyalty to the Communist cause exceeded his loyalty to the United States properly placed could do irreparable harm to our security'.[64]

To hunt out what might be just one disloyal person, Executive Order 9835 was announced in March 1947, just nine days after the Truman Doctrine itself, calling for a loyalty investigation of all federal employees on the grounds that '*any* disloyal or subversive person constitutes a threat to our democratic processes'.[65] In so doing the Order transformed the debate about loyalty in America. Whereas previously the dismissal of an employee would require definite proof, the new Loyalty Program was designed to preclude any *potential* subversion. The Program therefore came to define disloyalty not only through membership of communist parties and organisations, but also through association with members of such parties and organisations. It was thus the domestic equivalent of the Truman Doctrine, once more merging domestic and international politics in the struggle for security. The Truman Doctrine's requirement that people choose between alternative ways of life implied that criticism of such a choice implied disloyalty. This would reach its apogee in what is loosely and misleadingly known as 'McCarthyism' and in particular the well-known cases of people in the culture industry 'naming names'. But we should not be distracted by the rise of McCarthy the man or the label 'McCarthyism' for both were in fact *products* of the Loyalty Program, which lasted much longer than McCarthy's own fifteen minutes of fame and extended well beyond the culture industry. What is called 'McCarthyism' was, in reality, merely one chapter in a much larger project concerning loyalty, identity and security.[66]

By the early 1950s loyalty pledges and oaths were common at both federal and state level. The initial Order brought over 2 million employees within its ambit, and later Orders increased the number exponentially, to the point at which loyalty pledges were needed not just to gain employment but also

> to obtain permits to fish in New York city reservoirs, to become a public accountant in New York state, to sell insurance or pianos in Washington, DC, to obtain unemployment compensation in Ohio, to box, wrestle, barber or sell junk in Indiana, to be licensed as a pharmacist in Texas or to become a veterinarian in the state of Washington.

Continuing in this vein, Robert Goldstein notes that in California 'the legislature required oaths for all state employees, for residents living in public housing and for organisations seeking to qualify for tax exemptions, including churches', while in Los Angeles 'a loyalty oath was incorporated into tax forms, so that it was impossible to pay taxes without swearing one's loyalty'. David Caute notes that in the District of Columbia a man was refused a licence to sell second-hand furniture because he had invoked the Fifth Amendment when questioned about Communism.[67] The ichthyologist at the Fish and Wildlife Service, the mine-safety engineer in the Department of the Interior, the oncologist at the National Cancer Institute, the sugar expert at the Bureau of Plant Industry, the wood-tick expert at the Rocky Mountain Laboratory of the National Institutes of Health, the person who discovered vitamin B_{12} at the Bureau of Dairy Industry – all these and many more came to have their political views scrutinised.[68]

The effects of the Loyalty Program, then, were huge. To understand why, we need to recognise that the Program was enacted for reasons other than simply unearthing communists in positions of power or influence. In fact the Program was concerned less with 'loyalty' and more with the subtle and ambiguous ways in which 'loyalty' might be expressed. Executive Order 9835 states that 'the standard for the refusal of employment or the removal from employment in an executive department or agency on grounds relating to loyalty shall be that, on all evidence, reasonable grounds exist for belief that the person involved is disloyal to the Government of the United States'. That is, the question of loyalty was in fact the question of *disloyalty*. And yet

'disloyalty' was as equally unclear as loyalty. First, 'disloyalty' is
understood here as a question of the display of opinion, thought or
behaviour that is indicative of disloyalty. Second, the real issue was
one particular form of disloyalty: a purported preference for communism. And third, it was in fact very much a question of trying to
identify the *potentially* disloyal as much as the actual disloyal – as
Truman let slip in a statement on the issue.[69] To this end, although
many commentators have criticised the Executive Order and thus the
Loyalty Program for the absence of any definition of what counted as
'disloyalty', the point is surely that a definition was neither possible
nor desirable, since the whole Program turned out to be a search for
modes of thought or opinion suggestive of someone who is at least
potentially disloyal and who might then become communist. Hence
the best that could ever be found, in the phrase of the Order, was any
'reasonable grounds' to believe that the person was disloyal; which
meant, in effect, that to some extent it was up to the accused to prove
their loyalty. Moreover, in April 1951 Executive Order 10241 changed
the standard for loyalty firings from 'reasonable grounds' to 'reasonable
doubt', a shift which also made its way into local legislation, so that all
that was now needed was for a hearing to establish reasonable doubt
as to someone's innocence. Eisenhower's Executive Order 10450 of
April 1953 signalled yet another shift to broader questions concerning
general character and conduct, including a more specific reference to
'sexual perversion' to which I return below.[70]

The only guidance given in the original Order for determining
disloyalty were six types of activities: (1) sabotage, espionage, prepar-
ation for these, or knowingly associating with spies or saboteurs; (2)
treason or sedition or advocacy of these; (3) advocacy of revolution or
force or violence to alter the constitutional form of government of the
United States; (4) intentional, unauthorised disclosure of documents
or information of a confidential or non-public character; (5) per-
forming or attempting to perform one's duties so as to serve the
interests of another government in preference to the interests of the
United States; and (6) membership in, affiliation with or sympathetic
association with any foreign or domestic organisation, association,
movement, group or combination of persons designated by the
Attorney General as totalitarian, fascist, communist, or subversive, or
as having adopted a policy of advocating force or violence to alter the
form of government of the US. As many pointed out at the time, the

first five categories were already grounds for criminal prosecution under existing laws and/or dismissal under civil service regulations.[71] This, combined with the fact that the sixth category concerned beliefs and associations, suggests that the Order and the Loyalty Program were concerned less with detecting genuine threats to national security and more with targeting beliefs, thoughts, opinions and associations considered by the Loyalty Boards to be close to communism. It was, in effect, a formal political attempt at eradicating ideas thought to be subversive and administering thoughts and opinions more generally. This took the issue way beyond the question of loyalty to the US government to one of loyalty to American ideals and institutions in general. That is, to the myth of America as an imagined community. For J. Edgar Hoover, the issue of loyalty concerned not the security of the government, but 'vigorous, intelligent, old-fashioned Americanism', Americanism as 'a way of life' centred on 'the sanctity of the home . . . faith in God . . . [and] respect for constituted authority'.[72] In raising these issues the Loyalty Program was, in effect, in the business of *shaping* forms of behaviour and belief around political order and national identity.

This can be seen in the questions asked and discussions that took place at Loyalty Boards. Many questions concerned immediately political subjects such as the Truman Doctrine, Marshall Plan, or the Berlin blockade, and the employee's connections to communist organisations. These included obvious questions about communism and/or the Soviet Union – 'Are you now or have you ever been a member of the Communist part?', 'When did you become a member of the Communist Party?' – to the less obvious, such as 'In your recollection, do you recall ever discussing any topic which might be sympathetic to Communist doctrine?' Questions such as these were often followed up with the usual Kafkaesque formulations:

Q: When did you become a member of the Communist Party?
A: I never became a member of the Communist Party.
Q: If you are, as you say, a loyal American, why do you persist in denying that you were a member of the Communist party?

The in-depth research, however, shows that very few members of communist organisations were found. This in part explains why so many questions were concerned less with formal membership or informal connections with such organisations, or even international affairs and political doctrines, and much more with a wide range of social and political beliefs, revealing an incredibly narrow and conservative vision of 'disloyal' tendencies:

> Which would you choose, freedom or security?
> There is a suspicion in the record that you are in sympathy with the underprivileged. Is this true?
> Have you ever made statements about the 'downtrodden masses' and 'underprivileged people'?
> Have you ever indicated that you favored a redistribution of wealth?
> Do you think that workers in the capitalist system get a relatively fair deal?
> Do you believe in government ownership of public utilities as a general proposition?
> The file indicates that you were quite hepped up over the One World idea . . . [and that] you were a strong advocate of the United Nations. Are you still?
> Have you provided any sort of religious training for your children?
> Do you think that Russian communism is likely to succeed?
> Have you ever discussed the subject of the dance in Russia?

Other questions concerned intellectual and cultural habits:

> What newspapers do you read?
> Do you read the *New Republic*?
> Do you have any favorite newspaper columnists of the day?
> In your newspaper reading, what headlines attract your attention? Do you follow the United Nations activities?
> What kinds of books did you get from them [the Literary Guild Book Club]?[73]
> Is it or is it not true that you attended a picnic of the Washington Bookshop Association?[74]
> How do you explain the fact that you have an album of Paul Robeson records?

Many questions focused on race as an indicator of dangerous and disloyal political tendencies:

Are you in favor of racial segregation?
Do you believe that white and colored races should intermarry?
Have you ever had Negroes in your home?
What were your feelings at the time concerning racial equality?
Did you ever write a letter to the Red Cross about segregation of blood?

Such questions about race, based on a conservative view of the 'right' position for loyal subjects to hold on the race question, were a common basis for branding people disloyal. Walter White, Executive Secretary of the National Association for the Advancement of Colored People, wrote to Truman on 26 November 1948 concerning the 'increasing tendency on the part of government agencies to associate activity on interracial matters with disloyalty'. Pointing to the fact that 'investigating agents have been asking white persons whether they associate with colored people' and 'colored people have been asked whether they have entertained white people in their homes', White also noted that 'there is considerable evidence before us that many colored government employees, who are now being charged with disloyalty, have such accusations brought against them because they have actively opposed segregation and discrimination'.[75] The reasoning was simple: those who opposed segregation or who spoke out on other racial matters must by definition be suspect. As the chairman of one Loyalty Board put it, 'the fact that a person believes in racial equality doesn't *prove* that he's a communist, but it certainly makes you look twice, doesn't it?'[76] A genuinely loyal American, in the eyes of the Loyalty Boards and in the ideology of national security, would be a racist one – despite the fact that the Cold War was, in theory at least, being fought with civil rights reforms as a way of warding off criticism along these lines from foreign powers.[77] This reiterates the point that it was organisations of the Left rather than the Right that were the real issue: the reason the Ku Klux Klan was never under investigation is because it was not 'un-American' and so could not be a security threat.

Further questions concerned sexuality and gender. Any expression or defence of sexual difference was deeply problematic. The Hoey Committee, established in 1950 to investigate homosexuality as a security threat, stated in its final report *Employment of Homosexuals and Other Sex Perverts in Government* that all of the intelligence agencies

'are in complete agreement that sex perverts in Government constitute security risks',[78] and Executive Order 10450 of April 1953
highlighted the dangers of 'sexual perversion'. 'Can you think of a
person who could be more dangerous to the United States of America
than a pervert?' asked one Senator.[79] Ostensibly, the fear was that
sexual perversion made someone susceptible to blackmail, and that
the Soviet Union would target 'susceptible' individuals. Thus one of
the leading witnesses to the Hoey Committee, CIA Director Admiral
Roscoe Hillenkoetter, reported on the case of Colonel Alfred Redl, the
homosexual head of Austrian intelligence before World War I who
turned out to be a double agent, turning over documents to the
Russians who had been blackmailing him. Ignoring the fact that this
single case was of an Austrian military officer rather than an American
civil servant and occurred a rather long time previously, Hillenkoetter
commented that this was an example of 'what can be done to a
country's security by a homosexual strategically placed'.[80] The Committee suggested that 'the social stigma attached to sex perversion
is so great that many perverts go to great lengths to conceal their
perverted tendencies', making them easy prey for blackmailers.
Moreover, communists and homosexuals were said to employ the
same kind of subversive secrecy in their practices and meetings. This
danger was supposedly compounded by the growing numbers of
homosexuals and 'perverts' in offices, homes, schools, churches, and
positions of power and influence – the Kinsey Report on male sexual
behaviour, published in 1948, had revealed not only the diversity of
sexual practices engaged in by Americans, but also the large number
of men who were willing to admit to some homosexual experience,
and hence encouraged the idea that homosexuals could indeed be
everywhere.

Such ideas were popularised in right-wing journalism, the best
example of which is *Washington Confidential* by journalists Jack Lait
and Lee Mortimer. Calculating 6,000 homosexuals on the government
payroll, Lait and Mortimer set out to reveal the way such people are
attracted by the security offered by the civil service, which becomes a
fertile breeding ground for illicit meetings and underhand forms of
communication, not only among themselves but also among the many
thousands who did not make it onto the payroll – 'hairdressers,
waiters, bartenders'. Lait and Mortimer reiterate the idea that homosexuality renders people vulnerable to blackmail, and so 'with more

than 6,000 fairies in government offices, you may be concerned about the security of the country'. After all, in Moscow 'young students are indoctrinated and given a course in homosexuality, then taught to infiltrate in perverted circles in other countries'. But perhaps even worse, given their love of illicit sex and the need to meet fellow homo-sexuals (Lait and Mortimer list many bars, restaurants and public areas), public places have been turned into 'cesspools of perversion'. Indeed, Washington is now nothing but a 'garden of pansies'.[81] Paraphrasing Kennan, we might say that homosexuality was thought to be one of the 'sources of Soviet conduct'.

It was not just muckraking journalists who conjured up such ideas. In *The Vital Center*, one of the key documents of post-war American liberalism, Arthur Schlesinger points to the conspiratorial nature shared by both communist subversion and homosexual subculture: with such a level of secrecy, communists could only interact either instinctively or 'by the use of certain phrases, the names of certain friends, by certain enthusiasms and certain silences'. 'It is reminiscent', says Schlesinger, 'of nothing so much as the famous scene in Proust where the Baron de Charlus and the tailor Jupien recognize their common corruption'. Similarly, 'the half-concealed exercises in penetration' practised by Communism are reminiscent of the furtive 'homosexuality in a boys' school'.[82] For Schlesinger, then, the 'vital center' was very much a masculine, virile and courageous one – as distant as possible from the disloyal communist-totalitarian man who enjoys 'the losing of self in masochism'. Similarly, in an essay on the Kinsey Report published in *Partisan Review* in April 1948, Lionel Trilling discussed the Report in terms of its presentation of homo-sexuality as somehow 'normal' within the developing 'community of sexuality'.[83]

In its final conclusions the Hoey Committee gave currency to the widespread myth that homosexuals and other 'perverts' constituted a security threat: they were susceptible to blackmail, they 'lack the emotional stability of normal persons' and they have a 'weak moral fiber'. Given their polluting nature, they offer the same danger as communists: just 'one homosexual can pollute an entire office'.[84] This view became formalised as part of government policy and across the mainstream political spectrum. Perhaps unsurprisingly given the role of key international organisations in cultivating economic order addressed in the previous chapter, the US pressured organisations

such as the UN, UNESCO, World Bank and IMF to treat homosexuality in the same way, often conducting its own investigations into
employees of those organisations,[85] and it has been said that 'US
irritation with British neutralism [among British liberals] was sometimes equated rhetorically with the heterosexual American male's
suspicion of effeminacy and bisexuality – both traits associated with
some of the Bloomsbury *literati* in CCF circles'.[86] Given the absence of
any real concrete evidence that homosexuals were being used in such
ways, however, and the obvious fact that it is only in the making of
homosexuality as a security risk, as something to be denied or covered
up, that homosexuals could be susceptible to blackmail anyway, there
was clearly also something at stake other than 'susceptibility'. Perhaps
it was just a sheer weakness that homosexuals were believed to have –
the assumption that 'when one played the role of subordinate partner
in the game of pleasure relations, one could not be truly dominant
in the game of civil activity'.[87] Hence much of the language and
assumptions in place both apes the language used to describe the
Soviet Union – where the Russian population were slaves to communism, the homosexual-pervert was a slave to their desires – and
replicates the Nazi fantasy of eradicating homosexuality in order to
secure the state and purity of the people.

The 'Red Scare', then, had a tinge of pink or lavender; the
Comintern was also thought of as a 'homintern'. 'We don't want
any Communists or cocksuckers in this library', as the Librarian of
Congress Luther Evans put it in 1947,[88] reflecting a persistent linking
of political radicalism with homosexual fellatio that runs through the
whole history of the US national security state, from Joe McCarthy's
quipping to reporters that 'if you want to be against McCarthy, boys,
you've got to be a Communist or a cocksucker' to Oliver North's
declaration following the bombing of US barracks in Beirut that it's
time to kill the 'cocksucker terrorists'.[89] As a result, it is perhaps not
surprising to find that more homosexuals and lesbians were expelled
from the federal government and public posts in the 1950s than were
Communists and 'fellow travellers'.[90]

But what else might be at stake is perhaps revealed in the vague
terminology in the debate about homosexuality, and because of the
perceived 'subversive' nature of sexual diversity more generally. The
fear of homosexuals as 'security risks' overlapped with the even looser
terminology of the time: 'persons of unconventional morality', 'misfits',

'moral risks', 'undesirables', 'moral weaklings', all terms that could be applied to women as well as men, heterosexuals as well as homosexuals, and all underpinned by a conception of instability – both emotional, sexual, political – said to arise with deviations from the 'normal'. Just as we saw in the case of law and violence in Chapter 2, 'normality' once again comes to act as the basis of a certain deployment of power.[91] It was therefore not only male–male sexual relations that were an issue, but sexuality more generally; even sexual liberty had to be subsumed under security. This can be seen in the kinds of questions asked of women.

> Have you had sexual relations with a man? Have you had sexual relations with a woman?
> When did you last have intercourse?
> Have you ever had sexual intercourse without being married?
> When did you last buy contraceptives?

One woman lost her job for 'immorality', because she had conceived a child outside marriage (despite subsequently marrying the father). But the best-known case concerned Marcelle Henry, who worked for the *Voice of America*. Having once been interviewed for potential communist sympathies, her sexual relations with various men meant she came under scrutiny again. After being accused by her personnel department of 'uncouth behaviour', Henry was brought in front of a televised hearing accused of being pro-Communist and un-American, but her actual dismissal two weeks later was made on the grounds of her 'disregard for the generally accepted standards of conventional behaviour'.[92] She herself pointed out that 'I am accused of loving the other sex too much', and was astute enough to note that, for security reasons, both homosexuality and heterosexuality can be construed as dangerous.[93]

Questions to men included the following:

> Did you not state to other individuals that because you were opposed to the institution of marriage you did not marry your wife at the time you assumed your marriage relation with her?
> Your wife is a church-goer?
> When you were in X's home, did X's wife dress conventionally when she received her guests?
> What do you think of female chastity?[94]

The concern over female sexuality was in part due to the critique of the family and women's oppression found within Marxism and feminism, and to the widespread assumption that in the Soviet Union women had been 'nationalised', forced to register at 'bureaus of free love' and to work in factories as opposed to realising themselves as true women at home.[95] But the 'logic' behind the questions was to link disloyalty – potential rather than actual – with a particular notion of what counted as (un)acceptable thoughts, views and behaviour, which in turn were thought to be communist or evidence of tendencies towards communism.

Moral surveillance has long been entwined with political surveillance; police power entwined with bourgeois morality; statecraft with soulcraft. What we have here is the conduct of conduct as a technology of power, manifested in the cult of domesticity; that is, in domesticity as a police power. As security is linked to a 'proper' morality and 'normal' sexuality, so the desire for security becomes a political technology for the securing of desire. Not a repressive strategy, but the mobilisation of sexuality for security, constantly reasserting a view on who might have sex with whom as a means of interpellating certain human pleasures as a security threat. Containment, the key to security, could function as a 'micro-physics of power' resonating through the personal lives of citizens, making the citizenry as much an active subject of *raison d'état* as its passive object.[96] National security was thus dependent not only on political loyalty, but also on a certain tactics of morality that, in turn, were taken to be indicative of one's loyalty. The outcome was a reassertion of the importance to national security of that privileged object of bourgeois subjectivity, the married heterosexual couple.

In constructing certain forms of sexuality as 'security risks', the loyalty oath could help shape subjectivity and identity. Thus while loyalty oaths have long been associated with sovereignty – a sign and symbol of one's subjection and obedience – they are also very much disciplinary.[97] Loyalty oaths instil discipline by fabricating a self-regulating subject, a *loyal* self-regulating subject who identifies with the state as the purported agent of security. (One might better say: is *faithful* to the state, as 'loyalty' oscillates here between conjugal and political fidelity.) At the same time, loyalty oaths come to constitute the collective identity of the group(s) in question, a form of mediated reciprocity in which swearing allegiance makes a claim on all members of the group that they will never become 'Other', constituting the unity and identity of the group and reaffirming these against the foreign and outside.[98] The mass of heterogeneous interests, desires and identities that makes up a society has to be condensed into a single national entity, a 'nationality', the order and security of which has to be constantly reiterated against the dangerous Other. The crudeness and simplicity of the images of ideological purity in defining the identity of the imagined communities in question only helps in driving home the central message: that it is to this identity that loyalty would be expected. This is loyalty as a search for conformity, an adherence to the status quo, an essentially conservative political discourse.[99] Outside of the obvious practices of, say, reading Marx or defending the Soviet Union in debates, the questions asked at the Loyalty Hearings were aimed at picking up on those views thought to be the central indicia of communism (that is, of a security threat): being committed to women's equality; pointing to the diversity of possible pleasures in the nature of human desire; suggesting a better deal for blacks; voicing dissatisfaction with any aspect of the social order; reading and thinking a little too much and in all the wrong ways.

'Loyalty' comes to mean an uncritical and unquestioning acceptance of the myth of the nation. Not only are the nation and its (security) state finished products, but so too are the range of socio-economic practices which they claim to be 'normal'. Anything remotely approaching 'critical', 'thoughtful' or 'intellectual' becomes immediately problematic. Alan Barth has suggested that the Loyalty Program applied 'a kind of intellectual means test under which only the indigent in ideas can qualify'.[100] So important was it for the population to be intellectually indigent – that is, as far from critical as possible – that when faced with a glowing recommendation from journalist Elmer Davis providing a reference for a prospective employee, which highlighted her intelligence as well as her loyalty, one security officer commented that 'these intelligent people are very likely to be attracted to Communism'.[101] Particularly heinous is any critical thinking about capital, correlated with 'liberty' and identified with 'Americanism'. 'Business' and 'patriotism' become inseparable. The pledge of allegiance to the flag is, in this context, a pledge of allegiance to the profit system, while any critique of capital automatically renders one a 'security risk'.

The culmination of this mutually constitutive relation between security, identity and loyalty is perhaps loyalty to the Loyalty Program itself. One reason why so many people went along with the Hearings at Loyalty Boards was because they accepted the legitimacy of loyalty practices. Perhaps the best-known example of this is the case of the scientist J. Robert Oppenheimer. Castigated by conservatives for being a fellow-travelling dupe and treated as a hero by liberals for being victimised on the flimsiest grounds and found 'guilty by association', the interesting details of Oppenheimer's case lie in his behaviour in front of the Loyalty Board. 'Oppenheimer was curiously passive throughout the proceedings and, under hostile questioning, even apologised rather pathetically for his earlier radical sympathies', notes Allen Weinstein. At the end, Oppenheimer actually thanked the Board for its patience and consideration despite the fact that it had browbeaten him, humiliated him and stripped his life bare.[102] The only explanation for such measured complicity in his own undoing lies in a fact neglected by contemporaries and historians: Oppenheimer entirely accepted the legitimacy of his own trial, because like his accusers, and like so many who came to be judged by the Loyalty Program, he entirely accepted the legitimacy of the security system itself.

In 1978, researching his father's involvement in the security politics of the period, the journalist Carl Bernstein interviewed Clifford Clark about the Loyalty Program. Clark had been Truman's counsel, meeting him on a daily basis during this period to discuss specifically the progress of the Program. Clark's views on the question of loyalty were as follows:

> My own feeling is that there was not a serious loyalty problem. I felt the whole thing was being manufactured. We never had a serious discussion about a real loyalty problem . . . The President didn't attach fundamental importance to the so-called Communist scare. He thought it was a lot of baloney . . . There was no substantive problem. It was a political problem. We did not believe there was a real problem. A problem was being manufactured. I don't believe any of us ever felt really threatened, Carl. I don't believe anything there constituted a genuine threat.[103]

In this sense, the Loyalty Program can be seen as yet another dimension of the manufacture of insecurity, helping to reinforce the view that this is a dangerously insecure world. On the one hand, the Loyalty Program did a good job of reinforcing any existing fears over national security and fabricated new fears where previously there were none. On the other hand, it also made quite a lot of people feel even more insecure over all sorts of other things – their jobs and liveli-hoods, betrayal by friends, surveillance, witch-hunts, over just about anything.

This is also why the standard criticism of the Program, that it spent a lot of money finding very few spies and saboteurs, while absolutely true, misses the real issue. Most critics of the Program noted at the time 'that the program . . . accomplished little in the way of security' and 'proved to be a miserable failure as far as security is concerned', having 'found no spies or security violations in sensitive areas or otherwise'.[104] Figures for 1950 suggested that of approximately 2.5 million employees investigated (at a cost of $21.5 million), only 97 had been discharged, despite the absurd and ambiguous nature of the meaning of '(dis)loyalty', while the Chairman of the Loyalty Review Board noted that during its first three years not one single case of espionage had been encountered. The FBI in the course of 10,000 full field investigations and 3 million examinations of records found no evidence even directing toward espionage. A later survey of the Loyalty Program in 1953 found that some 13.5 million people had been investigated, with just under 5 million persons checked for government employment and by 1957 the overall cost had risen to some $350 million, resulting in over 11,000 people losing their jobs. Significantly, no espionage or sabotage was uncovered. Yet to criticise the Program for failing to uncover espionage or sabotage and/or for being hugely expensive overlooks the fact that espionage needs to be understood in terms of its mythological function in preserving the political taboo of the state secret.[105] But more generally the Loyalty Program needs to be seen in terms of the *theatrics* of power, and in that sense, the theatrics of security. The high point of such theatrics was undoubtedly the act of suicide by leaping from a window. The extent to which this act of suicide was enjoyed by those in power is illustrated by a comment from Congressman Karl Mundt after Lawrence Duggan threw himself from a window in New York in 1948. Mundt announced that the reason for this was that Duggan had been named at a HUAC meeting as implicated in a communist spy ring. The committee would disclose the other names, Mundt said, 'as they jump out of windows'.[106] This is the accusation, confession and execution rolled into one, opening the way for perhaps the most theatrical of 'confessions' possible.

On a more mundane level, the huge number of televised Loyalty Hearings can be seen as theatrical degradation ceremonies, in the sense discussed by Harold Garfinkel and developed by Victor Navasky. As the first political trials to be televised to a mass audience, they took the theatre of power to a new stage, and in so doing helped sustain the culture of fear, not least the fear of disgrace, and used these in fomenting the political paranoia of the security state. The job was to secure the state, not by discovering subversives but by stigmatising those who might get anywhere near subversion, a process involving public denunciations and so producing a moral indignation among the viewers and others receiving the information about who had been 'named and shamed'. For security to work, the rites of degradation count for more than the rights of man. Designed 'to effect the ritual destruction of the person denounced', as Garfinkel puts it,[107] such rites help reaffirm the collective identity of the group as a whole. The process of stigmatising individuals as subversives, as disloyal to the state and to the American way, as agents of a foreign power, could thereby reassure those watching of their own identity, loyalty and security, while also nonetheless hinting at the continued insecurity which will require yet more rites of degradation.[108]

Far from being aimed at rooting out communists, then, the Hearings were designed to reassert the logic of (in)security and identity, and thereby consolidating the logic of security. The flipside of this is that betrayal of anything *other* than one's nation becomes a virtue. Betrayal loses any stigma and becomes the true test of loyalty, since without the willingness to 'name names' no oath is credible.[109] Betrayal of friends and lovers, partners and family, colleagues and neighbours; all become not only permissible, but actually required – a permissible 'transgression' in exchange for submission to authority and a brief glimpse of that longed-for security. The purity of one's loyalty and identity and a related sense of 'security' momentarily achieved and experienced – at the cost of genuine human relations. Loyalty and security become more or less synonymous.[110]

Synonymous? Barth reports an exchange between one Security Officer, Mr Robinson, and an employee, Mr Blank, during one hearing:

Mr. Robinson: What I would like to say for the record is that we carefully bear in mind in all these cases that there is a very definite difference between the word 'security' and the word 'loyalty'.

Mr. Blank: May I ask what the difference is? It's not clear to me.

Mr. Robinson: There's a vast difference between security and loyalty . . . I'll point out the difference. I think loyalty must necessarily be a conscious proposition. Security, or lack of it, might be conscious or unconscious. And I think that probably serves the purpose of what I am trying to do, but I am making the statement for the record without any implication as to any conclusion that you should draw from that statement, but you made several statements about that and I just want to make clear that this action was based, as the press release stated, as a matter of security.[111]

Thus if there is a distinction between loyalty and security, it lies in the fact that one can be consciously loyal, but unconsciously a security threat, which seems to be a way of saying that one can be a security threat without even knowing it. Better still, one might not know it, but *the state has ways of knowing it for you*, even if you think you are innocent (for in the logic of paranoia, no one is innocent).[112] So although the Loyalty Program could eventually be scrapped with the Eisenhower administration's shift of emphasis from '(dis)loyalty' back to 'security risks' (it is much easier to brand people a 'security risk' rather than a 'disloyal citizen') the focus on security risks did little to change the way the state operated since 'security risks' were people who were loyal or who *thought* they were loyal but whose character and habits might make them potentially liable – alcoholics, homo-sexuals, notorious womanisers, or just plain mercenaries who might become the dupes of real spies. 'Security risks' were thought in many ways to be more dangerous than 'disloyalty cases' if only because they were thought to be more common.[113] The procedural problems inherent in the Loyalty Program were simply repeated in the 'security risk' programme but, more importantly, the focus was still on 'good character' and the (re)shaping of identity rather than the immediate security from foreign invasion or military threat. That there was such continuity despite the shift in programme is unsur-prising, not least because no one seems to have really understood the difference between security and loyalty.

Synonymous, then? Maybe. But definitely intimately connected to fear and violence. The cult of loyalty helps sustain a climate of fear, in which the identity of the group can be (re)constructed through the fear of the outsiders: the Others, the disloyal, the ones who fail the test of loyalty or refuse to take the pledge. And these are the ones against which violence must be exercised. '*This* is precisely what a pledge is', Sartre comments: 'namely the common production, through mediated reciprocity, of a statute of violence'. Once the loyalty oath has been taken, the group claims the right to guarantee everyone's security at whatever cost. In the name of freely sworn loyalty, the security and liberty of the group and its members demands the violence of all against any Others.[114] The origin of the pledge, in other words, is the fear that arises from the fabrication of insecurity and the orchestrated violence carried out as a consequence. At the heart of the pledge, then, is nothing less than terror.

Huey Long is said to have once commented that if fascism came to America it would be on a programme of Americanism; notwithstanding my earlier reservations about the problems in the label 'McCarthyism', some people also worried that at the height of his power McCarthy would bring fascism to America: his early sympathy for *Mein Kampf* and an episode in his early Senatorial career in which his investigation of the prosecution of Nazis implicated in a massacre in Belgium gave rise to concerns of Nazi sympathising.[115] It is therefore unsurprising that more than a few commentators noted early on that the Loyalty Program surpassed the practices for consolidating loyalty, national identity and political unity used by fascist and authoritarian regimes. 'To enumerate the features of the loyalty program', Barth suggests, 'is to suggest the description of an authoritarian society'.[116] The parallels are obvious: lack of toleration of different political opinions in public life; the enforcement of rigid political orthodoxy through the use of vague and sweeping standards of loyalty; police incursions into personal lives; the proscription of lawful associations; Star Chamber proceedings on the basis of anonymous testimony; persecution for political beliefs entailing no criminal conduct. The authors of one report commented that 'no precedent is to be found in foreign experience, outside the totalitarian states, for a comprehensive, continuous system of loyalty surveillance similar to that instituted by the Loyalty Order in the United States'.[117] If not fascism, then the description certainly sounds remarkably like the 'totalitarian' regime from which America was supposedly being secured by the Loyalty Program.

Fascism aside, the attempt to secure the imagined community of the nation goes hand in hand with the politics of loyalty in reinforcing a system of symbolic representation of and concrete difference from the Other, the extensive policing of organisations and associations, and the political administration of human subjectivity. Thus alongside and as part of the national security state we find a security–identity–loyalty complex, held together by fear and violence. Deployed in the name of security, loyalty and identity help organise the political imagination around the state. Identity is mobilised for loyalty – to the state; loyalty is mobilised for identity – with the nation; and both loyalty and identity are thereby mobilised for security. It is as though identity could be borne only through the political cultivation of a devoted loyalty to the state and the 'values' it purports to defend, and only a permanently expressed loyalty to this identity will keep us secure.[118] 'Security' is thus always much more than a dimension of foreign policy, military technology and external defence. Rather, it is integral to the logic of (national) identity, a key moment in the cultivation of loyalty within the garden of security. And the real beauty of this security–identity–loyalty complex is that permanent emergency and the collapse of any distinction between war and peace mean that the constant testing of loyalty, reassertion of identity and improvement in security can be carried out by and across the whole social body: the police are everywhere.

Chapter 5

THE COMPANY AND THE CAMPUS

═══════════

In times of terror, when everyone is something of a conspirator,
everybody will be in the position of having to play detective.
                            Walter Benjamin, *The Paris of the Second Empire*
                                                in Baudelaire (1938)

'It was one of the worst things I've seen in my lifetime', commented
Carlton Brown, a commodities broker, about what he witnessed on
11 September 2001. 'All I could think about was getting them the hell
out', he says. 'Before the building collapsed, all we could think about
was, let's get those clients out'. Out of the buildings about to collapse,
presumably? No: Brown was concerned about clients becoming
trapped in the gold market, which he knew would close once the
World Trade Center towers collapsed. As the planes were hitting the
towers 'the first thing you thought about was "Well, how much is
gold up?"'. As fortune would have it, he adds, 'in the next couple of
days we got them all out'. And fortune really was smiling at some
people that day, because 'everybody doubled their money'. So for
some people 11 September 2001 turned out to be a real 'blessing in
disguise'. 'Devastating, you know, crushing, heart-shattering. But . . .
for my clients that were in the [gold] market, they all made money',
he says. 'In devastation there is opportunity. It's all about creating
wealth.'[1]

In devastation there is opportunity. And since one of the things
supposedly devastated on that day was the established notion of
security, the outcome of which has been the launching of a new global
war in the name of 'national security', perhaps there is also opportunity in security.

'National security is everybody's business', says Linda Millis. Millis works for a Washington-based organisation called Business Executives for National Security. The organisation claims to have 'only one special interest', namely to assist major corporations in their desire 'to help make America safe and secure'.[2] In this it tallies with the official US policy of securing the nation by uniting the power of the state and the power of capital. The *Roadmap for National Security* (February 2001) sought to encourage higher rates of investment in 'security projects' organised and carried out by private capital, and the *National Strategy for Homeland Security* (July 2002) stressed the embedded relationship between the public and private sectors in security. But the definitive statement is the *National Security Strategy* of September 2002, of which at least a third is spent on the role of a global *economic* strategy as part of the project of national security. This strategy is founded on the idea that 'if you can make something that others value then you should be able to sell it to them'.[3] And since, as Tony Blair puts it, 'security is life's most precious commodity',[4] who can doubt either the value of security or the belief that it could and should be sold. Security, in this sense, shares a fundamental unity with capital.

To grasp this fundamental unity we need to focus our attention on the security industry. The idea of a 'security industry' is aimed in part at undermining the illusion that the desire for security is something that somehow emerges spontaneously from people's needs. But it also draws attention to the way security products are tailored for consumption and, through this, the ways in which the security industry integrates its consumers into a wider culture of (in)security. In this sense I use the idea of a security industry to connote the production of security as a commodity and thus the role of capital in the more general security offensive. We saw in previous chapters how moves which appear initially as strategic 'security concerns' are in fact transacted by commercial struggles, how emergency powers have been used as a form of administering capitalist modernity, and the links between social security, national security and economic order. The idea of a security industry pushes this further, creating the possibility of exploring the ways in which the ideology of security has been governed as much by the process of capital accumulation as by state strategy against this or that enemy.

If security is indeed a commodity then it has to be understood through the most profound lens shaped for our understanding of the commodity, namely the critique of political economy. This requires us to read the security industry through the ideas of commodification and fetishism. Steps have been made along these lines, most notably by Steven Spitzer and George Rigakos,[5] but their insights need pressing and further developing. In particular, they need pressing and developing because much of the debate about security has been dominated by a focus on 'privatisation' and the growth of 'private security'. While this focus has some things going for it, it tends to rely on some dubious assumptions about the state. In particular, it relies on the assumption that the 'privatisation' of security is a feature and function of an increasingly 'hollowed-out' state. The argument here aims to develop an approach that eschews the somewhat problematic notion of privatisation, and aims at an analysis rooted more thoroughly in the critique of political economy by focusing on the ways in which the ideology of (in)security is central to the political logic of capital as well as the logic of the state. Rather than discuss the 'privatisation' of security based on the mythical notion of a 'hollowed-out' state, I aim instead to analyse the deadly *complicity* between security and capital, a complicity in which the security state and security industry collide and collude in a mutual bid to reinforce a political agenda structured ideologically around the security fetish.

The span of the security industry is vast, including the Baroque arsenal of the military-industrial complex, development centres, the oil industry, investment banks, multi-national corporations and an almost immeasurable number of smaller companies engaged in 'domestic' security. It also includes a significant amount of university research. For this reason I later turn to the ways in which the security project has shaped academic research, to the extent that whole disciplines have been constructed, and others restructured and re-focused, around the logic of security. I have elsewhere shown how the state is engaged in the constant production of new forms of knowledge, constructing certain categories for redefining reality according to the demands of state power and the political administration of civil society.[6] I want here to push this argument further by showing how the demands of national security helped the state historically in generating not just new categories, but also new disciplines – to show the way in which large numbers of intellectuals have succumbed to the fetish of security. To bring the production of commodities and the production of ideas together in this way may seem a little odd to some readers. But there must surely be a reason why the CIA is known as 'The Company' and its headquarters as 'The Campus'.

SECURITY FETISHISM

On 26 May 2003, following the successful military operation by the US and its allied forces, Paul Bremer, the US-appointed interim governor of Baghdad, announced that Iraq was 'open for business'. The corporate invasion of Iraq could now take place. This invasion had been fairly well planned by the Committee for the Liberation of Iraq, consisting of a combination of neocons, foreign-policy hawks and leading figures from major corporations such as Bechtel and Lockheed Martin. Major corporations were henceforth awarded huge contracts for the reconstruction of Iraq. One of Halliburton's subsidiaries, Kellogg, Brown & Root (KBR), was granted a non-competitive contract for up to $7 billion to extinguish oil-well fires and rebuild Iraq's oil operations. These contracts were later extended to include fuel supply, to the extent that by 2004 Halliburton or its subsidiary had received over $10 billion dollars for work in Iraq, including money for a range of activities not involving energy supplies, such as quarter-mastering US forces. KBR had also been given the task of constructing additional detention units at Guantánamo. For this reason Halliburton and KBR have become the focus of a lot of media attention, but more than 150 other US companies have also been awarded contracts for work in Iraq, worth some $48 billion. These include substantive contracts for organisations such as the Bechtel Group, which in April 2003 signed a $680 million contract for the design, construction or reconstruction of one port, five airports, the road network, rail system, municipal water and sanitation services, electric power systems, school and health facilities, select government buildings, and irrigation systems, to which was added a further $350 million in September of that year and then another $1.82 billion in January 2004. The corporations involved have performed incredibly well during this period: Bechtel's revenue increased from $11.6 billion in 2002 to $17.4 billion in 2004, while Halliburton's stock price nearly quadrupled in value between March 2003 and January 2006.[7]

A large amount of research has shown that the financial arrangements for projects such as these have often been highly dubious, less than transparent, and possibly illegal. Much of the money for reconstruction has never left the US, and much of the Iraqi's own money has also been paid to American firms on highly generous terms – KBR received $73 million for motor caravans to house the 101st Airborne Division, twice as much as the army said it would cost to build barracks itself, while a firm called Custer Battles was paid $15 million to provide security for civilian flights at Baghdad airport during a period in which no civilian planes were flying. 'Technological inflation' has also been very much at work: the costs of the Logistics Civil Augmentation Programme (LOGCAP), for example, rose from a projected yearly total of $5.8 billion in September 2003 to $8.6 billion in January 2004. Other costs not subject to such inflation were often either plain dubious (one official audit of some of the Halliburton contracts found $212 million in 'questionable costs', while KBR has been found to have overcharged the US military by about $60 million for fuel deliveries) or simply not known (eight other government audits of Halliburton were marked 'classified' and not released). And with the CPA keeping hundreds of millions of dollars in shrink-wrapped bundles of cash, money sometimes just went 'missing' – 19 billion of the new dinar (approximately $1.3 million) was found on board a plane in Lebanon sent from Iraq by the Interior Minister of Bremer's 'government'; some $8.8 billion from the Development Fund for Iraq remains unaccounted for. At the same time, the failure to actually fulfil contracts has not led to any loss of income – Bechtel's failure to repair the water treatment and distribution system in fifteen urban areas within six months and provide a potable water supply in all urban areas within twelve months led to neither cancellation of the contract nor loss of any money.

These practices are clearly due to the need to get the Iraqi people ready for a new life organised by and for capital, an Iraq which, in Rumsfeld's words, 'provides opportunities for its people through a market economy', following the policy developed by the US Agency for International Development under advice from BearingPoint Inc. (formerly KPMG), in their report 'Stimulating Economic Recovery, Reform and Sustained Growth in Iraq' (February 2003) specifying a liberalisation of the Iraqi economy.[8] The stress was and is very much on the market: 'Market systems will be favored – not Stalinist command systems – and the Coalition . . . will encourage moves to privatize state-owned enterprises'.[9] But this liberalisation of Iraq was to be conducted under a decidedly dictatorial political order. So from

May 2003, when Iraq was declared open for business, to June 2004, when the Coalition Provisional Authority (CPA) was dissolved, the new authoritarian liberalism in Iraq saw the introduction of 100 Orders fundamentally altering Iraqi law in order to implement a capitalist economic model. After first firing more than half a million employees of the 190 state-owned companies (Orders 1 and 2) and passing an Executive Order granting non-Iraqi companies (that is, American companies) immunity from prosecution for any acts undertaken in relation to oil exploration, production or sale, a raft of other Orders was set in place including a trade-liberalisation policy removing all protective barriers (Order 12), a flat-tax policy (Order 37), the opening of the Iraqi banking sector to foreign ownership (Order 4), the rewriting of the patent, trademark and copyright laws to ensure access to foreign producers (Orders 80, 81 and 83) and, most importantly, the selling off of all of Iraq's state-owned enterprises (Order 39). The only laws left intact were the previous regime's limitations on labour rights and trade union membership. All these Orders were then upheld with the passage of the constitution in October 2005, Article 25 of which requires that the State guarantee the reform of the Iraqi economy according to 'modern economic principles' and ensures the 'development of the private sector'. A commitment to capitalism is now a constitutional requirement.

Retort has called this a form of military neo-liberalism, and much has been said about the 'commodity whose geo-strategic significance had obsessed the American military establishment ever since World War Two', namely oil.[10] But the same establishment has also been obsessed with another commodity in the same period, namely security. Virtually all the Orders passed by Bremer and ratified as part of the new Iraqi constitution have been justified on the grounds and in the name of security. The justification is sometimes explicit, such as in the prohibition of certain forms of media activity (Order 14), prescribing who can run for or hold offices (Orders 62 and 97) and the placing of US representatives in key positions that last for five years (Orders 57 and 77). Or the justification is implicit: as part of the world historical project of imposing neo-liberal logic across the globe and calling it 'international security'. To this end a huge amount of the money intended for rebuilding Iraq has been siphoned off to companies trading in something called 'security'.

The US originally allocated $5.8 billion to build Iraqi security, and in February 2005 Bush asked Congress for another \$5.7 billion to go towards this task. Since most of this money has been spent on 'security personnel' employed by corporations rather than states, the security industry as such has emerged as the second largest member of the 'coalition of the willing'; one recent report estimates that there are approximately 48,000 security contractors working in Iraq.[11] There are now so many security contractors working in Iraq that the companies employing them have established their own association – the Private Security Company Association of Iraq (PSCAI). The personnel in question perform a range of tasks once carried out by military personnel, such as logistics, operational support and training. DynCorp, for example, has a \$50 million contract to help form Iraq's new police department, judicial branch and prison system, having performed a similar task in Haiti in 1994, Croatia and Bosnia in 1995 and Columbia in 2001. They also carry out far more controversial 'security' tasks, for example acting as 'interrogators' or 'translators': twenty-seven of the thirty-seven interrogators working at Abu Ghraib prison when the abuses being meted out there became known were employed by the private contractor CACI International. And far from providing for a national reconstruction that might go some way to satisfying real human needs, this security industry in Iraq is having the opposite effect: by the end of 2005, US officials were reporting that key building projects in Iraq were grinding to a halt because 'security' was diverting funds intended for electricity, water and sanitation, while the \$18.4 billion relief and reconstruction fund for Iraq has been reallocated to counter-insurgency warfare.

So if Iraq was indeed 'open for business' then it was especially open for the business of security. The reorganisation of the Iraqi working class, one of the central objectives of the war, was carried out under the label 'security'. What we are witnessing in Iraq, then, is an explicit illustration of the collusion between capital and security, a twenty-first-century version of the subsumption of 'liberty' under security and of liberal order-building. On the one hand we have the commercialization of security, in which security is to be achieved via the activities of capital; on the other hand we have the securitization of capital, in which capital accumulation is increasingly being conducted in the name of security.

Now, much of the literature in this field has suggested that this joint process is indicative of a significant historical shift arising from the disintegration of state power, a disintegration 'typical of a new era' in Eric Hobsbawm's words.[12] For a large number of commentators this 'disintegration' of state power has resulted in an extensive 'privatisation' of military practices and a massive growth in the market for security. In this era, it is suggested, we are witnessing a 'market for force' in the making.[13] The key issue for these writers is not security *per se*, but the fact that the money has gone to *private* security. This argument relies on a fundamental agreement that the end of the Cold War and/or the pressures exerted on the state through the development of neo-liberal post-Fordist practices signalled a growth of private security companies (PSCs).[14] The revenue of the global international market in security rose from $55.6 billion in 1990 to $100 billion in 2000, and is predicted to double again to $202 billion in 2010. At the same time, security companies with publicly traded stocks grew at twice the rate of the Dow Jones Industrial Average in the 1990s. The top thirty-five of these, including the Vinnell Corporation, Military Professional Resources, Inc. (MPRI), and KBR, are among the most profitable businesses in the US today. In January 2004 the influential think tank GlobalSecurity revealed that Bush's government had filtered more money into their Black Budget than any other administration in American history. Reports filed by other companies confirm this trend: the British-based company Control Risks Group, for example, working in Iraq for the UK government but also contracted by Bechtel and Halliburton, saw its turnover increase by fifteen times after 2003; Aegis's turnover increased from £554,000 in 2003 to £62 million in 2005, three-quarters of which was due to its Iraq contracts. Many of these companies have become major employers: DynCorp, for example, employs approximately 17,000 employees in over 550 operating facilities across the world, while BAE Systems is Europe's largest defence company, employing over 90,000 people with sales of over £13 billion (2004 figures).[15]

It is this use of security contractors, expansion of profits and increasing number of employees working 'in security' that has led many to argue that we have entered a new era of state sovereignty or seen a major shift in international power with the rise of the security industry. The 'privatisation' of security is almost universally taken to be indicative of a shift in the logic of sovereignty. Peter Singer, for example, argues that many states have been unable to live up to their side of the 'security promise', resulting in a profound reconceptualisation of the politics of security.[16] In other words, the position holds that as the state is said to have gradually abandoned or been stripped of its commanding heights so security has become more of a private enterprise; security as 'a growth industry *par excellence*' is only being achieved on the back of a shift in state power. In this it tallies with the literature on the 'new wars', which often talks about the 'de-statisation' of military force.[17] The outcome, Anna Leander suggests, is a 'considerable shift of authority from the public to the private'.[18] For Ken Silverstein, mercenaries are the foot soldiers of privatisation, transferring the responsibilities of government, while for Deborah Avant the privatisation of security deeply affects the entrenched concept of sovereignty.[19] The underlying assumption made is that security is a public good and thus is 'naturally' a function of the state. The 'privatisation' of security is thus assumed to be part of a wider shift in state power: the 'hollowing-out' of the state has resulted in the privatisation of security. A similar claim is made within the industry itself.[20]

These assumptions and claims overlap considerably with two parallel debates in the sociology of law. First, much of the current research on policing accepts, either openly or implicitly, that the boundary between 'public' and 'private' policing is becoming increasingly blurred. A grey area is said to have emerged, populated by private or quasi-public institutions which cannot be easily fitted into the category of 'public police' but which seem to exercise similar powers and carry out 'traditional' policing functions.[21] And this grey area is now quite substantial: in the UK, for example, there are approximately half a million 'security operatives' employed within the security industry, compared to approximately 136,000 'public' police officers; a similar if not higher ratio exists in other countries. Some individual security companies employ roughly the same number of staff as some state police organisations: the 1999 purchase of Pinkerton by Securitas created a security company employing 114,000 staff; the merger of Danish company Falk with the UK's Group 4 and then the takeover by the new Group 4 Falk of the US-based Wackenhut Corporation in 2002 created an organisation with over 200,000 employees and an annual turnover of around $3.7 billion; the further merger in February 2004 between Group 4 Falk and Securicor produced a new and even larger company, Group 4 Securicor. With companies as large as this it is unsurprising to find that the

Confederation of European Security Services estimates that its member organisations have over 1 million employees in the European Union.[22]

The ambiguity over what counts as 'security-spending' makes it difficult to gauge exactly how much is being spent on security domestically, or even what counts as spending on security. The regulatory body for the UK estimates the annual revenue of the UK's security industry in 2003 to be between £3 billion and £4 billion.[23] A recent estimate of the global security market cites a figure of £60 billion,[24] although 'according to *Fortune* magazine, the private sector will spend over $150 billion on homeland security-related expenses such as insurance, workplace security, logistics, and information technology'.[25] The Office of Homeland Security has suggested that the US alone spends roughly $100 billion per year on homeland security,[26] and some industry analysts have predicted that the US market will be worth $180 billion by 2015, adding that this figure could 'skyrocket' should there be further terrorist attacks.[27]

The second parallel debate concerns the monumental effort to lock up a sizeable percentage of the population. With a maximum-security prison costing up to $75 million, the practice of incarceration involves lucrative partnerships between capital and the state. Just one prison, Pelican Bay State Prison in the US, provides 1,500 jobs, an annual payroll of $50 million, and has a budget of over $90 million. And the number of such prisons is increasing: between 1985 and 1995 there was a 500 per cent increase in the number of private prisons in America, and plenty of other states are following suit. This and the continued maintenance of an institution which is like a hotel with a guaranteed occupancy, as one supplier of private prisons put it,[28] generates a range of support services such as the provision of food, medical supplies, transportation and furniture production, and a burgeoning 'speciality item' industry selling fencing, handcuffs, drug detectors, protective vests and other 'security' devices to prisons, all of which tempt a range of corporations into the world of the prison. And the real beauty of these hotels with guaranteed occupancy is that the residents are also compelled to work for their stay, with prison labour now used to make uniforms for McDonald's and lingerie for Victoria's Secret, motherboards and jeans, licence plates and furniture, and is increasingly involved in telemarketing, in drug-testing and on public works. With no strikes, no unions, no unemployment insurance to pay or compensation for industrial 'accidents', prison labour looks remarkably like slave labour for the New World Order, a pot of gold for corporations encouraged by politicians whose goal is to 'turn every federal prison . . . into a mini industrial park'.[29]

In this 'new era', then, we have what appears to be a transformation in policing and incarceration that parallels the transformation in the exercise of military violence. As with the military, the central institutions of law and order, discipline and punishment, are increasingly being described in terms of their 'privatisation'. And this description relies heavily on the same assumptions about shifts in sovereignty and government: practices and responsibilities assumed to be central to the modern state have supposedly been hived off to private agencies, evidence of a new era in sovereign power and the mode of rule. The domestic security industry is therefore said to 'plug the gaps' or 'fill the vacuums' left by a 'hollowed-out' state, gaps and vacuums that are sometimes traced back to the fiscal crisis of the state. On this view the growth of 'private security' constitutes a 'quiet revolution' issuing in a new era founded on a commercial compromise between the sovereignty of the state and commercial interests; 'private' forms of security seep more and more into the public realm just as certain forms of 'public' activities become increasingly privatised.[30] Since exercising violence and incarcerating people have long been seen as part and parcel of the legitimacy (and monopoly) of the state, changes to these practices are, unsurprisingly, said to have effected a transformation in the exercise of power in late modernity, a transformation towards a new 'nodal governance' in which the state is said to be merely one actor in security provision.[31] In other words, the predominant view is that where the state is thought to have failed or to have not performed sufficiently well, 'private' security forces and groups have stepped in. And once more this is the story that the industry likes to tell about itself, a story in which 'private' security is said to take off from the general security problematic, but which also reinforces it; capital is once more presented as making its own inimitable contribution to (national) security.[32]

Taken together then, these areas of research have tended towards the argument that we have entered a new era of 'private' or 'commercial' security, in which the state is somehow being ousted from one of its core tasks: of offering protection. But while there is obviously some mileage in the notion of 'privatisation' as capturing some of the changes taking place, the danger with 'privatisation' as a concept is that because the conceptual couplet public-private is part of the liberal tradition, its use runs the serious risk of liberal assumptions filtering into the analysis. This is perhaps best seen through the ways in which the claims about 'privatisation' almost always go hand in hand with seriously misleading claims about the 'hollowing-out' of the state or a transformation of state power. What I want to propose instead is an alternative analysis rooted in the idea of commodification and fetishism. Doing so will also allow me to suggest that what is happening is very far from being a transformation or hollowing-out of state power. Rather, the changes taking place help reinforce part of Marxism's insight into the *unity* of state and capital. Examining the ways in which both capital and the state benefit from the obsession with security, and thereby reading security as the basis for both a sustained capital accumulation and a constant political policing of civil society, takes us away from the liberal assumptions inherent in the public-private distinction and towards a different framework entirely, allowing us to focus more directly on the ongoing commodification of security. This enables us to develop the critique of security through the idea of the *security fetish* and thus to treat the security industry as a *partner* to the state, a partnership increasingly organised around the ideology of security. Reading security as a fetish, then, is intended to reassert the ways in which security is ideologically generated and developed as an interest of *both* capital and state.

In order to be 'productive' for capital, security has to undergo the reification universally applied across the bourgeois world; security must first be translated into the materiality of the commodity.[33] Security appears at first sight to be an obvious, even trivial thing. It thus appears even more trivial in the form of that apparently most obvious thing, the commodity, in which form it appears to be nothing other than an object satisfying a human need. But Marx notes of the commodity that 'as soon as it emerges as a commodity, it changes into a thing which transcends sensuousness'.[34] The commodity is thereby given a mystical value arising not from its use-value. If this is so for the commodity in general, then commodities presented in security terms are at an added advantage here, as they appear to serve the satisfaction of a very basic human need. But Marx's point is that commodity-production *per se* is far from obvious and trivial. Tracing the contours of the production of security commodities takes us to the heart of the security industry, a process whereby security becomes fetishistically inscribed in commodified social relations.

Security firms do not engage in the security industry because they have an interest in 'social control' or 'surveillance'. Rather, they engage in the industry because of a far more mundane interest in making a profit.[35] To make a profit the security industry must *sell* security. And to sell security it must first help generate insecurities. Like any industry, the security industry interpellates consumers as sovereign subjects – the customer is king. But it simultaneously interpellates them as fearful – the customer is insecure. In so doing it plays a key role in the fabrication of the much wider culture of fear used to shore up the national security project. But where the state uses such fear to sustain support for the national security project, the security industry aims to turn the feelings associated with (in)security into the consumption of commodities. It thus offers a 'solution' to fear and insecurity in entirely commodified forms. What is generated is a need for security – a need recognised by capital only as a need that can be satisfied by this or that commodity – and so the production of more and more commodities marketed in 'security' terms. The security industry thus uses its purported concern for human beings and their security to reinforce the logic of both security and the commodity form across the face of society.

In one sense, then, the industry solution to insecurity and fear, namely consumption, runs parallel to and complements the political solution. But as well as running parallel to the political solution, the security industry also offers a decidedly *apolitical* alternative to the political solution. For if the state can be said to be failing as guarantor of security, then the security industry position is clear: *only* consumption can save us now. With the production of (in)security, capital thereby finds itself once more aligned with the state and yet also able to offer a non-political solution to a problem once thought of as solely the preserve of the state. In this it chimes with the neo-liberal political agenda promulgated high and wide over recent years, an agenda used to both explain and legitimise the incursion of the security industry into the world of law, war and order-construction.

Because the need for security is so amorphous and ambiguous, the number and kind of commodities that can be invested with the 'aura' of security is almost limitless, embracing both the tangible and the less than tangible. At the same time, new commodities presented in 'security' terms have a constant presence in the media. Spitzer points out that the generalised levels of insecurity, fear and paranoia in modern capitalist societies make it ultimately impossible to distinguish between commodities which are more immediately concerned with 'security' and commodities which are merely invested with security 'attributes'.[36] But this is also very much because more and more commodities are simply marketed as solutions to one insecurity or another, from airbags to laptop bags; insurance for life and insurance for death; firewalls in the home to firewalls in the computer; surveillance cameras, personal monitors, motion detectors: ever more products marketed as solutions to this or that insecurity, all within a system of consumption in which the consumer-citizen moves from one bourgeois fortification to another – from the securitized shopping arcade and megastore to the security-oriented gated community and home, and in vehicles sold for their mythical security and modelled on military designs such as the SUV.[37] 'Domestic security' thus oscillates nicely between the intensely 'private' space of the home to the intensely 'public' realm of 'homeland' and 'national' security. Hence the relationship between the actual commodity and its uses is heavily mediated by its symbolic production. Security has a 'virtually limitless ability to absorb signifiers', suggests Spitzer, to the extent that commodity after commodity can be loaded with symbolic value.[38] And the result of this is the implication that only an ever-increasing consumption can make us secure: only consumption can *secure* us now. Consumption becomes a means of managing one's own protection via the endless stream of security products. This constant striving for security through the consumption of security goods, driven by the emergency mentality but focused on private 'readiness' for whatever attack is around the corner, contributes to the perpetual ratcheting-up of the level of expectation surrounding the goods and services in question.[39]

The broader socio-political and historical backdrop to this is of course the point first raised in Chapter 1: that it is the logic of a society founded on the commodity form that generates the vast range of insecurities in the first place. As Marx and Engels point out in the *Manifesto*, a social order which rests on the production of goods for exchange rather than the satisfaction of human need generates an everlasting uncertainty and constant agitation of all social conditions. For the security industry to thrive this broader backdrop has to be

suppressed or denied – 'all reification is a forgetting', says Adorno.[40]
And yet set alongside the paranoid state, this backdrop also places the
security industry in an envious position as the struggle for national
security joins in the fight for corporate security, environmental
security, bio-security, food security, and so on. There is no shortage of
insecurities, but all of them can be dealt with . . . if the money is right.
In creating an endless supply of raw material and hardly lacking a
demand or willingness to pay for its product, the industry's continued
existence and expansion is guaranteed. Moreover, the security industry
encourages the view that the solution to the insecurity that permeates
the whole of bourgeois society lies in an individualised consumption
of commodities seen for their security value, when of course the whole
point is that the insecurity in question is an inescapable feature of
bourgeois society.

To the extent that capital and the state live off the production of
insecurity, they must also ensure that security is never really achieved.
The constant iteration of insecurity after insecurity ensures that everyone is forced to keep striving for some form of security: in commodity
after commodity, insurance policy after insurance policy, and in
constant deference to the uniforms which police us. In this sense
the security industry, like the security state, must perpetually cheat its
consumers of what it promises. The promissory note is endlessly
prolonged, revealing that, ultimately, the promise is illusory: all that
is confirmed is that the real target will never be reached.[41] And so
new security commodities will be offered on the market just as new
security measures will be 'offered' by the state, and if ever one 'insecurity' might actually disappear, so more can be fabricated. Security,
then, has become part of the commodity fiction, the vital organising
principle of bourgeois society.[42] And yet what makes this particular
aspect of the commodity fiction so *real* is that security seems so
obviously integral to our being. Thus although the security industry
purports to satisfy the need for security, humans are ultimately merely
an object of calculation in the industry. And so the stronger the
security industry becomes, the more summarily it deals with real
needs: controlling them, disciplining them, transforming them. The
result is a security industry structurally integrated with consumer
culture and the fetishised world of commodity production.

To describe the products of the security industry in terms of the
fetish of commodities is not to suggest that they are simply objects of

desire. Rather, when Marx speaks of fetishism he is speaking about the character of the commodity itself and, in particular, the fetish character of its form – its *Fetischcharakter*. Fetishism 'attaches itself to the products of labour as soon as they are produced as commodities, and is therefore inseparable from the production of commodities'.[43] This is the basis of the mysterious nature and enigmatic character of the commodity, the object's suprasensible sensuousness (a 'sensible suprasensible thing'). This enigmatic and mysterious character of the commodity arises from the form of the commodity itself. 'The mysterious character of the commodity-form consists therefore simply in the fact that the commodity reflects the social characteristics of men's own labour as objective characteristics of the products of labour themselves, as the socio-natural properties of these things'.[44] In other words, the social relations between human subjects assume, under commodity production, the fantastic form of a relation between objects.

At the same time as he writes of the fetish character of the commodity, however, Marx also writes of fetishism (*Fetischismus*) as a form of ideology. This is the fetishism of political economy, for example, which 'becomes quite palpable when it deals with capital'.[45] Here Marx is using 'fetishism' to refer not to the character of the commodity, but to the system of beliefs about the commodity perpetuated by political economy. That is, he is referring to the *ideology* of commodity production. One of the most important dimensions of this ideology is its presentation of the historical as natural. Hence in the unpublished chapter on the 'Results of the Immediate Process of Production', Marx describes the economists' equation of production with commodity production as the 'fetishism of the political economists', a 'fetishism peculiar to the capitalist mode of production' which 'consists in regarding *economic* categories, such as being a *commodity* or *productive* labour, as qualities inherent in the material incarnations of these formal determinations or categories'.[46] The clearest statement of this use of 'fetishism' to capture an ideological process is perhaps in Volume 2 of *Capital*, where he comments on 'the fetishism peculiar to bourgeois economics, which transforms the social, economic character that things are stamped with in the process of social production into a natural character arising from the material nature of these things'.[47]

The idea of the fetish of commodities, then, is used by Marx to capture both the character of the commodity and the ideology surrounding the commodity in bourgeois thought. This is in part rooted in the phantasmagorical character of the commodity, a character which arises from the commodity itself but is perpetuated in the fetish as ideology. This phantasmagorical character ultimately depends on the erasure of the materiality of the socio-economic relations of production from social and political awareness (again: all reification is a forgetting). The security commodity is fetishistic in precisely this double sense. On the one hand, commodities presented as a solution to the problem of security possess an enigmatic and mysterious character, arising partly from the character of the commodity itself and partly from what they represent, and yet at the same time security is constantly rendered representationally material just as its materiality is vanishing. On the other hand, such commodities are organised and presented in terms of the wider ideology of the commodity that so dominates today's political language. Thus the wider ideology of the commodity form has come to coincide with, to run parallel to, to reinforce and legitimise the contemporaneous rise in the ideology of security.

Writing in 1842 of the attempt by the owners of the Rhineland forests to use the Rhineland Assembly to stop peasants and workers appropriating wood from the forests, Marx noted that 'the *savages of Cuba* regarded gold as a fetish of the Spaniards . . . If the Cuban savages had been present at the sitting of the Rhine Province Assembly, would they not have regarded *wood* as the *Rhinelanders' fetish?'*[48] We might add that had the Cuban savages been present in the first decade of the twenty-first century, they might well have regarded security as the ultimate fetish, its mysterious and enigmatic quality allowing it to take the form not only of wood, but also metal, plastic and sometimes as nothing material at all. They would also no doubt have marvelled at just how many commodities had this character. That this is so should not surprise us, since as I have been arguing, security is the supreme concept of bourgeois society and liberal thought. As such, it is perhaps unsurprising to find that in many ways security has become that society's supreme fetish. This fetish helps mask an agenda that is distinctly pro-capitalist, part of a strategy for managing the contradictions of a capitalism being constantly restructured according to the shifting levels of class confidence expressed by the ruling class. The intensification of the reification and fetishism surrounding security that we are now witnessing is thus an outcome of tendencies that have existed for some time.

In this sense, the security industry both feeds on and feeds the very ideology propagated by the security state (and, of course, a security-obsessed mass media and intelligentsia). The security industry is thereby integral to an imagined economy of insecurity, simultaneously relying on the range of social and political fears on which bourgeois society both depends and feeds, and yet dependent on the belief that more and more consumption, more and more commodification, can save us from our insecurities. Security has thus become a strategy for the expansion of capital, supplementing capital, deployed to shore it up and facilitate its flows. But far from implying or signalling any kind of shift in state power or sovereignty, this *reinforces* the logic of security around which the state is organised and helps put certain state capacities into motion, elaborating and constantly multiplying apparatuses of coercion, control and political administration. Fetishism protects capital, says G. A. Cohen.[49] But it also protects the state. Far from undermining or 'hollowing out' the state, the security logic helps sustain a key logic of state power, putting certain state capacities into motion. After all, and contra the 'privatisation of security' thesis, one of the few aspects of the capitalist state actually reinforced under neoliberalism is the security apparatus.[50] For as much as security has become a strategy for the expansion of capital, so conversely capital shores up the ideology of security and facilitates its flows. And in so doing it shores up rather than challenges the logic of state power.

Moreover, to think of these issues in terms of the idea of 'privatisation' runs the risk of implying that we need to resist such privatisation and 'return' security to its supposedly 'natural' home and guardian, namely the state. But this is a serious mistake. Rather than 'return' security to the state, we need to resist the security fetish *per se*, for it is partly this that blinds us to the ways in which we might intervene against the forms of domination and exploitation that take place under the label of security. This is what cannot be grasped in thinking about security in terms of its 'privatisation', but can be grasped in terms of the critique of security. If the movement against capital is a movement against fetishism, as it must be, then it must set as one of its targets the current fetishism surrounding security. In so doing it must aim at the combined overthrow of the security industry *and* the security state.

Such an overthrow, central to the critique of security, will, however, also have to tackle the extent to which the ideology of security has dominated modern thought, most notably in the key institution of intellectual labour, the university.

SECURITY INTELLECTUALS

In a letter of 3 August 1931, written from his fascist prison cell, Gramsci noted that delving deeply into the concept of the state requires delineating the history of intellectuals.[51] Nowhere is this truer than with the national security state, which employs a broad range of individuals who may be loosely grouped together as 'security intellectuals'. Of such intellectuals Robin Luckham notes:

> The majority are employed by the military, the police, and intelligence services. But there are others whose connection to the armament culture is less direct: academics on government contracts, analysts employed in quasi-independent 'think-tanks', or members of the research and security branches of political parties. Their most characteristic products are strategic, political, or economic assessments of current events and scenarios that spell out the likely consequences of future policies, decisions, and events.[52]

I want to expand Luckham's argument beyond armaments and explore the security intellectual, and to do so by situating their key institutional home, the university, within the broader configuration of a hegemonic and fetishistic ideology of security.

To make this argument requires a particular kind of focus, requiring us to leave aside several issues relating to the role of universities in the military-industrial complex. First, I shall focus on the social sciences, and so leave aside the question of the natural sciences and related fields such as computing, since much of the detail and debate concerning the role of 'mercenary science' in the national security state is well known. Intellectuals within the social sciences, in contrast, often like to think of themselves as situated at a more comfortable distance from the centres of power, retaining an autonomy which allows them to cast more critical judgement on key policy issues. Yet as we shall see, many of the disciplines within the social sciences have not only ended up operating within the same discursive practices that constitute an unreflective apology for the national security state and its imperialist drive, but they have often been forged by the national security state for that very purpose. Second, this will not be the place to spell out yet again the revolving door that exists between the world of academia and the world of national security. Third, I will avoid reiterating well-known details concerning the security services' use of 'liaison officers', 'officers-in-residence', and 'persons of trust' within universities, and the use of universities as recruiting grounds for the security services.[53] Fourth, I will forego discussing at any length the surveillance under which many academics have been placed, not just socialists and communists but also those involved in campaigns around civil liberties, peace, race and the environment. Finally, I will eschew the debate concerning the supposed fundamental disjuncture between academia and the security services, namely that while the former relies on openness, the latter relies on secrecy, and the idea that these distinct worlds have to be kept apart if intellectual work is to be accorded any respect. This goes without saying, but it barely scratches the surface of what is in fact a far deeper problem. But what then is there left to address?

In 1976 the US Senate revealed that well over a thousand books had been produced, subsidised or sponsored by the CIA before the end of 1967.[54] If we take this figure back to the official birth of the CIA, that works out at over a book a week, for twenty years. In many cases the books in question became important works in their academic fields. I want to explore the ways in which such a project allowed the security agencies to determine the central concepts, approaches and concerns adopted by intellectuals, shaping the work of those in key disciplines as well as the subjects about which the discipline claimed to be writing. This is indicative of a long-standing desire within the CIA to depend more on 'a community of scholars than on a network of spies' (George Bush), and thus a more general desire to appear to be more of an 'intellectual' organisation rather than a security-driven one. Speaking of attempts to work with academia during the 'war on terror', one CIA official commented that 'we don't want to turn [academics] into spies . . . We want to capture them intellectually',[55] part of a wider historical desire to make the CIA seem more like 'a university without students and not a training school for spies', as one figure put it.[56] And what better way to capture academics intellectually than to forge and shape the very disciplines required by the security state in the first place?

My interest, then, lies in the making and remaking of academic disciplines and sub-disciplines to further the security project. In other words, I am interested more in what has been prescribed rather than proscribed. This prescription is not about recruitment or surveillance; it is not even about 'collaboration'. Rather, it is about the *production* of knowledge at the highest level: the fabrication of intellectual disciplines or sub-disciplines through what Bruce Cumings describes as the displacement and reordering of the boundaries of scholarly research.[57] It is not just that the basic techniques of the security state employed by the FBI and CIA 'depended upon conceptual, methodological, and technological developments in which social scientists . . . were intimately involved'.[58] It is also that the conceptual, methodological and technological developments were actually shaped by the key security institutions. In other words, in the constant reshaping of society, the project of security colonised the minds of the intelligentsia – shaping disciplinary knowledge by forging the very disciplines themselves and thus, in the process, generating a guardian class of social scientists for the security of bourgeois order. What we are talking about, then, is the centrality of the security intellectual to the regimes of knowledge produced by and for the national security state and thus, given the importance of security knowledge to the ideology of security as a whole, the ways in which the security intellectual has provided a key role in establishing certain forms of discourse as the 'common sense' of politics. Canons, rather than cannons, are therefore the issue; research topics prescribed by national security, and thus research topics not covered; the invention of certain kinds of discourse and thus the proscription of others; the creation of disciplines and foci and thus the policing of others; a radical project of *Gleichschaltung* around the logic of security. The connection with more recent attempts to continue in this vein will hopefully be apparent.[59]

The original Eberstadt Report outlining the need for a unified National Security Council had stressed the importance of educational institutions as channels of communication between the military and civilian population, and the National Security Act 1947 subsequently established a research and development board to stimulate research and development programmes in the armed forces, with the 'behavioural sciences' specifically included in the mandate. The significant differences between the 'Cold War' and previous confrontations required a new approach to political intelligence, especially the social, psychological, economic, political and cultural differences between those committed to 'freedom' and 'security' and the totalitarian other. The first requirement, then, was knowledge of Russia.

In mid-1947 the Carnegie Corporation was in touch with a number of universities about the state of knowledge of Russia, in particular on the part of social scientists, noting that the state itself lacked the personnel to conduct inquiries into long-term research on issues of a social, psychological and anthropological nature pertaining to Russia and its people. The outcome was a proposal of July 1947, called 'Russian Studies', exploring the possibility of an institute in this field based in one of the major universities, with Harvard as first choice. In discussions later that year it was made clear that the argument for the research and centre 'is admirably set forth in the recent article on Sources of Soviet Conduct by X in Foreign Affairs'.[60] James J. Angleton had already established a Soviet Division in the CIA in late-1947, one of the main purposes of which was to reach out to universities providing money for language study and area training, and the developing Center at Harvard coincided with the push by William Donovan, director of the Office of Strategic Services (OSS) and in some ways the founder of the CIA, George Kennan and John Patton Davies, to bring large amounts of state and corporate funding to the universities through what was originally intended to be an institute of Slavic studies.[61] On the one hand, then, the Russian Research Center had all the trappings of academic gravitas. Based in one of the world's leading universities, it could also boast of the involvement of highly rated intellectuals such as Talcott Parsons, one of the original members of the Center's Executive Committee. On the other hand, for both Harvard and the individuals, the Center was never just an intellectual arena. The fact that none of the four members of the founding Executive Committee had studied Russian affairs or had knowledge of Russian, that its Director was an OSS veteran who had worked on the anthropology of Japan, and that Secretary of State George Marshall sat on the Board of Trustees of the Carnegie Corporation, is perhaps telling. More important than their 'expert' knowledge was the willing-ness of academics to break down any barriers between the university and the security state. This had been especially true of Parsons, who strongly approved of either overtly or covertly attaching universities to the intelligence apparatus, to the extent of using Harvard connections to help ease the entry to the US of people accused of collaborating with the Nazis.[62] Concomitantly, those involved in the Center were often responsible for denouncing other scholars to the security services due to doubts about their loyalty. The point, however, is that the Russian Research Center was deeply involved with the security agencies from the outset and that several Foundations, not only Carnegie but also Rockefeller and Ford, worked with the Center in the funding of projects. As we shall see, as key institutions of the American ruling class the Foundations would play an important role, not only in developing Russian studies, but also the other key disciplines that will become part of the security project.

From such a model other such centres emerged as universities elsewhere followed suit, across the world as well as in the US. Out of such institutes and their collaboration – with each other as well as with the security services – a new discipline was being formed: Russian studies (or 'Soviet studies' – the terms were thought inter-changeable). By 1965 more than two dozen American universities had Soviet or East European centres, while more than three thousand scholars identified themselves as interested principally in Soviet or Slavic concerns.[63] As such, Russian/Soviet studies was not just a means for universities to liaise with the security services, it was in fact a *product* of the security project. To be sure, what eventually came to pass as Russian/Soviet studies would include scholars with a variety of views,[64] but the main point is clear: the academic study of the Soviet Union not only shadowed the rise of the national security state, but also the US national security state shaped Soviet studies politically and intellectually. 'American Sovietology', Stephen Cohen comments, 'was created as a large academic profession during the worst years of the cold war'.[65]

This is clear from the model through which the Soviet Union was understood, namely 'totalitarianism', which coincided neatly with the wider development of the term outside of the academy. As developed initially by Friedrich and Brzezinski, 'totalitarian' was taken to mean a one-party state, organised through terroristic police control, with a monopoly or near-monopoly over the means of communication and the military, centralised control of the economy, and an official ideology.[66] We have seen in previous chapters how this simply ignores the real history of states and movements which genuinely thought themselves 'totalitarian'. The point here is that the model simply describes certain features of the Soviet regime, building them into a definition of 'totalitarianism' such that the Soviet Union emerges as the epitome of the totalitarian regime. 'Totalitarianism' thereby became the dominant category in Russian/Soviet studies, the consensus underpinning vast swathes of Sovietology. It was also quickly taken up and turned into a key analytic tool within political science more generally. This is a paramount, though by no means the only, example, as we shall see, of political science as ideology, in which a whole research agenda was built around what was essentially an anti-communist slogan.[67] A term that had been used in official and popular discourse now had the air of intellectual gravitas, as more and more scholars working within the Institutes and Centers used it without question. And if they did not genuinely believe it, then the Loyalty Program encouraged them not to ask too many critical questions.[68]

The logic of totalitarianism as used in Russian/Soviet studies had as its corollary the logic of freedom being propagated by the US state as its own version of the good society. 'It is obvious that in using the totalitarian model', comments Alfred Meyer, 'American scholars were also celebrating Americanism'.[69] This then became the driving force behind the invention of American studies. By 1948 some sixty US institutions were offering undergraduate degrees in the field, compared with just seven institutions during the war. Postgraduate programmes similarly expanded, and American studies programmes began to be launched in other countries, such as the 'Americanistics' programme at Amsterdam from 1947 and the Salzburg Seminar in American Studies launched by Harvard students in the city in the same year. Key journals in the field began to be published in this period, such as *American Quarterly* from 1949, and key organisations were launched such as the American Studies Association in 1951.[70] While Paul Bové is right to argue that compared to other area studies, American studies had no integral links to the security state,[71] in focusing very much on 'American identity' and the 'American way of life' the emerging discipline nonetheless performed an important ideological function. Witness, for example, the report of a conversation between Richard Hoggart and a young American Fulbright scholar who was trying to explain what the discipline of American studies was all about. Hoggart was having difficulty grasping the idea until his interlocutor, after repeated efforts, finally blurted out: 'but you don't

understand, I *believe* in America'.[72] In peddling such belief and pan-
dering to the myth of consensus, freedom and democracy found in the
security–identity–loyalty complex, American studies offered a neat
contrast with the image of the totalitarian Soviet Union emerging
from within Russian studies, a contrast which reinforced the notion of
American exceptionalism and fitted comfortably with the imperialist
and authoritarian ideology then being more widely propagated.
Unsurprisingly, it too attracted corporate and state funding.[73]

At issue here, however, is not simply the generation of Russian or
Soviet studies on the one hand and American studies on the other.
Both were part and parcel of the growing trend for the national
security state to shape intellectual labour within the university. Out
of such 'schools for strategy'[74] emerged the key concepts of Cold
War confrontation and a justification for the logic and policy of
containment. Since the security project had by now become nothing
less than a project for the reshaping of global order, knowledge of all
problematic or potentially problematic nations, states and regions
became necessary. The security of the new global American empire
required an intellectual infrastructure producing the kind of
knowledge of the various 'areas' of the globe which were, or might
become, an issue. And since most major nations, states and regions
were either political enemies, potential enemies, or economic com-
petitors and therefore possibly just as dangerous, rather a lot of 'areas'
needed to be covered – more or less the whole world, in fact. 'How
shall we build this national program for area studies?' asked a report
produced by the Social Science Research Council in 1947. 'First, we
must work toward complete world coverage.'[75]

'Area studies' *per se* thus came to the fore, with Russian/Soviet
studies quickly followed by Asian studies, South Asian studies,
Japanese studies, Middle Eastern studies, African studies, West
European studies, Latin American studies, and so on, multiplying from
a mere handful before the war to 191 by 1968, to the extent that no
self-respecting university could get by without a range of area studies
centres. Given the close intellectual connection between area studies
and national security problems it is no surprise to note that many of
these new institutes were funded via new foundations established for
that purpose by the CIA, such as the Asia Foundation, or through new
journals, such as the *China Quarterly*, originally established with a CIA
subvention. The Ford Foundation alone provided $270 million to

thirty-four universities for area and language studies in the thirteen year period from 1953.[76] As a way of presenting the new area studies as highly innovative, involving interdisciplinary work against the 'conservatism' of traditional departments and their disciplines, the idea of 'behavioural science' came to the fore, pushed initially by the National Security Act. The Ford Foundation even had its own behavioural sciences division, which alone distributed $43 million in the seven years following its inception in 1951, most of which was to train more behaviouralists.[77] 'Behavioural science' was intended to flag up a multidisciplinary and thus intellectually radical coalition of sociologists, political scientists, psychologists and anthropologists, being brought together in area studies. It was also meant to skirt around any use of the word 'social', as in 'social sciences', which for many connoted the idea of radical change embodied in the 'social' of 'socialism'. (It is worth noting that the same purported intellectual radicalism behind such interdisciplinary work was strangely absent when other academics came to suggest the introduction of 'studies' which equally required interdisciplinary labour, such as 'Black studies'; the generosity towards interdisciplinary area studies was also hardly forthcoming towards interdisciplinary Black studies.[78])

Speaking at the School of Advanced International Studies at the Johns Hopkins University in 1963, McGeorge Bundy, originally of Harvard's Center for International Affairs and later JFK's national security advisor, spoke of the 'curious fact' of academic history, namely that 'in very large measure the area studies programs developed in American universities in the years after the war were manned, directed, or stimulated by graduates of the OSS', adding that 'there is a high measure of interpenetration between universities with area programs and the information-gathering agencies of the government of the United States.[79] Note: 'manned, directed, or *stimulated* by graduates of the OSS'. Regardless of the relative slowness in moving into certain areas, it is still reasonable to say that the growth of 'area studies' as a cross-disciplinary university enterprise grew out of the interests and needs of the security services. As Robin Winks has shown, area studies programmes in American universities came to reflect the relative strengths of the area-related staffs in the national security state. So the weakest for some time was Latin America and the security agencies were slow to move into Near- and Middle-Eastern studies.[80] With no real epistemological position or even method to speak of outside of a concern with 'security', area studies simply became a means of gathering information of use to the national security state. Because of this, pre-existing centres for the study of a particular area had to be either subsumed under the logic of security or pushed aside. For example, although the security services lacked real strength and intelligence in Latin American studies, they nonetheless ignored the expertise in the independent Institute of Hispanic American and Luso-Brazilian Studies under the leadership of Rodney Hilton at Stanford, and shunned its monthly *Hispanic American Report*. When Stanford was offered money to put together a Latin American studies programme via a Ford Foundation grant in 1963 and driven more explicitly by the demands of the national security state, the *Report* was suspended and the Hispanic Institute put on 'teaching only' duties.[81]

In stimulating and pursuing research in this way the national security state could shape the very concepts and methods to be used in its exercise.[82] Reflecting on his own experiences within area studies, Bruce Cumings comments that

> Countries inside the containment system, like Japan or South Korea, and those outside it, like China or North Korea, were clearly placed as friend or enemy, ally or adversary. In both direct and indirect ways the U.S. government and the major foundations traced these boundaries by directing scholarly attention to distinct places and to distinct ways of understanding them (for example, communist studies for North Korea and China; modernization studies for Japan and South Korea). To be in 'Korean studies' or 'Chinese studies' was to daily experience the tensions that afflicted Korea and China during the long period of the Cold War.[83]

Different concepts and discursive strategies were forged, giving rise to two key tropes: on the one hand, 'Pacific Rim' – a term helping to transform a former enemy into a friend but also invoking a community of the free, a huge historical forgetting, and a new-born world to which anyone could belong so long as they committed themselves wholeheartedly to the capitalist cause, transforming the general sensibility concerning nations such as Japan through the projection of more 'peaceable' philosophies such as Zen; on the other hand, 'Red China' – a nasty red blotch on the map.[84] Where it wasn't perpetuating a security-driven epistemology with categories such as 'Pacific Rim', area studies reified yet other categories, such as 'national character' or 'national culture', and even created new objects of analysis, such as the one based on an age-old cartographer's fantasy known as 'Asia'.[85] None of this mattered so long as it worked as a means of knowledge-production and -dissemination. The process of naming as such was sufficient to give the thing enough substance for the political work to be done: classification is a form of power, a means of generating the categories which then shape perceptions of the world.[86]

It is fair to say that to the extent that the American security state shaped the field of area studies, it had a profound impact on the intellectual research into those areas of the world seen to be communist or potentially so. But since this was a decidedly international project, area studies was accompanied at an early stage by 'international studies', incorporating international relations and languages as well as what was coming to pass as strategic studies and what would eventually emerge as security studies. The first significant centre for international studies was Massachusetts Institute of Technology's Center for International Studies (CENIS), which during its early years was underwritten by the CIA almost as a subsidiary enterprise funded via the Ford Foundation. CENIS's roots lie in a series of brainstorming sessions at MIT during 1950–1 involving military and security elites and social scientists and focusing on the problem of strategy and tactics for the Cold War, in particular concerning how to defeat the Soviet jamming of the *Voice of America*. The final report, delivered to the Secretary of State in February 1951, noted that although the initial problem posed to them appeared to be merely technical, 'the technical problem constitutes only one of a collection of inseparable conditions'. The questions to ask were not so much about technology and much more about psychology and propaganda: 'What is the nature of the people to whom the United States' messages are and ought to be directed? What ultimate effects are to be desired? What sort of messages ought to be sent?' As such, the final report made a range of recommendations concerning propaganda and communications, issues to which I turn in detail below. But one of its most influential recommendations concerned the recruitment of competent researchers, for which it pointed to universities as security resources, proposing a new kind of university

research institute which 'could carry out government research programs in the field of political warfare utilizing university personnel'.[87]
This report from 'Project Troy' was, according to Allan Needle, 'crafted
to help cement lasting relations between American academics
(specifically, natural scientists, social scientists, and historians) and
the American foreign and intelligence bureaucracies',[88] and led to the
creation of CENIS under the directorship of Max Millikan, who before
his appointment had been assistant to the director of the CIA.

Like area studies, then, the discipline of international studies was
also very much a product of the security project, developing in tandem
with area studies in general and Russian/Soviet studies in particular,
as CENIS became an archetype for government-sponsored imitators
at the universities of Washington, Illinois, Columbia, Princeton,
George Washington, Michigan, and dozens of others. Most were
'manned, directed or stimulated' by members or former members of
the security services, and key texts to emerge from the centres were
often funded by the CIA. Walt Rostow's *Dynamics of Soviet Society*
(1953), for example, appeared in two versions, one classified for the
CIA and others within the political establishment, and one un-
classified for the public. Both versions had the same central thesis –
that the Soviet Union was an imperialist power bent on world
domination and that the US had responsibility to fight this. The 'public'
version eventually became a key textbook in the field, but makes no
mention of the backing or financing of the book.[89] But to make the
point more fully, however, requires an illustration of the major themes,
concepts and foci of the discipline, most obviously with the categories
of 'development' and 'modernisation' and the associated notion of the
'Third World'.

'Development' and 'modernisation' (interchangeable terms for
many) had a role in rearticulating knowledge about the Pacific Rim
and Red China, with one a prime example of successful development
and the other the prime example of failed development. But the real
achievement of these concepts was to shape the research agenda
for the 'Third World', part of the schema for dividing the globe
conceptually into three 'worlds' which emerged at this time.[90] The
'Third World' was used to describe 'underdeveloped' or 'pre-modern'
nations as a group, but captures part of the insecurity surrounding the
'Second World' of socialist nations. This helped to simultaneously
demarcate research on communism from area studies, only to bring

them together politically through the question of communist infiltration and insurgency in the Third World. For in the schema, the Third
World was destined to become part of the First World – to modernise,
to develop – unless thwarted from doing so and directed into an
alternative modernity by communism. The logic of the 'three worlds'
was thus always much more than describing different parts of the
planet. Rather, it was a key concept for thinking about the relationship
between the First and Second Worlds, with the Third World a key site
of capitalist-communist confrontation. Thus in one sense the concept
of the Third World had nothing to do with relative poverty and
everything to do with absolute security: it was a term used to describe
non-aligned nations which could either become incorporated into the
order of international capital or become a security threat. And given
how common the 'three worlds' model became, to the extent that its
meaning was thought to be both self-evident and unmistakable, it is
safe to say that whole swathes of social science research were shaped
by this problematic.[91]

The key to this problematic of 'developing', 'modernising' the Third
World into the First rather than the Second was identified in a set of
'Pentagon Talks' in 1947 in which American and British officials agreed
on the need to stem widespread discontent in Africa and the Middle
East by improving living standards there, and was then pursued
by Truman in his 1949 inauguration speech in which he identified
'underdeveloped areas' as central to the unfolding security strategy.
Building on such prompts the CIA through the Social Science
Research Council and the Ford Foundation funded Rostow and others
to provide an anti-Communist grand narrative of history around
which a security strategy for the 'Third World' could be built. This
narrative was modernisation theory and the concept of development:
the belief that 'underdeveloped' areas suffered from a fundamental
lack, a fundamental *incapacity* which might be exploited as a political
weakness by communism. Their 'development' or 'modernisation' was
to be their salvation and, concomitantly, was to be the First World's
security. In one of the key texts of this new discipline, Daniel Lerner
comments that where once the talk had been of 'Europeanisation',
and then 'Americanisation' and so to 'Westernisation', Europe, America
and the West now offer an even broader notion: modernisation. Yet
this modernity is in conflict with an alternative: the modernity of communism.[92] At the same time, Lerner astutely noted that whereas some

political leaders found it easy to denounce the West, denouncing 'modernisation' was a much harder trick to pull off. Who could be *against* development, other than primitives and traditionalists?[93]

'Modernisation'/'development' studies, and the politics implicit within them concerning the superiority of America/Europe/the West in general and the nation-state and capital as the political forms of modernity, quickly became a key metanarrative surrounding the notion of security. And since this narrative incorporated an economic dimension, in the shift from subsistence economies to industrial-sation (a.k.a. 'growth'); a political dimension, in the shift from authori-tarian and tradition-bound systems to democratic and participatory systems; a social dimension, in the notion of a rise of individualism and social mobility; and a socio-religious dimension, in the notion of a shift towards secularisation, so the model had broad interdisciplinary appeal. Thus the work of Rostow on the Soviet Union, Gabriel Almond on psychological warfare, Harold Lasswell on public opinion, and Daniel Lerner on postwar Europe could provide both information and legitimisation for the security project being meted out across the globe, while the more overt attacks on the radicalism of Third World intellectuals put forward by Edward Shils and James Burnham could also offer a suitable level of polemical and rhetorical support.[94] And social scientists more generally were drawn in increasingly large numbers to the new field, for just as it didn't matter that the key intellectuals in Harvard's Russian Research Center had no prior knowledge of Russia, so it was equally unimportant that social scientists working in development studies also had little knowledge of the places that were said to need 'developing' – the key issue was less the 'Third World' itself and much more a commitment to the broad model of change and security implicit in the development/modernisation idea.

Since the key issue was how to prevent the Third World from 'falling' towards communism (from being 'failed states' *avant la lettre*), academics taken with this idea came to focus on the mechanisms for integrating these nations into the system of global capital, and to thus entrench capital into those same nations (socially and culturally as well as economically), a refinement of eighteenth-century liberal internationalism coordinated to the needs of the postwar international trading system established by the national security state and global capital.[95] The nature of the project is apparent from the sidelining of key radical thinkers in the field such as Gunnar Myrdal, Paul Baran or Barrington Moore Jr., but is perhaps most obvious in the body of economic theory that grew up around these ideas, which reproduces faithfully the liberal-imperialist assumption that 'developed' countries are in no way responsible for 'underdevelopment', says nothing about capitalist exploitation, and repeats the injunction that all countries work together towards 'social harmony'.[96] This does not mean that change was to be prevented. Rather, the question was the way in which change was to come about and the political direction or nature of the change. As an alternative to the revolutionary praxis of Marxism, development studies offered a version of Social Darwinism reworked through a structural-functionalist lens: identifying 'the requirements for modernisation' means 'defining social evolution in institutional terms'.[97] This is apparent from Rostow's *Stages of Economic Growth*. Subtitled *A Non-Communist Manifesto*, the book treats the economic field as essentially biological and so offers a non-Marxist materialism, arguing for the Third World to be allowed 'to enjoy the blessings and choices opened up by the march of compound interest' and mass consumption rather than the unmitigated misery of universal human freedom.[98] Moreover, in thinking about 'development' in these ways, development studies could then reinforce that fetish of area studies, the national model. As Harry Harootunian puts it, 'what eventually would be offered as both a representation of and a prescription for development was an evolutionary model of growth, against a putatively revolutionary one that, if followed, would promise the realization of the peaceful development of capitalism'.[99] 'Development' thus constituted an evolutionary adaptation to capital, reconfigured as 'modernisation'. At the same moment that western modernity was being restructured in all its capitalist glory, the 'underdeveloped' world was formed as a new deployment of power for the security of liberal order-building.

We can trace this from a report written by members of staff at CENIS and backtrack from there. Written under the direction of Max Millikan, and involving Daniel Lerner, Walt Rostow and Lucian Pye, the report was presented to the Senate Committee on Foreign Relations in January 1960. Called 'Economic, Social, and Political Change in the Underdeveloped Countries and Its Implications for United States Policy', the report was published the following year as *The Emerging Nations*.[100] As a means of understanding social change in colonial societies, the report offered a classification of the Third World in terms of 'traditional societies', 'modern oligarchies' and 'potentially democratic' formations. Each of these felt the pressures generated by the push to modernisation, since 'virtually all individuals everywhere want some of the fruits of modernization'.[101] These 'fruits' lay in economic development, which was in turn thought to be the condition of democratisation. But the key question was how to maintain stability and order in the context of development, for such instability leads to guerilla operations and encourages people 'to accept in desperation the unity and discipline that Communist and other totalitarian forms of social organization hold out to them'.[102] Here development studies leant intellectual weight to counter-insurgency practices: since the rationality of capitalist modernity was taken as read, so the necessity and rationality of eliminating oppositionist movements needed to be explained and justified. Counter-insurgency practices carried out by military elites and newly emerging security forces were thought to be crucial to maintaining order and authority under the process of modernisation and development. The report thereby articulated a set of views that had emerged from CENIS, facilitated by the security elites, and which then filtered through other developing centres for international studies, helping to create a *de facto* agenda for development studies in which the conjunction of national security and economic order were integrally connected to intellectual, political and cultural understandings of America's place in the world and its modernising mission.[103] Indeed, a major text in the literature edited by Gabriel Almond and James S. Coleman concluded that 'Anglo-American qualities most closely approximate the model of the modern political system'.[104]

These general ideas permeated the more specific texts within the disciplines. For example, Lerner's *The Passing of a Traditional Society: Modernizing the Middle East*, published in 1958 following research conducted since 1950 under joint sponsorship by CENIS and the Bureau of Applied Social Research (BASR) at Columbia, became a hugely influential text. In it Lerner suggested that while in Turkey and Lebanon modernisation and stability and tended to go together, in countries such as Iran and Syria this had not been the case. While Turkey and Lebanon were 'democratising', Iran and Syria were 'bolshevising'. In frustrating the course of modernisation by cultivating political 'extremism', the 'bolshevising' tendencies were said to act as a block on the 'right' form of political development, the direction and tempo of which was meant to be overseen by a new elite committed to modernisation.

In conforming to US policy in particular and the bourgeois conception of development in general, it is not difficult to see what took place more as 'underdevelopment' or 'maldevelopment', a direct result of pursuing US security interests at the expense of genuine improvements in people's lives and standards of living, carrying with it brutal violence in the form of counterinsurgency and destabilisation, again organised by 'First World' security agencies for the benefit of international capital.[105] This gave radical new life to the idea of 'police' and 'military assistance', which increasingly allowed states to exercise violence in the name of development: 'police' and 'military' assistance were thought necessary as counters to the insurgencies generated by the struggles over the modernisation process, but were to be offered only to those nations 'developing' in the appropriate ways.[106] 'Development' thus became a means of extending 'security', while 'security measures' became necessary due to the upheavals and resistance caused by development. Security intellectuals working in this field were deeply complicit in this process, providing the key information for the security agencies, legitimising the system, and peddling the key notions and concepts used in a range of books and reports. Contrary to recent accounts trying to 'humanise' security by merging it with development,[107] development and security have always been merged; indeed, development is a security concept.

Out of the question of how to maintain political order in the context of modernisation, elite formation and political culture came to the fore. Because 'modernity is a style of life' as well as an economic project the crux of the matter was *how* one might move from traditional ways towards modern life-styles.[108] The focus on political culture naturally meant a focus on the main forms of cultural transmission and, in particular, the practices of participation. Lerner suggests that whereas traditional society is non-participant, modern society involves a culture of participation: formal schooling, reading newspapers, expressing an opinion, changing jobs, voting in elections of competing candidates.[109] This is clear from the defining text on political culture, Almond and Verba's *The Civic Culture* (1963). This book is now regarded as a classic of comparative politics and for putting the concept of political culture onto the map of political science. But it should in fact be read as a contribution to the American national security state, for which Gabriel Almond served: its central argument is congruent with the strategy being employed by the national security state, in which the whole machinery of government in 'developing' states, including 'the people' themselves, was found wanting compared to those of liberal democracies, and which therefore needed the winning of hearts and minds through a psychocultural security project.[110] In their book Almond and Verba state that 'new world political culture will be a political culture of participation', which they take to mean 'the belief that the ordinary man is politically relevant' (the ordinary woman presumably not expected to enjoy the same level of participation or relevance). The term 'belief' is important here, since the authors accept that much of the argument about participation is based on the myth of participation: that citizens see themselves as potentially active. Indeed, actual participation is not really desirable for good order, since participation was more often than not a cause for concern: the ideal order is one in which 'the ordinary citizen be relatively passive, uninvolved, and deferential'.[111] The ideal citizen is a docile body. The other side of this argument is that the passive, uninvolved and deferential citizen be led by 'modernising elites' who by definition possess 'modern' habits and characteristics. 'Modernisation' was in this way part of the battle over identity discussed in the previous chapter, one in which the security intellectuals were more than willing to take sides armed with classically liberal notions of individuality, rationality and the standard justifications for the severe inequalities between nations. At the same time, modernisation theory also coincided with some of the main assumptions of elite theory. The real issue, however, is that since the participatory state can be either democratic or totalitarian, the project is to ensure that only one of these wins out – or, to put it another way, to ensure that one of the myths is more successful.[112] 'In American Cold War-era scholarship on political culture', notes Ida Oren, 'the boundaries between the study of political culture and the politics of U.S. foreign policy were porous at best'.[113] In fact, what emerges from the academic study of political culture is an argument for extending the security project into the Third World, a reinforcement of the prevailing economic and political orthodoxy around capital, and thus an apology for counterinsurgency tactics, all dressed up in the garb of 'comparative politics'.[114]

Almond and Verba suggest that ensuring the victory of the democratic myth – of any myth – means ensuring that leaders in developing nations use the right psychological and cultural tactics. Shifting the focus of discussion onto questions of psychology in this way involves an important ideological shift of the focus away from questions of the process or underlying structural issues of socioeconomic change to one of the actors involved and the cultures in which they are immersed.[115] This simultaneously reinforces a set of arguments within international studies about mass psychology and communications. For Almond and Verba (the former having served as external consultant to the Psychological Strategy Board) the central feature of political culture is *'psychological orientation toward social objects'*.[116] As well as playing on dubious claims about 'national character' which Almond had developed in his book *The American People and the Foreign Policy* (in which he sought to assess the 'psychological potential' of the American people in the struggle for world leadership),[117] this argument overlaps nicely with modernisation theory: in Rostow's argument, cultivating the appropriate psychological outlook is a way for societies to be jolted into modernisation. In the final chapter of *The Stages of Economic Growth*, on 'Marxism, Communism, and the Stages-of-Growth', the fundamental difference between the Communist and non-Communist analyses is said to lie in the view of human motivation. Marx's analyses fail to explain historical transformation because they fail to grasp human motivation and psychology.[118] Arguments such as these made questions of psychology a security issue. Ellen Herman notes that many psychologists in the early Cold War thought that there was little point in assisting abstractions like 'developing societies'. But 'personalities', on the other hand, were concrete entities, and concrete entities about which psychology claimed to know. Thus psychologists were increasingly used within the intellectual programmes generated by the national security state, which after all had been aiming for an interdisciplinary approach; they could also justify their inclusion on the grounds of national security. Herman writes that the concept of political culture thereby injected a new appreciation for psychology into the study of comparative politics, though we might just as easily say that psychology's politicisation came via its incorporation into the disciplinary shifts registered by the rhetoric of national security.[119]

Part of the point about the discussion of the 'psychological orientation' of individuals within the political culture is that their 'personalities' could be shaped through political intervention. One of the 'appeals of communism', as Gabriel Almond argued in a book with that title, lay in the personal deviance and psychological maladjustment on the part of social misfits, expressed in social forms of resentment, alcoholism and, as we saw in the previous chapter, sexual promiscuity.[120] This needed psychological work on the part of elites, in yet another attempt at the conduct of conduct. In an essay on 'Political Culture and Political Development' Lucian Pye suggested that 'the concept of political culture assumes that each individual must, in his own historical context, learn and appropriate into his own personality the knowledge and feelings about the politics of his people and his community. This means in turn that the political culture of a society is limited but given firm structure by the factors basic to dynamic psychology'.[121] For other contributors to the book, psychological orientation towards ones political culture was a form of national identity: a sense of belonging, a form of patriotism, and thus the foundation of loyalty. According to Verba, for example, 'the question of national identity is the political culture version of the basic problem of self-identity', whereby physical and legal membership of a system should coincide with psychological membership. As well as legitimising the activities of national elites, this psycho-political affect also perpetuates feelings of loyalty among the members.[122]

This helped develop the discipline of 'mass communication', since it was widely assumed that modernisation involved not just industrialisation, secularisation and urbanisation, but also a well-developed communications system. Lerner's argument, for example, was that in certain developing societies, 'psychological participation' through opinion was spreading before genuine economic and political participation, creating a mass of people relatively well-informed through the mass media but politically disenfranchised and economically struggling, and therefore susceptible to communist insurgents.[123] To control this situation required elite management of the media and communications systems. This reinforced the importance of 'communications research' in the field of international studies and facilitated the rise of 'mass communications research' as a distinct disciplinary activity. Lerner's book therefore became and remained a foundational text in communication studies as well as development theory.

Christopher Simpson has shown how 'mass communications' has its origins in 'psychological operations' used in World War Two and then further intensified with a multi-million-dollar bureaucracy for conducting clandestine psychological warfare during the Cold War. NSC 4 (December 1947) established measures for 'the immediate strengthening and coordination of all foreign information measures . . . to counteract effects of anti-U.S. propaganda', following which emerged funding for the *Voice of America*, scholarly exchange programmes, cultural centres abroad, and other means of propaganda. NSC 4-A, a 'top secret' document issued on the same day as NSC 4, was even more explicit about the necessity for covert psychological operations along with the overt ones encouraged by NSC 4.[124] The psychological operations programme was then expanded in March 1949 with NSC-43, again a year later with NSC-59 (March 1950), and then again with NSC 129/1 (April 1952). The language around 'psychological warfare' – and even the term itself – involved a multi-layered, euphemistic and often contradictory terminology 'that permitted those who had been initiated into the arcana of national security to discuss psychological operations and clandestine warfare in varying degrees of specificity depending on the audience, while simultaneously denying the very existence of these projects when it was politically convenient to do so'.[125] Part of this euphemism and fudging lay in the very term 'mass communications research' itself, which sounds less underhand than 'propaganda' and less violent than 'psychological warfare'. Sounds, in fact, like an academic discipline.

To this end the security services, military intelligence and propaganda agencies helped bankroll all the large-scale communications research projects by US scholars, including the research into techniques of persuasion, opinion measurement, interrogation, political and military mobilisation and the propagation of ideology. At least six of the most important centres of communication studies, including the Survey Research Center (SRC, later to become the Institute for Social Research) at the University of Michigan, BASR at Columbia, and CENIS, developed as *de facto* adjuncts of government psychological warfare programmes, with the US allocating between $7 million and $13 million annually for university and think-tank studies into communications. The reliance of such centres on psychological warfare money 'was so extensive as to suggest that the crystallisation of mass communications studies into a distinct scholarly field might not have come about during the 1950s without substantial military, CIA, and USIA [US Information Agency] intervention'.[126]

The point, again, is not about contacts and money *per se*; nor is it about the *use* of the discipline of communication studies. Rather it is that the discipline was actively *constructed* by the national security state. If the critical point of leverage in intellectual work lies in the formation of agendas, models, perspectives and concepts, then the extent to which this discipline was shaped by the logic of security becomes clear. Take for example the key journal and key textbook in the field, *Public Opinion Quarterly* (POQ) and *The Process and Effects of Mass Communication* (1954), edited by Walter Schramm. The editors of and main contributors to *POQ* all had close links to the security services, with many dependent on such government funding for their livelihood. Simpson shows that between 1945 and 1955 the case studies, research reports and polemics in *POQ* were all in favour of expanded psychological operations, with the journal publishing articles that tended to reinforce the official US position on relations with the Soviet Union, the 1948 election in Italy, and the Middle East. The journal offered repeated publication, editorial slots, book excerpts and book reviews to those working in the new field, such as Daniel Lerner, W. Phillips Davison and Harold Lasswell. *POQ* thus managed to articulate and defend particular preconceptions about mass communication. To give just one example, a special issue of *POQ* on 'International Communications Research' in 1952 contained essays on psychological policy, the international impact of *Voice of America*, resistance to propaganda, the comparative study of communications, and some case studies of techniques and countries. Many of the essays, such as Charles Y. Glock's 'Comparative Study of Communications and Opinion Formation', were underwritten by the Department of State (and virtually all US research into 'national communication systems' during the decade that followed was underwritten by the Department of State or the military). They helped forge the idea of 'national communication systems' and implied that propaganda and communication management are characteristic of all states. While suggesting that what was different was the degree or style of control, this normalised the concept being articulated. At the same time, the journal marginalised those it saw as 'outside' the discipline, those critical theorists and others who wrote with more radical views about the topic of communication: *POQ* had no space for articles by or on critical theorists working on themes concerning mass communication, such as Adorno, Horkheimer or C. Wright Mills, and ridiculed any widely read critical work on the subject, such as Vance Packard's *The Hidden Persuaders*.[127]

Schramm's book, said by some to be the springboard for the launch of communications research as an autonomous academic discipline,[128] replicated and reinforced this tendency. Schramm founded the first independent Department of Communications at Iowa and in 1947 established the Institute of Communications Research at the University of Illinois, which formed the basis of the first doctoral programme in mass communications.[129] Many of the essays in the book had state backing, which the book nowhere mentions. Nor does it mention the fact that the book was prepared originally as training material for US propaganda programmes. More important is the way that the book helped forge a key set of agreed concepts for the discipline, such as the idea of a 'national communications system', the 'opinion leader', 'reference groups', and the distinction between 'elite' and 'mass' audiences. Schramm's own work had already placed the idea of 'personal influence' on the research agenda of the discipline.

Schramm's research on Korea, funded by USIA and published as a commercial book co-written with John Riley, called *The Reds Take a City: The Communist Occupation of Seoul, with Eyewitness Accounts* (1951), translated into twelve languages and distributed throughout the world by the US Information Service, had led him to argue that the effect of communications messages was more a function of the psychological and social status of the recipient rather than the message itself. The real test of this, he believed, was the effect of communications in a 'Soviet' society, such as Korea. (It didn't seem to matter that Korea was not a 'Soviet' society.) Through this test Schramm came to distinguish between 'authoritarian' and 'Soviet totalitarian' communication systems, with the latter reducible to three basic elements: monopoly, concentration, and reinforcement. From this Schramm could argue that authoritarian but anti-communist states are inherently better than communist states because of the structure of their communication systems – one is more 'free' than the other.[130] At the same time, however, he also argued that Soviet experts were aware of the limits of persuasion through the national communication system and so employed 'personal influence' via respected members of a person's social network and 'face-to-face indoctrination' via 'opinion leaders'. And so the concept of 'personal influence' became a dominant paradigm in media sociology.[131] This then reinforced assumptions about the inevitability and appropriateness of elite control of mass communication, especially in 'managing' the modernisation process, 'winning' targeted audiences and, by distorting unauthorised communication, helping ensure that indigenous radical and democratic movements did not achieve their goals. This helped effect a highly convenient shift in language as, for example, 'deception' could be recast as 'perception management'. Beyond communication research this paradigm was one in which the purported 'study' of power by social scientists was in fact a rationalisation of that power, in which all that mattered was to improve its efficiency and effectiveness.[132]

I have been arguing, then, that the ideology of security shaped a whole tranche of academic work within the social sciences, which then reinforced the very project being undertaken in the name of security, to the extent that dominant paradigms within the social sciences concerning development, modernisation, mass communication and political culture were in fact part and parcel of the *paradigm of domination*, as Simpson puts it. This is not to say that every scholar in these disciplines was some kind of political lackey – the US state's role in Vietnam came under fire from some Southeast Asia specialists, its policy concerning Pakistan came under fire from some within South Asian studies, its role in Latin America came under fire from some of those working in Latin American studies, and the same can be said for its role in Middle East politics.[133] My point, rather, is that most of the major and many of the minor concepts used within the disciplines I have been discussing were shaped by a political project that under its broadest label could be called the search for security. Far from being autonomous disciplines, never mind ones founded with a critical political edge, these disciplines were central to the ideological growth of the logic of security, part of the discursive economy built up to project the logic of security across the face of the globe. They became crucial capillaries for the dissemination and articulation of the meaning, production and spread of a certain kind of knowledge oriented around the idea of security, and their key thinkers became the 'organic intellectuals' of the security state, accepting, parroting and legitimising the official security policy of the hegemonic power, the political economy of security, and the logic of security as a whole. They were well equipped to serve in this way because their categories of analysis, particularly their conceptions of power, knowledge and order were no different from those found in the political rhetoric of the state itself.

This was parallelled in shifts in other more established disciplines, which were encouraged to rethink their approaches and assumptions. In economics, game theory, linear programming and mathematical approaches came to dominate the field as the national security state made available large amounts of research funding to those willing to work in these areas, due to their focus on conflict and decision-making within the context of constrained maximums or minimums. The same is true of rational choice theory, which came to dominate political science.[134] And anthropological research was also reshaped in ways of interest to the national security state.[135] But the security intellectuals were to find their real home in that newest of new disciplines: 'security studies'.

Security studies became a decisive field in western intellectual labour with the birth and growth of the security state. A whole profession devoted to 'security' quickly emerged, initially as a subdiscipline of International Relations (with its own supine relation to the state)[136] and gradually in its own right in the university – and now in the twenty-first century the growth discipline *par excellence*. Security studies, like its sister discipline strategic studies, emerged as part of the discursive economy built up around a politics driven by the logic of security and dominated by the concerns of the hegemonic powers. Existing from its birth as far as could be imagined from the idea of critique, security studies easily adopted some of the key categories of imperial confrontation, especially those which over-lapped with international and area studies, such as 'deterrence'. 'Most academics in national security studies were concerned with various issues of deterrence broadly conceived', reports Deborah Welch Larson, 'such as the development of strategies to deter Soviet aggression'.[137] As such it became an important factor in the dissemination and articulation of security concerns on the part of such powers, not least because its central categories and key conceptions of power, subjectivity and knowledge were no different from those of the rhetoric of hegemonic powers themselves. In its fetish for security and the state, and the geopolitical project being carried out in their name, security studies quickly came to act as a 'celebratory' enterprise,

valorising liberal values, institutions and political economy and entrenched in a defence of a distinct historical and cultural achievement,
sometimes known as 'the West' but better understood as capitalist
modernity.[138] Its central presumption, that the state provides the
legitimate framework for negotiating the insecurities of the modern
world and capital the basis for this negotiation, makes less sense than
it ever did.

Anyone well versed in history or with experience of university life
will know about the shameful ways in which large numbers of
academics have elevated venality into the cardinal academic virtue,
complying with the demands of those in power and the wishes of
those with money: witness the political scientists, historians, anthro-
pologists, geographers, cartographers, sociologists, linguists and many
others who reworked their disciplines according to the principles and
myths, and the principle myths, of fascism.[139] 'Academic life under
fascism', notes Christopher Hutton, 'is a dismal . . . episode in an
unedifying story of relations between the modern academic and the
state, and between academics and power both within and outside the
university'.[140] But this part of the history of fascism is merely the worst
moment in the wider and equally unedifying story of relations
between academics and the state more generally, merely one way in
which intellectuals have kowtowed to the principles and myths, and
the principle myths, concerning security and the state. Spouting
the jargon of security and enthralled by the trappings of power, their
intellectual labour consists of nothing less than attempts to write hand-
books for the princes of the new security state. The death of countless
numbers in a more 'efficient' bombing of a city, the stationing of troops
halfway around the world in order to bring to an end any attempt at
collective self-determination, the use of military machines against
civilians, the training of police forces in counter-insurgency practices,
but more than anything the key concepts and categories used to
explain and justify these things – all defended, supported and even
'improved' by security intellectuals for whom, ultimately, intellectual
labour boils down to little more than the question of the most efficient
manner in which to achieve the security demanded by the state and
bourgeois order. In rationalising the political and corporate logic of
security, the security intellectual conceals the utter irrationality of the
system as a whole. The security intellectual, then, is nothing less than
the security ideologue, peddling the fetish of our time.

CLOSING GAMBIT: RETURN THE GIFT

The only way out of such a dilemma, to escape the fetish, is perhaps to eschew the logic of security altogether – to reject it as so ideologically loaded in favour of the state that any real political thought other than the authoritarian and reactionary should be pressed to give it up. That is clearly something that can not be achieved within the limits of bourgeois thought and thus could never even begin to be imagined by the security intellectual. It is also something that the constant iteration of the refrain 'this is an insecure world' and reiteration of one fear, anxiety and insecurity after another will also make it hard to do. But it is something that the critique of security suggests we may have to consider if we want a political way out of the impasse of security.

This impasse exists because security has now become so all-encompassing that it marginalises all else, most notably the constructive conflicts, debates and discussions that animate political life. The constant prioritising of a mythical security as a political end – as *the* political end – constitutes a rejection of politics in any meaningful sense of the term. That is, as a mode of action in which differences can be articulated, in which the conflicts and struggles that arise from such differences can be fought for and negotiated, in which people might come to believe that another world is possible – that they might transform the world and in turn be transformed. Security politics simply removes this; worse, it removes it while purportedly addressing it. In so doing it suppresses all issues of power and turns political questions into debates about the most efficient way to achieve 'security', despite the fact that we are never quite told – never could be told – what might count as having achieved it. Security politics is, in this sense, an anti-politics,[141] dominating political discourse in much the same manner as the security state tries to dominate human beings, reinforcing security fetishism and the monopolistic character of security on the political imagination. We therefore need to get beyond security politics, not add yet more 'sectors' to it in a way that simply expands the scope of the state and legitimises state intervention in yet more and more areas of our lives.

Simon Dalby reports a personal communication with Michael Williams, co-editor of the important text *Critical Security Studies*, in which the latter asks: if you take away security, what do you put in the hole that's left behind? But I'm inclined to agree with Dalby: maybe there is no hole.[142] The mistake has been to think that there is a hole and that this hole needs to be filled with a new vision or revision of security in which it is re-mapped or civilised or gendered or humanised or expanded or whatever. All of these ultimately remain within the statist political imaginary, and consequently end up re-affirming the state as the terrain of modern politics, the grounds of security. The real task is not to fill the supposed hole with yet another vision of security, but to fight for an alternative political language which takes us beyond the narrow horizon of bourgeois security and which therefore does not constantly throw us into the arms of the state. That's the point of critical politics: to develop a new political language more adequate to the kind of society we want. Thus while much of what I have said here has been of a negative order, part of the tradition of critical theory is that the negative may be as significant as the positive in setting thought on new paths.

For if security really is the supreme concept of bourgeois society and the fundamental thematic of liberalism, then to keep harping on about insecurity and to keep demanding 'more security' (while meekly hoping that this increased security doesn't damage our liberty) is to blind ourselves to the possibility of building real alternatives to the authoritarian tendencies in contemporary politics. To situate ourselves against security politics would allow us to circumvent the debilitating effect achieved through the constant securitising of social and political issues, debilitating in the sense that 'security' helps consolidate the power of the existing forms of social domination and justifies the short-circuiting of even the most democratic forms. It would also allow us to forge another kind of politics centred on a different con-ception of the good. We need a new way of thinking and talking about social being and politics that moves us beyond security. This would perhaps be emancipatory in the true sense of the word. What this might mean, precisely, must be open to debate. But it certainly requires recognising that security is an illusion that has forgotten it is an illusion; it requires recognising that security is not the same as solidarity; it requires accepting that insecurity is part of the human condition, and thus giving up the search for the certainty of security and instead learning to tolerate the uncertainties, ambiguities and 'insecurities' that come with being human; it requires accepting that 'securitizing' an issue does not mean dealing with it politically, but bracketing it out and handing it to the state; it requires us to be brave enough to return the gift.[143]

NOTES

INTRODUCTION

1. Cited in David Lister, 'Two Wheels: Good. Two Legs: Terrorist Suspect', *The Times*, 17 October 2005.
2. MI5, *Protecting Against Terrorism* (HMSO, 2005), p. 11.
3. Michael J. Shapiro, *Reading the Postmodern Polity: Political Theory as Textual Practice* (Minneapolis: University of Minnesota Press, 1992).
4. *Iraq: Law of Occupation*, House of Commons Research Paper 03/51, 2 June 2003, pp. 7–8.
5. Michael Dillon, *Politics of Security: Towards a Political Philosophy of Continental Thought* (London: Routledge, 1996), p. 14; Michael Dillon, 'Culture, Governance, and Global Politics', in François Debrix and Cynthia Weber (eds), *Rituals of Mediation: International Politics and Social Meaning* (Minneapolis: University of Minnesota Press, 2003), p. 136; David A. Baldwin, 'The Concept of Security', *Review of International Studies*, Vol. 23, No. 1, 1997, pp. 5–26, p. 26.
6. *AUT Look* [Newsletter of the former Association of University Teachers in Britain], November 2004, p. 9; Food Security Ltd, 'Factsheet', no date [Spring 2006]; tiger case cited in James Randerson, 'Tigers on the Brink of Extinction', *The Guardian*, 21 July 2006, p. 3.
7. Bradley S. Klein, 'Conclusion: Every Month is "Security Awareness Month"', in Keith Krause and Michael C. Williams (eds), *Critical Security Studies: Concepts and Cases* (London: UCL Press, 1997).
8. See Joseph J. Romm, *Defining National Security* (New York, 1983); Emma Rothschild, 'What is Security?', *Daedalus*, Vol. 124, No. 3, 1995, pp. 53–98; Mohammed Ayoob, 'Defining Security: A Subaltern Realist Perspective', in Krause and Williams (eds), *Critical Security Studies*.
9. Lester Brown, *Redefining National Security*, Worldwatch Papers No. 14 (Washington, 1977); Richard Ullmann, 'Redefining Security', *International Security*, Vol. 8, No. 1, 1983, pp. 129–53; Jessica Tuchman Mathews, 'Redefining Security', *Foreign Affairs*, Vol. 68, No. 2, 1989, pp. 162–77.

10. J. Ann Tickner, 'Re-visioning Security', in Ken Booth and Steve Smith (eds), *International Relations Theory Today* (Cambridge: Polity Press, 1995).

11. Bradley S. Klein, 'Politics by Design: Remapping Security Landscapes', *European Journal of International Relations*, Vol. 4, No. 3, 1998, pp. 327–45.

12. J. Ann Tickner, *Gender in International Relations: Feminist Perspectives on Achieving Global Security* (New York: Columbia University Press, 1993); Jill Steans, *Gender and International Relations* (Cambridge: Polity Press, 1997), pp. 104–29; Miranda Alison, 'Women as Agents of Political Violence: Gendering Security', *Security Dialogue*, Vol. 35, No. 4, 2004, pp. 447–63.

13. Anthony Burke, 'Aporias of Security', *Alternatives*, Vol. 27, No. 1, 2002, pp. 1–27; *Beyond Security, Ethics and Violence: War Against the Other* (London: Routledge, 2007), pp. 52–3, 78.

14. Lucia Zedner, 'Too Much Security?', *International Journal of the Sociology of Law*, Vol. 31, No. 3, 2003, pp. 155–84.

15. Ian Loader and Neil Walker, *Civilizing Security* (Cambridge: Cambridge University Press, 2007).

16. Michael Williams, 'Words, Images, Enemies: Securitization and International Politics', *International Studies Quarterly*, Vol. 47, No. 4, 2003, pp. 511–31; William Walters, 'Figuring Security: Notes on Power, In/Security and Territory', paper presented at the Global Norms Under Siege Symposium, Queens University Belfast, May 2005.

17. Mark Neocleous, *Imagining the State* (Maidenhead: Open University Press, 2003); *The Monstrous and the Dead: Burke, Marx, Fascism* (Cardiff: University of Wales Press, 2005). The best work on this aspect of security is David Campbell, *Writing Security: United States Foreign Policy and the Politics of Identity* (Manchester: Manchester University Press, 1992).

18. Ole Waever, 'Securitization and Desecuritization', in Ronnie D. Lipshutz (ed.), *On Security* (New York: Columbia University Press, 1995), p. 75.

19. Didier Bigo, 'The Mobius Ribbon of Internal and External Security(ies)', in Mathias Albert, David Jacobson and Yosef Lapid (eds), *Identities, Borders, Orders: Rethinking International Relations Theory* (Minneapolis: University of Minnesota Press, 2001), p. 95.

20. André Gorz, 'Security: Against What? For What? With What?', *Telos*, 58, 1983–4, pp. 158–68; Giorgio Agamben, 'Security and Terror', *Theory and Event*, Vol. 5, No. 4, 2002.

21. Corey Robin, 'Protocols of Machismo', *London Review of Books*, 19 May 2005, pp. 11–14.

22. Dillon, *Politics of Security*, p. 16.

23. Mark Neocleous, *The Fabrication of Social Order: A Critical Theory of Police Power* (London: Pluto Press, 2000).

24. Ken Booth, 'Security and Emancipation', *Review of International Studies*, Vol. 17, No. 4, 1991, pp. 313–26, pp. 319, 323. Also Richard Wyn Jones,

Security, Strategy, and Critical Theory (Boulder, CO: Lynne Rienner, 1999); Ken Booth (ed.), *Critical Security Studies and World Politics* (Boulder, CO: Lynne Rienner, 2005).

25. For some bizarre reason Loader and Walker, *Civilizing Security*, p. 83, lump me in with 'critical security studies', a lumping which is even more bizarre when one realises that their understanding of 'critical security studies' is that it involves 'a leftist articulation of Carl Schmitt's characterization of modern politics'. This is a lazy and misleading description of my work, since I have been arguing against leftist articulations of Schmitt for well over a decade now – see 'Friend or Enemy? Reading Schmitt Politically', *Radical Philosophy*, 79, 1996, pp. 13–23. I carry on this argument in Chapter 2 below.

26. United Nations Development Programme, *Human Development Report 1994* (Oxford: Oxford University Press, 1994), p. 23.

27. Simon Dalby, *Environmental Security* (Minneapolis: University of Minnesota Press, 2002), p. xxvi.

28. Letter to Lassalle, 22 February 1858, in Karl Marx and Frederick Engels, *Collected Works, Vol. 40* (London: Lawrence and Wishart, 1983), p. 270.

29. Louis Althusser, 'Ideology and Ideological State Apparatuses' (1969), in *Lenin and Philosophy and other Essays*, trans. Ben Brewster (London: New Left Books, 1971), p. 161.

30. The model here is Theodor Adorno, 'Culture Industry Reconsidered' (1964), trans. Anson Rabinbach, in *The Culture Industry: Selected Essays on Mass Culture*, ed. J. M. Bernstein (London: Routledge, 1991).

31. Michel Foucault, 'What is Critique?', Lecture at the Sorbonne, 27 May 1978, trans. Kevin Paul Geiman, in James Schmidt (ed.), *What is Enlightenment?* (Berkeley, CA: University of California Press, 1996), p. 384.

32. Michel Foucault, 'Practicing Criticism' (1981), trans. Alan Sheridan, in Lawrence D. Kritzman (ed.), *Michel Foucault: Politics, Philosophy, Culture. Interviews and Other Writings, 1977–1984* (New York: Routledge, 1988), p. 154.

33. Michel Foucault, 'Rituals of Exclusion', in *Foucault Live: Collected Interviews, 1961–1984*, trans. Lysa Hochroth and John Johnston (New York: Semiotext(e), 1996), p. 68.

34. I use the term 'national security state' at times to refer to the specific entity which emerged in post-war America. At other times, however, I also use it as a cover term for the complex of networks which operates through the state in general, a network which includes the security and intelligence services but also a range of state and parastate apparatuses.

35. Williams, 'Words, Images, Enemies', p. 523; Bradley S. Klein, *Strategic Studies and World Order: The Global Politics of Deterrence* (Cambridge: Cambridge University Press, 1994), p. 140; Kanishka Jayasuriya,

'September 11, Security, and the New Postliberal Politics of Fear', in Eric Hershberg and Kevin W, Moore (eds), *Critical Views of September 11* (New York: New Press, 2002).

36. Jef Huysmans, 'Defining Social Constructivism in Security Studies: The Normative Dilemma in Writing Security', *Alternatives*, Vol. 27, Special Issue, 2002, pp. 41–62, p. 43.

37. Harry Harootunian, 'The Imperial Present and the Second Coming of Fascism', *boundary 2*, Vol. 34, No. 1, 2007, pp. 1–15, p. 11.

38. Mark Neocleous, *Fascism* (Maidenhead: Open University Press, 1997); Theodor Adorno, 'The Meaning of Working Through the Past', in *Critical Models: Interventions and Catchwords*, trans. Henry W. Pickford (New York: Columbia University Press, 1998); Harry Harootunian, 'The Future of Fascism', *Radical Philosophy*, 136, 2006, pp. 23–33; Samir Amin, *Capitalism in the Age of Globalization* (London: Zed Books, 1997), pp. 102–3; Nikhil Singh, 'The Afterlife of Fascism', *South Atlantic Quarterly*, Vol. 105, No. 1, 2006, pp. 71–93, p. 79.

CHAPTER 1: 'THE SUPREME CONCEPT OF BOURGEOIS SOCIETY'

1. See, for example, the British Home Office document *Counter-Terrorism Powers: Reconciling Security and Liberty in an Open Society: A Discussion Paper* (Cm 6147, February 2004), and Paper by the UK Presidency [of the EU], *Liberty and Security: Striking the Right Balance* (2005).

2. Ronald Dworkin, 'The Threat to Patriotism', *New York Review*, 28 February 2002, pp. 44–9, building on his questioning of the metaphor in *Taking Rights Seriously* (London: Duckworth, 1978), p. 198; Andrew Ashworth, *The Criminal Process: An Evaluative Study* (Oxford: Oxford University Press, 1998), p. 30; 'Security, Terrorism and the Value of Human Rights', in Benjamin J. Goold and Liora Lazarus (eds), *Security and Human Rights* (Oxford: Hart Publishing, 2007). Also Jeremy Waldron, 'Security and Liberty: The Image of Balance', *Journal of Political Philosophy*, Vol. 11, No. 2, 2003, pp. 191–210; Laura K. Donohue, 'Security and Freedom on the Fulcrum', *Terrorism and Political Violence*, Vol. 17, No. 1, 2005, pp. 69–87.

3. Ian Loader and Neil Walker, *Civilizing Security* (Cambridge: Cambridge University Press, 2007), p. 55, emphasis added.

4. Michel Foucault, 'Governmentality' (1978), in Graham Burchell, Colin Gordon and Peter Miller (eds), *The Foucault Effect: Studies in Governmentality* (London: Harvester Wheatsheaf, 1991); '"Omnes and Singulatim": Toward a Critique of Political Reason', in *Power: The Essential Works, Vol. 3* (London: Penguin, 2000); 'The Risks of Security' (1983), in *Power: The Essential Works, Vol. 3* (London: Penguin, 2000);

Security, Territory, Population: Lectures at the College de France, 1977–1978, ed. Michel Senellart (Basingstoke: Palgrave Macmillan, 2007).

5. Thomas Hobbes, *Leviathan* (1651), ed. Richard Tuck (Cambridge: Cambridge University Press, 1991), p. 120; also pp. 117–19.

6. John Locke, *Two Treatises* (1690), ed. Peter Laslett (Cambridge: Cambridge University Press, 1988), II, sections 4, 8, 17.

7. Locke, *Two Treatises*, II, sections 95, 220.

8. For discussions see Larry Arnhart, '"The God-Like Prince": John Locke, Executive Prerogative, and the American Presidency', *Presidential Studies Quarterly*, Vol. 9, No. 2, 1979, pp. 121–30; Harvey C. Mansfield, *Taming the Prince: The Ambivalence of Modern Executive Power* (Baltimore: Johns Hopkins University Press, 1989); Sheldon Wolin, *The Presence of the Past: Essays on the State and the Constitution* (Baltimore: Johns Hopkins University Press, 1989); Pasquale Pasquino, 'Locke on King's Prerogative', *Political Theory*, Vol. 26, No. 2, 1998, pp. 198–208; Clement Fatovic, 'Constitutionalism and Contingency: Locke's Theory of Prerogative', *History of Political Thought*, Vol. 25, No. 2, 2004, pp. 276–97.

9. Locke, *Two Treatises*, II, sections 6, 13.

10. Locke, *Two Treatises*, II, sections 159, 160, 164.

11. Locke, *Two Treatises*, II, section 210; Robert Filmer, *The Anarchy of a Limited or Mixed Monarchy* (1648), in Sir Robert Filmer, *Patriarcha and Other Writings*, ed. Johann P. Somerville (Cambridge: Cambridge University Press, 1991).

12. Locke, *Two Treatises*, II, section 158; Hobbes, *Leviathan*, p. 231.

13. Locke, *Two Treatises*, II, sections 3, 147.

14. Wolin, *Presence of the Past*, p. 168.

15. Mansfield, *Taming the Prince*, p. 200.

16. Locke, *Two Treatises*, II, sections 145, 147.

17. Locke, *Two Treatises*, II, section 98.

18. Leo Strauss identified the extent of Locke's Hobbesian tendencies in *Natural Right and History* (Chicago: University of Chicago Press, 1953), pp. 227–33. For context see Peter Laslett, 'Introduction' to Locke, *Two Treatises*, p. 72.

19. John Locke, 'An Essay on Toleration' (1667), in *Political Essays*, ed. Mark Goldie (Cambridge: Cambridge University Press, 1997), p. 142.

20. John Dunn, *The Political Thought of John Locke: An Historical Account of the Argument of the 'Two Treatises of Government'* (Cambridge: Cambridge University Press, 1969), p. 150.

21. Francesco Guicciardini, *Dialogue on the Government of Florence* (1521–4), trans. Alison Brown (Cambridge: Cambridge University Press, 1994), p. 159.

22. Niccolò Machiavelli, *Discourses on the First Decade of Titus Livius*

(1513–17), in *Chief Works, Vol. 1*, p. 218.

23. Niccolò Machiavelli, *The Prince* (1532), in *The Chief Works and Others, Vol. 1*, trans. Allan Gilbert (Durham: Duke University Press, 1958), p. 66.

24. Mark Neocleous, *Imagining the State* (Maidenhead: Open University Press, 2003), pp. 40–6.

25. Locke speaks of sovereignty almost entirely in relation to God, Adam's power and paternalism. As Franz Neumann notes, Locke's system is therefore a typically Whig system and the expression of a genuine national liberalism: 'His system, which claims to know no sovereignty, proves to be a typical bourgeois system of state and law, in which sovereignty is not called sovereignty but prerogative' – *The Rule of Law: Political Theory and the Legal System in Modern* Society (1936) (Leamington Spa: Berg, 1986), p. 125. Also see Arthur Selwyn Miller, *Democratic Dictatorship: The Emergent Constitution of Control* (Westport, CT: Greenwood Press, 1981), pp. 81, 97.

26. Dunn, *Political Thought of John Locke*, p. 163. Dunn adds (pp. 161, 199) that although Locke was interested in this style of writing, there is no way in which he saw himself as writing any kind of 'mirror for princes'. Yet he nonetheless concedes (p. 39) that the essay on toleration contains an explicit assertion of the primacy of reason of state.

27. Richard Ashcraft, *Revolutionary Politics and Locke's Two Treatises of Government* (Princeton, NJ: Princeton University Press, 1986), pp. 382–3.

28. Geraint Parry, *John Locke* (London: George Allen and Unwin, 1978), p. 130.

29. Locke, *Two Treatises*, II, sections 161–6.

30. Locke, *Two Treatises*, II, section 171, emphasis added.

31. Locke, *Two Treatises*, II, section 168.

32. Michael Ignatieff suggests that this is Locke's way of implying that people should take up arms to defend their freedom, but gives no textual evidence for this or an explanation for the interpretation – *The Lesser Evil: Political Ethics in an Age of Terror* (Markham, ON: Penguin Canada, 2004), p. 43. In paragraph 21 of the *Second Treatise* Locke does suggest that the absence of any appeal but to Heaven is equal to the state of war, which might imply the taking up of arms. And yet one might equally argue that the opposite is the case: the idea that 'may the Lord judge between me and you' is found in the Bible (in 1 Samuel, 24: 12), but there it is explicitly set *against* the taking up of arms: 'may the Lord judge between me and you, may the Lord avenge me; but my hand shall not be against you'.

33. Locke, *Two Treatises*, II, sections 147, 148, 154, 156, 159.

34. Locke, *Two Treatises*, II, sections 42, 164, 165, 166.
35. See Christopher Anderson, '"Safe Enough in His Honesty and Prudence": The Ordinary Conduct of Government in the Thought of John Locke', *History of Political Thought*, Vol. 13, No. 4, 1992, pp. 605–30.
36. Locke, *Two Treatises*, II, sections 162, 164.
37. Mansfield, *Taming the Prince*, p. 184; also 188, 200; Leo Strauss, *What is Political Philosophy?* (New York: Free Press, 1959) p. 218. Also note Laslett's comment, in his 'Introduction' to the *Two Treatises* (p. 88), that Locke 'could perhaps be looked upon as Machiavelli's philosopher', though Locke himself was of course resistant to any idea that he might be thought as having anything in common with Machiavelli. Nathan Tarcov has also traced an underlying Machiavellianism in Locke's *Thoughts Concerning Education* (1690), not least in Locke's recommendation for government by means of reverence, his attack on precepts and his recommendation that punishment be carried out by someone other than the parent who gives the orders. Nathan Tarcov, *Locke's Education for Liberty* (Chicago: University of Chicago Press, 1984).
38. Locke, *Two Treatises*, II, section 158, emphasis added.
39. As we will see in Chapter 3, this becomes the basis for a conception of 'economic security' that becomes central to liberal order-building in the twentieth century.
40. William Blackstone, *Commentaries on the Laws of England, Vol. 1* (1865), (London: Dawsons, 1966), pp. 230, 239, 244.
41. Montesquieu, *The Spirit of the Laws* (1748), trans. Anne Cohler, Basia Miller and Harold Stone (Cambridge: Cambridge University Press, 1989), Pt 2, Bk 11, Ch. 6; Pt 2, Bk 12, Ch. 19. Montesquieu here pre-empts Attorney General John Ashcroft's need to veil the statue of Justice in his office during the 'war on terror'. But in some senses John Ashcroft is more interesting than Montesquieu, at least on this occasion. His purported reason for veiling the statue was that he found it too revealing – although more than one person has guessed that maybe he just couldn't stand the sight of justice. There is a common interpretation of Montesquieu which suggests that his aim was to do away with prerogative or discretionary power. For example, see Bernard Manin, 'Checks, Balances and Boundaries: The Separation of Powers in the Constitutional Debate of 1787', in Biancamaria Fontana (ed.), *The Invention of the Modern* Republic (Cambridge: Cambridge University Press, 1994), p. 41. My point is that although this may appear to be the case, he ultimately concedes the need for such powers.
42. Peter N. Miller, *Defining the Common Good: Empire, Religion and Philos-*

ophy in Eighteenth-century Britain (Cambridge: Cambridge University Press, 1994), pp. 9, 23, 127.

43. Montesquieu, *Spirit of the Laws*, Pt 5, Bk 26, Ch. 23; David Hume, *An Enquiry Concerning the Principles of Morals* (1751), in *Enquiries Concerning the Human Understanding and Concerning the Principles of Morals* (Oxford: Clarendon Press, 1951), Sect. III, Pt II.

44. David Hume, 'Of Passive Obedience', in *Essays Moral, Political and Literary*, ed. Eugene F. Miller (Indianapolis: Liberty Fund, 1985), p. 489.

45. Jean-Jacques Rousseau, *The Social Contract* (1762), Book IV, Ch. VI, in *The Social Contract and Discourses*, trans G. D. H. Cole (London: Dent, 1973), p. 264.

46. Adam Smith, *Inquiry into the Nature and Causes of the Wealth of Nations* (1776), ed. R. H. Campbell, A. S. Skinner and W. B. Todd (Indianapolis: Liberty Fund, 1979), p. 539.

47. Also see James Madison, Alexander Hamilton and John Jay, *The Federalist Papers* (1787–8), No. 8 (Harmondsworth: Penguin, 1987), p. 114.

48. As we will see in Chapter 2, nothing could be further from the truth than Carl Schmitt's suggestion that liberalism ignores the problem of emergency.

49. Smith, *Wealth of Nations*, pp. 707, 787.

50. Adam Smith, *Lectures on Jurisprudence*, ed. R. L. Meek, D. D. Raphael and P. G. Stein (Indianapolis: Liberty Fund, 1982), pp. 405, 412, 540, 722.

51. Smith, *Lectures*, p. 944.

52. Smith, *Wealth of Nations*, pp. 706–7.

53. Smith, *Wealth of Nations*, p. 787.

54. Smith, *Wealth of Nations*, p. 921.

55. Jeremy Bentham, *Principles of the Civil Code*, in *The Works of Jeremy Bentham, Part II* (Edinburgh: William Tait, 1838), pp. 302–7, 311.

56. Montesquieu, *Spirit of the Laws*, Pt 2, Bk 12, Chs 1 and 2; Pt 2, Bk 11, Ch. 6. Note too that for Montesquieu the death penalty for murder or attempted murder is justified not because the murderer has taken away someone's liberty, but because they have 'violated security' – Pt 2, Bk 12, Ch. 4.

57. David Hume, *A Treatise of Human Nature* (1740), ed. L. A. Selby-Bigge (Oxford: Clarendon Press, 1978), p. 550; also see p. 485 where he comments on the centrality of security to the purpose of society, and pp. 538 and 541 on security as the foundation of justice.

58. Adam Ferguson, *An Essay on the History of Civil Society* (1767) (Edinburgh: Edinburgh University Press, 1966), p. 143; Thomas Paine, *Common Sense* (1776), in *Rights of Man, Common Sense and Other Political Writings*, ed. Mark Philp (Oxford: Oxford University Press, 1995), p. 7;

Joseph Priestly, 'An Essay on the First Principles of Government' (1771), in *Political Writings* (Cambridge: Cambridge University Press, 1993), p. 32; William Paley, *The Principles of Moral and Political Philosophy* (London: R. Faulder, 1785), pp. 444–5; *Federalist Papers*, 70, p. 402; Wilhelm von Humboldt, *The Limits of State Action* (1792) (Indianapolis: Liberty Fund, 1993), p. 84; George Washington, 'Farewell Address, 19 Sept., 1796', in *Writings* (New York: Library of America, 1997), p. 969.

59. [Benjamin Newton], *Another Dissertation on the Mutual Support of Trade and Civil Liberty* (London: T. Payne, 1756), p. 18.

60. Henry Care, *British Liberties, or the Free-born Subject's Inheritance* (London: Edward and Charles Dilly, 1766), pp. iii, vii–viii. The earlier text was *English Liberties; or, the Free-born Subject's Inheritance* (London: Sara Hares, 1691).

61. Graham Burchell, 'Peculiar Interests: Civil Society and Governing "The System of Natural Liberty"', in Burchell, Gordon and Miller (eds), *Foucault Effect*, p. 139. This subsumption of liberty under security runs through a whole range of contemporary projects supposedly rooted in liberal visions. On the one hand we find documents about liberty that are in fact documents about security. The Schengen Convention of 1990, for example, was intended to assert the principle of liberty (a new community founded on the principle of the free movement of persons across borders within the EU) but established the very grounds for restricting such movement – the grounds of national security (in Articles 2.2 and 96). The principle of liberty is thereby subsumed under the logic of securing 'Fortress Europe'. On the other hand, documents about security are often presented as documents about liberty. The French *Projet de loi sécurité intérieure* (PLSI) launched in October 2002 and intended to address the four million or so crimes recorded in the previous year by improving the internal security forces, modernising the French legal system and strengthening the authority of public agents to restore security, rests on one fundamental assumption: that security is 'the first of all liberties'.

This also somewhat undermines the project of critical security studies which, as noted in the Introduction, relies on linking security and emancipation, both theoretically and empirically. As can now be seen more clearly, this is far closer to classical liberalism than to twentieth-century critical theory.

62. Foucault, 'Lecture of 18 January 1978', and 'Lecture of 5 April', in *Security, Territory, Population*, pp. 48, 348; Colin Gordon, 'Governmental Rationality: An Introduction', in Burchell et al. (eds), *Foucault Effect*, p. 20.

63. Mitchell Dean, 'Powers of Life and Death Beyond Governmentality',

Cultural Values, Vol. 6, Nos 1 and 2, 2002, pp. 119–38.

64. In *Utilitarianism, On Liberty and Considerations on Representative Government* (London: Dent and Sons, 1972), p. 50.

65. Mill, *Representative Government*, in *Utilitarianism*, p. 355.

66. John Stuart Mill, *On Liberty* (1859) (Harmondsworth: Penguin, 1974), p. 175.

67. Mill, *Representative Government*, p. 188.

68. Michel Foucault, 'History of Systems of Thought, 1979', *Philosophy and Social Criticism*, Vol. 8, No. 3, 1981, pp. 353–9, p. 355.

69. Bentham, *Principles of the Civil Code*, p. 308.

70. Michael Dillon, *Politics of Security: Towards a Political Philosophy of Continental Thought* (London: Routledge, 1996), p. 16; Sheldon Wolin, *Politics and Vision*, Expanded Edition (Princeton, NJ: Princeton University Press, 2004), pp. 282–97; Judith N. Shklar, 'The Liberalism of Fear', in Nancy L. Rosenblum (ed.), *Liberalism and the Moral Life* (Cambridge, MA: Harvard University Press, 1989), p. 29.

71. John Locke, *An Essay Concerning Human Understanding* (1690), ed. John W. Yolton (London: Everyman, 1961), Bk 2, Ch. 20, section 6.

72. John Stuart Mill, 'Nature', in *Three Essays on Religion* (1874), (London: Watts and Co., 1904), pp. 17–18.

73. Adam Smith, *The Theory of Moral Sentiments* (1759), ed. D. D. Raphael and A. L. Mackie (Indianapolis: Liberty Fund, 1982), pp. 12, 13.

74. Karl Marx and Frederick Engels, *The Manifesto of the Communist Party* (1848), in Karl Marx and Frederick Engels, *Collected Works, Vol. 6* (London: Lawrence and Wishart, 1984), p. 487.

75. I have pursued this in a different direction in *The Fabrication of Social Order: A Critical Theory of Police Power* (London: Pluto Press, 2000).

76. Bentham, *Principles of the Civil Code*, p. 308; Jeremy Bentham, 'Method and Leading Features of an Institute of Political Economy' (1801–4), in *Jeremy Bentham's Economic Writings, Vol. 3*, ed. W. Stark (London: George Allen and Unwin, 1954), pp. 309–11, 318, 324.

77. Locke, *Two Treatises*, II, section 124.

78. Smith, *Wealth of Nations*, p. 715.

79. Smith, *Wealth of Nations*, p. 910.

80. Smith, *Wealth of Nations*, p. 833.

81. Smith, *Wealth of Nations*, p. 540.

82. Bentham, 'Institute of Political Economy', p. 310.

83. Mill, *Representative Government*, p. 188. Also see J. S. Mill, *Principles of Political Economy* (1848) (London: Longmans, 1904), Bk III, Ch. XVII.

84. Smith, *Wealth of Nations*, p. 944; also see pp. 456 and 710. William Blackstone, *Commentaries on the Laws of England*, p. 125; Paine, *Rights of Man*, p. 162; French Declaration, Clause II; Newton, *Dissertation on*

Mutual Support, pp. 12–13, 17.

85. Karl Marx, 'On the Jewish Question' (1844), Karl Marx and Frederick Engels, *Collected Works, Vol. 3* (London: Lawrence and Wishart, 1975), p. 163, translation modified.

86. Karl Marx, *Capital: A Critique of Political Economy, Vol. 1*, trans. Ben Fowkes (1867) (Harmondsworth: Penguin, 1976), p. 801.

87. On the question of the 'person' see Neocleous, *Imagining the State*, pp. 72–97.

88. Wendy Brown has shown the extent to which toleration also functions as regulatory and depoliticising power for liberalism in *Regulating Aversion: Tolerance in the Age of Identity and Empire* (Princeton, NJ: Princeton University Press, 2006).

89. Mitchell Dean, *The Constitution of Poverty: Toward a Theory of Liberal Governance* (London: Routledge, 1991), p. 196; *Governmentality: Power and Rule in Modern Society* (London: Sage, 1999), p. 117.

90. See my *Fabrication of Social Order*. On the question of security in relation to absolutism see Stephen Holmes, *Passions and Constraint: On the Theory of Liberal Democracy* (Chicago: University of Chicago Press, 1995), pp. 246, 258.

91. Dean, *Governmentality*, p. 137. Also Mitchell Dean, 'Liberal Government and Authoritarianism', *Economy and Society*, Vol. 31, No. 1, 2002, pp. 37–61.

92. Dershowitz first pushed this argument on TV and in print media in early 2002. The argument appears in *Why Terrorism Works: Understanding the Threat, Responding to the Challenge* (New Haven: Yale University Press, 2002), pp. 131–63. Bentham laid the liberal grounds for this in his manuscripts on torture. These can be found in W. L. and P. E. Twining, 'Bentham on Torture', *Northern Ireland Legal Quarterly*, Vol. 24, No. 3, 1973, pp. 305–56. Dershowitz is pleased to note (p. 142) that Bentham constructed a 'compelling hypothetical case to support his utilitarian argument against an absolute prohibition on torture'.

In June 2004, the Law faculty at Harvard, including Dershowitz, circulated a petition signed by 481 prominent professors of law and politics from 110 American universities condemning the abuses of detainees. Yet the real thrust of the letter was not in fact an attack on all forms of torture, but a call for 'a coercive interrogation policy' made 'within the strict confines of a democratic process'. In other words, and in typical liberal fashion, the problem lay not in the torture but in which body sanctions it – it should be sanctioned by the legislature rather than the executive. One can only hope that the tortured are reassured that their pain and misery are ratified by due process. Following this, funding from Homeland Security helped forge a project by the Law School and Kennedy School of Government to draw up a code for coercive interrogation. I will have more to say about the role of academics in the security complex in Chapter 5.

93. Ignatieff, *Lesser Evil*, pp. 138–41.

94. Ignatieff, *Lesser Evil*, pp. ix, 21.

95. Mariano Aguirre suggests that Ignatieff provides conservative arguments to the liberal audience and liberal alibis to the conservatives. See 'Exporting Democracy, Revising Torture: The Complex Missions of Michael Ignatieff', *openDemocracy*, 15 July 2005. This is in one sense true, though as I have been suggesting, the alibis in question involve far less 'smuggling' of concepts than Aguirre suggests – they are in fact part of the history of liberalism.

96. Bruce Ackerman, 'The Emergency Constitution', *Yale Law Journal*, Vol. 113, No. 5, 2004, pp. 1029–91, p. 1037; Michael Walzer, 'Emergency Ethics' (1988), in *Arguing About War* (New Haven: Yale University Press, 2004), pp. 33–50, building on an earlier argument concerning 'supreme emergency' in *Just and Unjust Wars: A Moral Argument with Historical Illustrations* (Harmondsworth: Penguin, 1977). The 'supreme emergency exemption' is also defended by John Rawls, *The Law of Peoples* (Cambridge, MA: Harvard University Press, 1999), pp. 98–9, and constitutes the basis of the argument in Ignatieff's *Lesser Evil*. I will have much more to say about 'emergency' in the chapter which follows. Waldron, 'Security and Liberty', p. 207. Also Richard Posner, 'Security versus Civil Liberties', *The Atlantic Monthly*, December 2001, pp. 46–7.

97. Michael Ignatieff, 'If Torture Works', *Prospect*, April 2006, p. 35.

98. See Colin Dayan, *The Story of Cruel and Unusual* (Cambridge, MA: MIT Press, 2007).

99. Hannah Arendt, *On Revolution* (New York: Viking Press, 1963), p. 3.

100. Ian Brownlie, *International Law and the Use of Force by States* (Oxford: Clarendon Press, 1963), p. 42.

101. H. W. Fowler, *Dictionary of Modern English Usage* (Oxford: Clarendon Press, 1965), p. 168.

102. Foucault, 'Lecture of 15 March 1978', in *Security, Territory, Population*, p. 262; Miller, *Defining the Common Good*, pp. 43, 46; Johann Sommerville, 'Ideology, Property and the Constitution', in Richard Cust and Ann Hughes (eds), *Conflict in Early Stuart England: Studies in Religion and Politics 1603–1642* (London: Longman, 1989), pp. 47–71.

103. Locke, *Two Treatises*, II, section 160.

104. Speech to the First Protectorate Parliament, 12 September, 1654, in *Oliver Cromwell's Letters and Speeches, Vol. III* (Leipzig: Bernhard Tauchnitz, 1861), p. 263.

105. A. V. Dicey, *Introduction to the Law of the Constitution* (1885) (London:

Macmillan, 1959), p. 202.

106. L. J. Roskill in *Laker Airways Ltd v. Department of Trade, All England Law Reports*, 1977, Vol. 2, pp. 196–7.

107. *Council for Civil Service Unions v. Minister for the Civil Service, World Law Reports*, 1984, Vol. 3, p. 1203.

108. This was Richard Nixon's view, adding that 'actions which otherwise would be unconstitutional, could become lawful if undertaken for the purpose of preserving the Constitution and the Nation' – television interview with David Frost, 19 May 1977, http://www.landmarkcases. org/nixon/nixonview.html.

109. Ernst Fraenkel, *The Dual State: A Contribution to the Theory of Dictatorship*, trans. E. A. Shils (Oxford: Oxford University press, 1941), pp. 65, 71.

110. David Dyzenhaus, 'Deference, Security and Human Rights', in Benjamin J. Goold and Liora Lazarus (eds), *Security and Human Rights* (Oxford: Hart Publishing, 2007), p. 132.

CHAPTER 2: EMERGENCY? WHAT EMERGENCY?

1. Carl Schmitt, *Political Theology* (1922), trans. George Schwab (Cambridge, MA: MIT Press, 1985), p. 5.

2. President Bush, 'Address to a Joint Session of Congress and the American People', 20 September 2001; Cheney, '56th Annual Alfred E. Smith Memorial Foundation Dinner', 18 October 2001; Tony Blair, 'Speech on Defence Policy to the Armed Forces', 12 January 2007.

3. Colin Powell described it as a long war on 14 September 2001, cited in Bob Woodward, *Bush at War* (New York: Simon and Schuster, 2002), p. 65. The phrase is repeated in US Department of Defense *Quadrennial Defense Report*, 6 February 2006; 'lengthy campaign' is President Bush, 'Address to a Joint Session of Congress and the American people', 20 September 2001; 'unknown duration' is in *The National Security Strategy of the United States of America* (Washington: The White House, September 2002), Preface; Cheney called the emergency the 'new normalcy' in 'Remarks to the Republican Governor's Association', 25 October 2001.

4. Walter Benjamin, 'On the Concept of History' (1940), trans. Harry Zohn, in *Selected Writings, Vol. 4: 1938–1940*, ed. Howard Eiland and Michael W. Jennings (Cambridge, MA: Belknap/Harvard, 2003), p. 392.

5. Giorgio Agamben, *Homo Sacer: Sovereign Power and Bare Life* (1995), trans. Daniel Heller-Roazen (Stanford, CA: Stanford University Press, 1998); *Means Without End: Notes on Politics*, trans. Vincenzo Binetti and Cesare Casarino (Minneapolis: University of Minnesota Press, 2000); *State of Exception* (2003), trans. Kevin Attell (Chicago: University of

Chicago Press, 2005); 'Form-of-Life', trans. Cesare Casarino, in Paolo Virno and Michael Hardt (eds), *Radical Thought in Italy: A Potential Politics* (Minneapolis: University of Minnesota Press, 1996).

6. Michael Hardt and Antonio Negri, *Empire* (Cambridge, MA: Harvard University Press, 2000), pp. 18, 39.

7. Michael Hardt and Antonio Negri, *Multitude: War and Democracy in the Age of Empire* (New York: Penguin, 2004), p. 7. In a review of *State of Exception*, Negri declares that there is no difference between the state of exception and constituent power and links the state of exception to the current permanent civil war. 'The Ripe Fruit of Redemption', *Il Manifesto*, 26 July 2003, trans. Arianna Bove and available at http://www.generation-online.org/t/negriagamben.htm.

8. Leo Panitch, 'Violence as a Tool of Order and Change: The War on Terrorism and the Anti-Globalization Movement', *Options politiques*, September 2002, pp. 40–4, p. 42.

9. Tony Bunyan, 'The Exceptional and Draconian Become the Norm', *Statewatch Report*, March 2005.

10. Jean-Claude Paye, 'Antiterrorist Measures, a Constituent Act', *Telos*, 128, 2004, p. 171–82.

11. Savas Michael-Matsas, 'Capitalist Decline, Nation State and State of Emergency', *Critique*, 36–7, June 2005, pp. 49–59.

12. Vivienne Jabri, 'War, the Politics of Security, and the Liberal State', in ELISE Collective Volume, *Counter-Terrorism: Implications for the Liberal State in Europe* (ELISE, 2005), p. 23.

13. Alex Callinicos, *The New Mandarins of American Power: The Bush Administration's Plans for the World* (Cambridge: Polity Press, 2003), p. 6.

14. Wendy Brown, *Edgework: Critical Essays on Knowledge and Politics* (Princeton, NJ: Princeton University Press, 2005), p. 10; Judith Butler, *Precarious Life: Powers of Mourning and Violence* (London: Verso, 2006), pp. 80.

15. See, for example, Franz Schurmann, 'Emergency Powers – the New Paradigm in Democratic America', *New California Media*, 23 December 2002; Jess Whyte, 'The New Normal', *Signature*, March 2005.

16. Benjamin J. Goold and Liora Lazarus, 'Introduction: Security and Human Rights', in Benjamin J. Goold and Liora Lazarus (eds), *Security and Human Rights* (Oxford: Hart Publishing, 2007), pp. 2–4.

17. Bulent Diken and Carsten Bagge Lausten, *The Culture of Exception: Sociology Facing the Camp* (London: Routledge, 2005).

18. Paul Virilio, *City of Panic* (2004), trans. Julie Rose (London: Verso, 2005), p. 74.

19. Paul Gilroy, *After Empire: Melancholia or Convivial Culture?* (Abingdon: Routledge, 2004), p. 65.

20. 'Permanent War, Permanent State of Emergency', *The Black Commen-*

tator, No. 14, 2002, identifying the permanent state of emergency as 'a permanent state of siege for Black America'.

21. Russell Jacoby, *Picture Imperfect: Utopian Thought for an Anti-Utopian Age* (New York: Columbia University Press, 2005), p. ix.

22. Joanna Apap and Sergio Carrera, 'Maintaining Security Within Borders: Toward a Permanent State of Emergency in the EU?', *Alternatives*, Vol. 29, 2004, pp. 399–416.

23. Robert Tracinski, 'War Powers Without War', *Ayn Rand Institute, Op-Eds*, 3 December 2001; Robert Higgs, 'In the Name of Emergency', *The Independent Institute*, 17 October 2001.

24. Agamben, *State of Exception*, p. 51.

25. Many commentators have opted to talk of the state of exception rather than emergency, usually on the grounds that not all states of emergency constitute a threat to the norm or a challenge to sovereignty – the influence of Schmitt again shows itself. In one sense, this is true – one only has to think of states of emergency called on the grounds of 'natural' disaster to see the point. Agamben opts for exception on the grounds that exception connotes being 'taken outside' (*ex capere*), which lays on the thematic of the camp, although he sometimes oscillates between exception and emergency. Except on a few occasions I will be using 'emergency', for political reasons to which I shall allude towards the end of this chapter.

26. See here Jef Huysman, 'Minding Exceptions: The Politics of Insecurity and Liberal Democracy', *Contemporary Political Theory*, Vol. 3, No. 3, 2004, pp. 321–41.

27. Barry Buzan, Ole Waever and Jaap de Wilde, *Security: A New Framework for Analysis* (Boulder, CO: Lynne Rienner, 1998).

28. See J. V. Capua, 'Early History of Martial Law in England from the Fourteenth Century to the Petition of Right', *Cambridge Law Journal*, Vol. 36, 1977, pp. 152–73.

29. Sir Matthew Hale, *The History of the Common Law of England* (1713), ed. Charles M. Gray (Chicago: University of Chicago Press, 1971) pp. 26–7.

30. Charles Fairman, *The Law of Martial Rule* (Chicago: Callaghan and Co., 1930), pp. 52–3; Nasser Hussain, *The Jurisprudence of Emergency: Colonialism and the Rule of Law* (Ann Arbor: University of Michigan Press, 2003); Charles Townsend, 'Martial Law: Legal and Administrative Problems of Civil Emergency in Britain and the Empire, 1800–1940', *The Historical Journal*, Vol. 25, No. 1, 1982, pp. 167–95; David Bonner, *Emergency Powers in Peacetime* (London: Sweet and Maxwell, 1985).

31. Henry Hallam, *Constitutional History of England From the Accession of Henry VII to the Death of George II, Vol. 1*, (London: John Murray, 1827), p. 258.

32. *Hansard*, Third Series, 17 March–10 April, 1851. Hence some claim that

'the expression martial law is not known to English law' – Leon Radzinowicz, *A History of English Criminal Law and its Administration from 1750, Vol 4* (London: Stevens and Sons, 1968), p. 143.

33. Fairman, *Law of Martial Rule*, pp. 29–30; Charles Fairman, 'The Law of Martial Rule', *American Political Science Review*, Vol. 22, No. 3, 1928, pp. 591–616.

34. Sir David Dundas responding to questions from Peel and Gladstone about the case of Ceylon, cited in Sir James Fitzjames Stephen, *A History of the Criminal Law of England, Vol. I* (1883) (London: Burt Franklin, 1973), p. 213.

35. Michel Foucault, *"Society Must be Defended": Lectures at the College de France, 1975–76*, trans. David Macey (London: Penguin, 2003), p. 103.

36. Michael A. Conron, 'Law, Politics, and Chief Justice Taney: A Reconsideration of the Luther v. Borden Decision', *American Journal of Legal History*, Vol. 11, 1967, pp. 377–88.

37. Frederick M. Watkins, 'The Problem of Constitutional Dictatorship', *Public Policy*, Vol. 1, 1940, pp. 324–79; Clinton Rossiter, *Constitutional Dictatorship: Crisis Government in the Modern Democracies* (1948) (New York: Harbinger Books, 1963); Carl Friedrich, *Constitutional Government and Democracy: Theory and Practice in Europe and America* (Boston: Ginn and Co., 1950), pp. 575–6; Lieutenant Colonel Joseph B. Kelly and Captain George A. Pelletier, Jr, 'Theories of Emergency Government', *South Dakota Law Review*, Vol. 11, 1966, pp. 42–69; Brian Loveman, *The Constitution of Tyranny: Regimes of Exception in Spanish America* (Pittsburgh: University of Pittsburgh Press, 1993); Oren Gross and Fionnuala Ni Aolain, *Law in Times of Crisis: Emergency Powers in Theory and Practice* (Cambridge: Cambridge University Press, 2006), p. 27.

38. J. H. Morgan, 'Martial Law', in *Encyclopaedia Britannica, Fourteenth Edition, Vol. 14* (London: Encyclopaedia Britannica Co., 1929), p. 984.

39. A. V. Dicey, *An Introduction to the Study of the Law of the Constitution* 288, 291 (10th ed. 1959); Stephen, *History of the Criminal Law*, pp. 208, 215; F. W. Maitland, *The Constitutional History of England* (Cambridge: Cambridge University Press, 1950), p. 491.

40. Fredrick Pollock, 'What is Martial Law?', *Law Quarterly Review*, Vol. 18, 1902, pp. 152–8, at 156. For other positions on the case see W. S. Holdsworth, 'Martial Law Historically Considered', *Law Quarterly Review*, Vol. 18, 1902, pp. 117–52; H. Erle Richards, 'Martial Law', *Law Quarterly Review*, Vol. 18, 1902, pp. 153–42.

41. George M. Dennison, 'Martial Law: The Development of a Theory of Emergency Powers, 1776–1861', *American Journal of Legal History*, Vol. 18, No. 1, 1974, pp. 52–79; Jason Collins Weida, 'A Republic of Emergencies: Martial Law in American Jurisprudence', *Connecticut Law Review*, Vol. 36, 2004, pp. 1397–1438.

42. For discussion see Ballentine, 'Qualified Martial Law, A Legislative Proposal', *Michigan Law Review*, Vol. 14, 1915–16, pp. 102–8 (Pt 1) and 197–218 (Pt 2); F. David Trickey, 'Constitutional and Statutory Bases of Governors' Emergency Powers', *Michigan Law Review*, Vol. 64, 1965–6, pp. 290–307.

43. Fabian Tract, *Emergency Powers: A Fresh Start* (An Informal Group Fabian Tract), No. 416, 1972, p. 5.

44. *Parliamentary Debates: House of Commons*, Vol. LXXXIV, 31 July 1916, col. 2143.

45. Harold M. Bowman, 'Martial Law and the English Constitution', *Michigan Law Review*, Vol. 15, 1916, pp. 93–126, p. 98.

46. Morgan, 'Martial Law', p. 985.

47. Cornelius P. Cotter, 'Constitutionalizing Emergency Powers: The British Experience', *Stanford Law Review*, Vol. 5, 1952–3, pp. 382–417, p. 384.

48. Cited in Charles Townshend, *Political Violence in Ireland: Government and Resistance since 1848* (Oxford: Clarendon Press, 1983), p. 311.

49. Cited in Thomas Jones, *Whitehall Diary, Vol. III: Ireland 1918–1925* 19–20 (Oxford: Oxford University Press, 1971). Jones was Deputy Secretary to the Cabinet.

50. Memo by Prime Minister, 19 May 1916, cited in Townshend, *Political Violence*, p. 310.

51. Letter from the JAG to Chief Secretary for Ireland, 19 July 1920, cited in Colin Campbell, *Emergency Law in Ireland, 1918–1925* (Oxford: Clarendon Press, 1994), p. 134.

52. Cited in K. D. Ewing and C. A. Gearty, *The Struggle for Civil Liberties: Political Freedom and the Rule of Law in Britain, 1914–1945* (Oxford: Oxford University Press, 2000), p. 184.

53. This was also the pattern in the colonies, as martial law gradually came to be superseded by 'emergency powers'. See, for example, the discussion of the shift in Egypt between 1914 and 1958 in Nathan Brown, *The Rule of Law in the Arab World: Courts in Egypt and the Gulf* (Cambridge: Cambridge University Press, 1997), pp. 82–3. For India see Venkat Iyer, *States of Emergency: The Indian Experience* (New Delhi: Butterworths, 2000).

54. William E. Scheuerman, 'Globalization and Exceptional Powers: The Erosion of Liberal Democracy', *Radical Philosophy*, 93, 1999, pp. 14–23.

55. William E. Scheuerman, 'The Economic State of Emergency', *Cardozo Law Review*, Vol. 21, 1999–2000, pp. 1869–94, p. 1877. Also see E. P. Thompson, 'The Secret State' (1978), in *Writing by Candlelight* (London: Merlin, 1980), p. 163

56. See the House of Commons Library Research Division, *Emergency Powers* (Background Paper, No. 66, n.d. [Jan. 1979]), p. 3.

57. Agamben, *State of Exception*, p. 2.

58. Cited in Hans Boldt, 'Article 48 of the Weimar Constitution, Its Historical and Political Implications', in Anthony Nicholls and Erich Matthias (eds), *German Democracy and the Triumph of Hitler: Essays in Recent German History* (New York: St. Martin's Press, 1971), p. 91.

59. Frederick Mundell Watkins, *The Failure of Constitutional Emergency Powers under the German Republic* (Cambridge, MA: Harvard University Press, 1939), p. 82.

60. Watkins, *Failure of Constitutional Emergency Powers*, pp. 75–8, 91–5; Boldt, 'Article 48', pp. 90–2; Lindsay Rogers, Sanford Schwarz and Nicholas S. Kaltchas, 'German Political Institutions II: Article 48', *Political Science Quarterly*, Vol. 47, 1932, pp. 566–601.

61. Ernst Fraenkel, *The Dual State: A Contribution to the Theory of Dictatorship*, trans. E. A. Shils (Oxford: Oxford University Press, 1941), p. 3.

62. See James K. Pollock and Harlow Henman (eds), *The Hitler Decrees* (Ann Arbor: George Wahr, 1934), p. 10.

63. 'Address Delivered at Democratic State Convention', 29 September 1936, in *The Public Papers and Addresses of Franklin D. Roosevelt, Vol. 5* (New York: Random House, 1938), pp. 386.

64. Reflecting back in 1936, Roosevelt commented that the crisis of 1933 to 1934 was 'made to order for all those who would overthrow our form of government' – 'Address Delivered at Democratic State Convention', 29 September 1936, in *Public Papers, Vol. 5*, pp. 385–6. On 1934 as a crucial year in American labour history see Irving Bernstein, *Turbulent Years: A History of the American Worker, 1933–1941* (Boston: Houghton Mifflin and Co., 1971), p. 217.

65. William E. Leuchtenburg, 'The New Deal and the Analogue of War', in John Braeman, Robert H. Brenner and Everett Walters (eds), *Change and Continuity in Twentieth-Century America* (Ohio: Ohio State University Press, 1964).

66. Franklin D. Roosevelt, 'Radio Address, Albany, NY, April 7, 1932', in *The Public Pages and Addresses of Franklin D. Roosevelt, Vol. 1* (New York: Random House, 1938), p. 624.

67. For example in Roosevelt, 'Radio Address, Albany, NY, April 7, 1932', p. 625.

68. Franklin D. Roosevelt, *On Our Way* (New York: John Day Co., 1934), p. 35.

69. See Jane Perry Clark, 'Emergencies and the Law', *Political Science Quarterly*, 49, 1934, pp. 268–83; Relyea, *Brief History of Emergency Powers*, p. 59; Michael R. Belknap, 'The New Deal and the Emergency Powers Doctrine', *Texas Law Review*, 62, 1983, pp. 67–109.

70. Francis Sejersted has shown the extent to which enabling acts were fundamental to economic modernisation and the development of cor-

poratism in Norway following the war – 'From Liberal Constitutionalism to Corporate Pluralism: The Conflict over the Enabling Acts in Norway after the Second World War and the Subsequent Constitutional Development', in Jon Elster and Rune Slagstad (eds), *Constitutionalism and Democracy* (Cambridge: Cambridge University Press, 1998).

71. Hussain, *Jurisprudence of Emergency*. Also see B. O. Nwabueze, *Constitutionalism in the Emergent States* (London and Enugu, Nigeria: C. Hurst and Co., in association with Nwamife Publishers, 1973), pp. 173, 180.

72. Denys C. Holland, 'Emergency Legislation in the Commonwealth', *Current Legal Problems,* Vol. 13, 1960, pp. 148–70.

73. Schmitt, *Political Theology*, pp. 13–14. See here Franz Neumann, 'Approaches to the Study of Political Power' (1950), in *The Democratic and the Authoritarian State: Essays in Political and Legal Theory* (New York: Free Press, 1957). What Schmitt and contemporary Schmittianism fail to grasp is that the 'state of exception' is not exceptional. On the contrary, as I am arguing here, in the guise of emergency powers it permeates the everyday functioning of modern states, even those which consider themselves 'democratic'.

74. Report by Daniel O'Donnell for the International Commission of Jurists, Series B, No. 9, June 10 1987; Daniel O'Donnell, 'States of Exception', *International Commission of Jurists Review*, 21, 1978, p. 52–3.

75. The author of that report, Joan Fitzpatrick, was also author of two other reports for the International Law Association on the same theme. The research is found in Joan Fitzpatrick, *Human Rights in Crisis: The International System for Protecting Rights During States of Emergency* (Philadelphia: University of Pennsylvania Press, 1994).

76. *Report by the UN Special Rapporteur, Mr. Leandro Despouy, on the question of Human Rights and States of Emergency*, United Nations, 1997 [hereafter 'Despouy Report'], paras 180–1. In a separate report from a year earlier, the same Special Rapporteur found 87 states having declared an emergency since 1985 – United Nations, Economic and Social Council, *The Administration of Justice and the Human Rights of Detainees: Questions of Human Rights and States of Emergency* (United Nations, 1996).

77. International Commission of Jurists, *States of Emergency: Their Impact on Human Rights* (1983), p. 413.

78. Cited in Daniel P. Franklin, *Extraordinary Measures: The Exercise of Prerogative Powers in the United States* (Pittsburgh, PA: University of Pittsburgh Press, 1991), p. 55.

79. Special Committee on the Termination of the National Emergency, United States Senate, *Emergency Powers Statutes: Provisions of Federal Law Now in Effect Delegating to the Executive Authority in Time of National*

Emergency. Senate Report 93–549, 93rd Congress, 1st Session, November 1973.

80. See *National Emergency Powers*, Congressional Research Service Report 98-505, 18 September 2001, pp. 13–16; *Terrorist Attacks and National Emergencies Act Declarations*, Congressional Research Service Report, RS21017, 7 January 2005, pp. 5–6.

81. Merlyn Rees in the House of Commons, 9 July 1974 – *Parliamentary Debates: House of Commons,* Vol. 876, 1974, col. 1273.

82. Roy Jenkins in the House of Commons, 28 November 1974 – *Parliamentary Debates: House of Commons,* Vol. 882, 1974–5, col. 642.

83. Fionnuala Ni Aolain, *The Politics of Force: Conflict Management and State Violence in Northern Ireland* (Belfast: Blackstaff Press, 2000); Laura Donohue, *Counter-Terrorist Law and Emergency Powers in the United Kingdom, 1922–2000* (Dublin: Irish Academic Press, 2001); Ewing and Gearty, *Struggle for Civil Liberties*, p. 331; Paddy Hillyard, 'The Normalization of Special Powers: From Northern Ireland to Britain', in Nicola Lacey (ed.), *A Reader on Criminal Justice* (Oxford: Oxford University Press, 1994).

84. Ewing and Gearty, *Struggle for Civil Liberties*, pp. 161–8, 272; Ni Aolain, *Politics of Force*, p. 64.

85. Oren Gross, 'Providing for the Unexpected: Constitutional Emergency Provisions', *Israeli Yearbook on Human Rights*, Vol. 33, 2003, pp. 1–31; Oren Gross, 'Chaos and Rules: Should Responses to Violent Crises Always Be Constitutional?', *Yale Law Journal*, Vol. 112, No. 5, 2003, pp. 1011–134; Menachem Hofnung, *Democracy, Law and National Security in Israel* (Aldershot: Dartmouth, 1996).

86. John Dugard, *Human Rights and the South African Legal Order* (Princeton, NJ: Princeton University Press, 1978), p. 112. Also see A. S. Mathews and R. C. Albino, 'The Permanence of the Temporary: An Examination of the 90- and 180-Day Detention Laws', *South African Law Journal*, 83, 1966, pp. 16–43; Nicholas Haysom, 'States of Emergency in a Post-Apartheid South Africa', *Columbia Human Rights Law Review*, Vol. 21, No. 1, 1989, pp. 139–62.

87. Cited in Stephen P. Marks, 'Principles and Norms of Human Rights Applicable in Emergency Situations', in Karel Vasak (ed.), *The International Dimensions of Human Rights, Vol. 1* (Westport, CT and Paris: Greenwood Press/UNESCO, 1982), pp. 184–5. More generally, see Nwabueze, *Constitutionalism in the Emergent States*, p. 173.

88. Inter-American Commission on Human Rights, *Report on the Situation of Human Rights in Paraguay* (Washington, January 1978).

89. Despouy Report, para. 127. Also see Claudio Grossman, 'States of Emergency: Latin America and the United States', in Louis Henken and

Albert J. Rosenthal (eds), *Constitutionalism and Rights: The Influence of the United States Constitution Abroad* (New York: Columbia University Press, 1990).

90. See United Nations, Economic and Social Council, *The Administration of Justice and the Human Rights of Detainees: Questions of Human Rights and States of Emergency* (United Nations, 1996).

91. Harold D. Lasswell, *National Security and Individual Freedom* (New York: McGraw-Hill, 1950), p. 29; Rossiter, *Constitutional Dictator*ship, p. 13; Albert L. Sturm, 'Emergencies and the Presidency', *The Journal of Politics*, 1, 1949, pp. 121–44, p. 141–2; Arthur S. Miller, 'Constitutional Law: Crisis Government Becomes the Norm', *Ohio State Law Journal*, Vol. 39, 1978, pp. 736–51; Gross and Aolain, *Law in Times of Crisis*, p. 175.

92. Adi Ophir, 'A Time of Occupation', in Roane Carey and Jonathan Shainin (eds), *The Other Israel: Voices of Refusal and Dissent* (New York: New Press, 2002), p. 60.

93. Note, for want of a recent example but which eschews the myth of temporariness, that just a few weeks after the attacks on the World Trade Center Dick Cheney commented that the changes being made for 'Homeland Security' are 'not a temporary measure just to meet one crisis' but 'will become permanent in American life . . . think of it as the new normalcy', 'Remarks to the Republican Governors Association', 25 October 2001.

94. H. P. Lee, *Emergency Powers* (Sydney: The Law Book Company, 1984), p. 4; Despouy Report, para. 20; Ergun Ozbudun and Mehmet Turhan, *Emergency Powers* (Strasbourg: Council of Europe, 1995), pp. 7–9.

95. William Gaillard, quoted in *The Guardian*, 5 April 2007.

96. United States Department of Health and Human Services, *Child Abuse and Neglect: Critical First Steps in Response to a National Emergency* (Washington: US Government Printing Office, August 1990).

97. On the latter see Aaron Perrine, 'The First Amendment Versus the World Trade Organization: Emergency Powers and the Battle in Seattle', *Washington Law Review*, 76, 2001, pp. 635–8.

98. The term 'emergency situation' or 'state of emergency' is now so overused that one expects that shortly we will find a new concept on the political market, something along the order of 'ultra-emergency'. The pattern has been set by the Department for Homeland Security starting to use 'ultra-catastrophe' to describe certain kinds of events. The ultra-catastrophe must surely constitute an ultra-emergency which in turn will necessarily generate ultra-emergency powers. For the Department's use of the term see 'Remarks by the Secretary of Homeland Security', 9 March 2006.

99. Gross, 'Providing for the Unexpected', p. 17.

100. Paul Virilio, 'The State of Emergency', in *The Virilio Reader*, ed. James Der Derian (Oxford: Blackwell, 1998), p. 52.
101. George Bush, News Conference at Sea Island, Georgia, 10 June 2004, in Mark Danner, *Torture and Truth: America, Abu Ghraib, and the War on Terror* (London: Granta, 2004), p. 46. The 'kick some ass' comment is reported by Richard A. Clarke, *Against All Enemies: Inside America's War on Terror* (New York: Free Press, 2004), pp. 23–4. The denial of knowledge of international law was at a press briefing, 11 December 2003. Rumsfeld's comment was at a press briefing in January 2002.
102. *Iraq: Law of Occupation*, House of Commons Research Paper 03/51, 2 June 2003, p. 25.
103. George Bush, Memorandum, 7 February 2002, in Danner, *Torture and Truth*, pp. 105–6.
104. Fleur Johns, 'Guantánamo Bay and the Annihilation of Exception', *European Journal of International Law*, Vol. 16, No. 4, 2005, pp. 613–35.
105. Chris af Johnick and Roger Normand, 'The Legitimation of Violence: A Critical History of the Laws of War', *Harvard International Law Review*, Vol. 35, No. 1, 1994, pp. 49–95, p. 50.
106. David Dyzenhaus, *The Constitution of Law: Legality in a Time of Emergency* (Cambridge: Cambridge University Press, 2006).
107. Jules Lobel, 'Emergency Power and the Decline of Liberalism', *Yale Law Journal*, 98, 1989, pp. 1385–433.
108. E. P. Thompson, *Whigs and Hunters: The Origin of the Black Act* (Harmondsworth: Penguin, 1977), pp. 265–6. I have subjected this to longer critique in *The Fabrication of Social Order: A Critical Theory of State Power* (London: Pluto Press, 2000).
109. Hussain, *Jurisprudence of Emergency*, p. 124.
110. 'The best thing in the world is a command' – Schmitt, *Legality and Legitimacy* (1932), trans. Jeffrey Seitzer (Durham: Duke University Press, 2004), p. 9.
111. David Dyzenhaus, 'The Permanence of the Temporary: Can Emergency Powers be Normalized?', in Daniels et al. (eds), *Security of Freedom*, p. 25.
112. Neocleous, *Fabrication of Social Order*, pp. 106–18; China Miéville, *Between Equal Rights: A Marxist Theory of International Law* (Leiden: Brill, 2005), p. 194.
113. Walter Benjamin, 'Critique of Violence' (1921), trans. Edmund Jephcott, in *Selected Writings, Vol. 1: 1913–1926*, ed. Marcus Bullock and Michael W. Jennings (Cambridge, MA: Belknap/Harvard, 1996), pp. 239, 252. For Schmitt, in contrast, the sovereign may stand outside the normally valid legal system, but 'nevertheless belongs to it' (*Political Theology*, p. 7). Thus Schmitt never rejects the need for a legal system of some kind. It is not legality itself that is problematic for Schmitt.

CHAPTER 3: FROM SOCIAL TO NATIONAL SECURITY

1. Cited in Daniel Yergin, *Shattered Peace: The Origins of the Cold War* (Harmondsworth: Penguin, 1980), pp. 194, 195.
2. Cited in Yergin, *Shattered Peace*, p. 195. In fact, the term itself was not entirely new. In Chapter 1 we saw it pop up very briefly in Smith's work. Moreover, a 'National Security League' had been established in 1914 by major companies such as US Steel and the Rockefeller oil companies, though it was concerned more with national identity than national security – a relationship I take up in Chapter 4. We might also point to a series of articles on foreign policy by Edward Mead Earle, such as 'American Military Policy and National Security', *Political Science Quarterly*, Vol. 53, No. 1, 1938, pp. 1–13, and 'National Security and Foreign Policy, *Yale Review*, Vol. 29, No. 3, 1940, pp. 444–60, along with Walter Lippmann's suggestion that 'the ideal of peace had diverted our attention from the idea of national security' – *U.S. Foreign Policy* (London: Hamish Hamilton, 1943), p. 30. But what is significant is that although the term appears in these texts there is little substantive analysis of what it is or might mean.
3. This point had already been made in 1941 in terms of the distinction between security and defence – for example: 'Security is a broad concept; as distinguished from mere defense', Edward Mead Earle, 'The Threat to American Security', *Yale Review*, Vol. 30, No. 3, 1941, pp. 454–80, p. 469. Also see his 'American Security: Its Changing Conditions', *Annals of the American Academy of Political and Social Science*, Vol. 218, 1941, pp. 186–93. But at this stage the notion of *national* security had not been attached to it.
4. Yergin, *Shattered Peace*, p. 194; Emily S. Rosenberg, 'Commentary: The Cold War and the Discourse of National Security', *Diplomatic History*, Vol. 17, No. 2, 1993, pp. 277–84; Michael S. Sherry, *In the Shadow of War: The United States since the 1930s* (New Haven: Yale University Press, 1995), p. 126.
5. *International Encyclopedia of the Social Sciences* (London: Macmillan, 1968), entry for 'national security', p. 40.
6. Arnold Wolfers, '"National Security" as an Ambiguous Symbol', *Political Science Quarterly*, Vol. 67, No. 4, 1952, pp. 481–502, p. 483.
7. Morton Berkowitz and P. G. Bock (eds), *American National Security: A Reader in Theory and Policy* (New York: Free Press, 1965).
8. P. G. Bock and Morton Berkowitz, 'The Emerging Field of National Security', *World Politics* 19, 1966, pp. 122–36. But note that this article was in fact a long review of four edited collections, none of which used the notion of 'national security' in either title or subtitle. Rather, the

books were *Components of Defense* (1965), *International Stability* (1964), *Analysis for Military Decisions* (1964), and *International Behavior* (1965).

9. Yergin, *Shattered Peace*, pp. 193–6. Saul Landau, *The Dangerous Doctrine: National Security and U.S. Foreign Policy* (Boulder, CO: Westview Press, 1988), p. xiii.

10. Robert Latham, *The Liberal Moment: Modernity, Security, and the Making of Postwar International Order* (New York: Columbia University Press, 1997), p. 94. Rosenberg, 'Cold War and the Discourse of National Security', p. 283.

11. Barry Buzan, Ole Waever and Jaap de Wilde, *Security: A New Framework for Analysis* (Boulder, CO: Lynne Rienner, 1998); pp. 7, 21, 131. Ole Waever, 'Securitization and Desecuritization', in Ronnie D. Lipshutz, ed., On Security (New York: Columbia University Press, 1995), pp. 65–71.

12. R. B. J. Walker, *Inside/Outside: International Relations as Political Theory* (Cambridge: Cambridge University Press, 1993); Didier Bigo, 'The Mobius Ribbon of Internal and External Security(ies)', in Mathias Albert, David Jacobson and Yosef Lapid (eds), *Identities, Borders, Orders: Rethinking International Relations Theory* (Minneapolis: University of Minnesota Press, 2001), pp. 91–116.

13. Simon Dalby, *Environmental Security* (Minneapolis: University of Minnesota Press, 2002), p. 7.

14. Didier Bigo, 'Internal and External Aspects of Security', *European Security*, Vol. 15, No. 4, 2006, pp. 385–404, p. 391.

15. Buzan, Waever and de Wilde, *Security*, p. 24; also Waever, 'Securitization and Desecuritization'.

16. See Crauford D. Goodwin (ed.), *Economics and National Security: A History of Their Interaction* (Durham: Duke University Press, 1991); Jonathan Kirshner, 'Political Economy in Security Studies After the Cold War', *Review of International Political Economy*, Vol. 5, No. 1, 1998, pp. 64–91; Michael Mastanduno, 'Economics and Security in Statecraft and Scholarship', *International Organization*, Vol. 52, No. 4, 1998, pp. 825–54; Patrick J. DeSouza (ed.), *Economic Strategy and National Security: A Next Generation Approach* (Boulder, CO: Council on Foreign Relations/ Westview Press, 2000); Norrin M. Ripsman, 'The Political Economy of Security: A Research and Teaching Agenda', *Journal of Military and Strategic Studies*, Spring 2000, pp. 1–7; Peter Dombrowski (ed.), *Guns and Butter: The Political Economy of International Security* (London: Lynne Rienner, 2005).

17. For example, Edward Mead Earle, 'Adam Smith, Alexander Hamilton, Friedrich List: The Economic Foundations of Military Power', in Edward Mead Earle (ed.), *Makers of Modern Strategy: Military Thought from Machiavelli to Hitler* (Princeton, NJ: Princeton University Press, 1943);

Albert Hirschman, *National Power and the Structure of Foreign Trade* (Berkeley, CA: University of California Press, 1945); Jacob Viner, 'Power Versus Plenty as Objectives of Foreign Policy in the Seventeenth and Eighteenth Centuries', *World Politics*, Vol. 1, No. 1, 1948, pp. 1–29; Bernard Brodie, 'Strategy as a Science', *World Politics*, Vol. 1, No. 4, 1949, pp. 467–88. Paul A. Samuelson also rewrote the second edition of his major textbook *Economics* to take account of the shift in emphasis away from mass unemployment and towards 'a national-security economy' – *Economics: An Introductory Analysis*, Second Edition (New York: McGraw-Hill, 1951), p. vi.

18. Joseph S. Nye and Sean M. Lynn-Jones, 'International Security Studies: A Report of a Conference on the State of the Field', *International Security*, Vol. 12, No. 4, 1988, pp. 5–27, p. 25.

19. On 21 January 1993, for example, President Clinton increased the membership of the National Security Council (NSC) to include the Secretary of the Treasury and the new position of Assistant to the President for Economic Policy. Four days later Clinton issued Executive Order 12835 establishing a National Economic Council, some of the staffing of which would be shared with the NSC.

20. Barry Buzan, *People, States and Fear: An Agenda for International Security Studies in the Post-Cold War Era, 2nd Edition* (Hemel Hempstead: Harvester Wheatsheaf, 1991), pp. 232, 237, 241, emphasis added.

21. The focus on America should not be misconstrued. The US is being examined as the prime example of, and key agent in, a much broader historical phenomenon in which the whole world order gets cast under the shadow of security.

22. Franklin D. Roosevelt, 'Message to Congress Reviewing the Broad Objectives and Accomplishments of the Administration', 8 June 1934, in *The Public Papers and Addresses of Franklin D. Roosevelt, Vol. 3: The Advance of Recovery and Reform* (New York: Random House, 1938), pp. 287–92.

23. Franklin D. Roosevelt, 'The Initiation of Studies to Achieve a Program of National Social and Economic Security. Executive Order No. 6757', 29 June 1934, in *Public Papers and Addresses, Vol. 3*, pp. 321–2.

24. Franklin D. Roosevelt, *On Our Way* (New York: John Day Co., 1934), pp. 182, 230.

25. Frances Fox Piven and Richard A. Cloward, *Regulating the Poor: The Functions of Public Welfare* (London: Tavistock Publications, 1972), p. 88.

26. Abraham Epstein, *Insecurity: A Challenge to America* (New York: Harrison Smith and Robert Haas, 1933). Epstein would continue using this notion of 'insecurity' as a stick even during the debates about what became the Social Security Act – see for example 'Our Social Insecurity Act', *Harper's Magazine*, 172, December 1935, pp. 55–66. I. M. Rubinow,

The Quest for Security (New York: Henry Holt and Co., 1934).

27. See Isaac Kramnick and Barry Sheerman, *Harold Laski: A Life on the Left* (London: Hamish Hamilton, 1993). For Laski's defence of emergency powers see *The American Presidency: An Interpretation* (New York: Harper and Brothers, 1940), p. 154.

28. Harold J. Laski, *Liberty in the Modern State* (Harmondsworth: Penguin, 1937), pp. 50–1. Note also his reiteration of security as the condition of human satisfaction, and the state as the condition of security, in a work from the same period – *The State: In Theory and Practice* (London: George Allen and Unwin, 1935), pp. 16–17.

29. Abraham Epstein, 'Security for Americans, I: Social Insurance Comes to the Fore', *The New Republic*, 21 November 1934, pp. 37–9; I. M. Rubinow, 'Security for Americans, II: The Ohio Plan of Unemployment Insurance', *The New Republic*, 28 November 1934, pp. 64–6; Elizabeth Brandeis, 'Security for Americans, III: Wisconsin's Start on Job Insurance', *The New Republic*, 5 December 1934, pp. 94–7; Mary Van Kleeck, 'Security for Americans, IV: The Workers' Bill for Unemployment and Social Insurance', *The New Republic*, 12 December 1934, pp. 121–4; Paul Douglas, 'Security for Americans, V: Unemployment Insurance and Relief', *The New Republic*, 19 December 1934, pp. 160–3; Abraham Epstein, 'Security for Americas, VI: A Program for Old-Age Security', *The New Republic*, 2 January 1935, pp. 212–15; George Soule, 'Security for Americas, VII: Can We Provide Security?', *The New Republic*, 16 January 1935, pp. 266–9.

30. For example by Frances Perkins, who would eventually be Chair of the CES. See 'Toward Security', *Survey Graphic*, Vol. 23, No. 3, March 1934, pp. 116–17 and p. 144; Frances Perkins, 'The Way of Security', *Survey Graphic*, Vol. 23, No. 12, December 1934, pp. 620–2 and p. 629.

31. Soule, 'Security for Americas, VII', p. 266.

32. Van Kleeck, 'Security for Americans, IV', p. 123.

33. For example, Raymond Gram Swing, 'Social Security in a Hurry', *The Nation*, Vol. 139, No. 3611, 19 September 1934, pp. 318–20.

34. Harold D. Lasswell, 'The Psychology of Hitlerism', Vol. 4, No. 3, 1933, pp. 373–84; Harold D. Lasswell, *World Politics and Personal Insecurity* (1934), republished as the first part of Harold D. Lasswell, E. Merriam and T. V. Smith, *A Study of Power* (Glencoe, IL: The Free Press, 1950), pp. 8–9, 25–6; Herbert Hoover, *The Challenge to Liberty* (New York: Charles Scribner's Sons, 1934), p. 178.

35. Cited in Donald Fisher, 'The Role of Philanthropic Foundations in the Reproduction and Production of Hegemony: Rockefeller Foundations and the Social Sciences', *Sociology*, Vol. 17, No. 2, 1983, pp. 206–33, p. 222.

36. It was also in this period that one can start to identify a certain style of writing about a 'golden age' defined by its security, an age usually taken to be prior to the First World War. In *Coming Up for Air* (1939) Orwell's character writes: 'Christ! What's the use of saying that one oughtn't to be sentimental about "before the war"? I *am* sentimental about it . . . The houses had no bathrooms, you broke the ice in your basin on winter mornings, the back streets stank like the devil in hot weather, and the churchyard was bang in the middle of the town, so that you never went a day without remembering how you'd got to end. And yet what was it that people had in those days? A feeling of security' (Harmondsworth: Penguin, 1962), pp. 106–7. Similarly, Stefan Zweig's biography *The World of Yesterday* (1943) begins thus: 'When I attempt to find a simple formula for the period in which I grew up, prior to the First World War, I hope that I convey its fulness by calling it the Golden Age of Security' (London: Cassell, 1943), p. 13. And note Hannah Arendt's comment that 'we must also admit a certain nostalgia for what can still be called a "golden age of security"' prior to 1914 – *The Origins of Totalitarianism* (1951), New Edition with Added Prefaces (San Diego: Harcourt Brace and Co., 1973), p. 123.

37. Franklin D. Roosevelt, 'Second "Fireside Chat" of 1934', 30 September 1934, in *Public Papers and Addresses, Vol. 3*, p. 413. The theme was followed up in many more fireside chats. See for example 'Fireside Chat' of 14 April 1938, where he describes security as the first line of the defence of liberty, and insecurity as the basis of non-democratic regimes – *Public Papers and Addresses, 1938: The Continuing Struggle for Liberalism* (New York: Macmillan, 1941), pp. 236–49.

38. Franklin D. Roosevelt, 'Address to the Advisory Council of the Committee on Economic Security on the Problems of Economic and Social Security', 14 November 1934, in *Public Papers, Vol. 3*, p. 454.

39. Franklin D. Roosevelt, 'Message to the Congress on Social Security', 17 January 1935, in *The Public Papers and Addresses of Franklin D. Roosevelt, Vol. 4: The Court Disapproves* (New York: Random House, 1938), p. 43.

40. Daniel Béland, *Social Security: History and Politics from the New Deal* (Kansas: University of Kansas Press, 2005), p. 100.

41. Alan Wolfe, *The Limits of Legitimacy: Political Contradictions of Contemporary Capitalism* (New York: Free Press, 1977), p.147.

42. Jennifer Klein, *For All These Rights: Business, Labor, and the Shaping of America's Public-Private Welfare State* (Princeton, NJ: Princeton University Press, 2003), pp. 78–9, 115, 138, 204; Piven and Cloward, *Regulating the Poor*, p. 92.

43. Cited in Klein, *For All These Rights*, p. 78.

44. It is pertinent to note in this context that F. A. von Hayek's attack on welfare systems and things 'social' takes the form in part of an attack on 'economic security' in *The Road to Serfdom* (London: Routledge, 1944), pp. 89–99.

45. See, for example, François Ewald, 'Insurance and Risk', and Daniel Defert, '"Popular Life" and Insurance Technology', both in Graham Burchell, Colin Gordon and Peter Miller (eds), *The Foucault Effect: Studies in Governmentality* (Hemel Hempstead: Harvester, 1991); Pat O'Malley, *Risk, Uncertainty and Government* (London: Glasshouse Press, 2004), pp. 38–47.

46. O'Malley, *Risk, Uncertainty and Government*, pp. 43–4, 125.

47. Richard Ericson, Aaron Doyle and Dean Barry, *Insurance as Governance* (Toronto: University of Toronto Press, 2003), p. 72.

48. Sir William Beveridge, *Social Insurance and the Allied Services* (London: HMSO, 1942), pp. 6–7, emphasis added.

49. See here Ewald, 'Insurance and Risk'; O'Malley, *Risk, Uncertainty and Government*; and Waever, 'Securitization and Desecuritization'.

50. Ericson, Doyle and Barry, *Insurance as Governance* , p. 50.

51. Mark Neocleous, *Administering Civil Society: Towards a Theory of State Power* (Basingstoke: Macmillan, 1996), pp. 131–40. On Roosevelt's wider policy here see Kees Van Der Pijl, *The Making of an Atlantic Ruling Class* (London: Verso, 1984).

52. Klein, *For All These Rights*, pp. 5–11, 78–115.

53. Franklin D. Roosevelt, 'Campaign Address on Progressive Government at the Commonwealth Club', San Francisco, 23 September 1932, in *The Public Papers and Addresses of Franklin D. Roosevelt, Vol. 1: The New Deal* (New York: Random House, 1938), pp. 742–56.

54. Klein, *For All These Rights*, p. 98.

55. Address at the Bond Club, 23 May 1943, cited in Klein, *For All These Rights*, p. 207.

56. Klein, *For All These Rights*, p. 207.

57. Klein, *For All These Rights*, pp. 101–2; Peter A. Swenson, 'Varieties of Capitalist Interests: Power, Institutions, and the Regulatory Welfare State in the United States and Sweden', *Studies in American Political Development*, Vol. 18, 2004, pp. 1–29.

58. Winthrop W. Aldrich, *An Appraisal of the Federal Social Security Act: Address Before the Institute of Public Affairs* (Charlottesville, 1936), p. 3, emphasis added.

59. Van Der Pijl, *Making of an Atlantic Ruling Class*, p. 93. Also see Richard E. Holl, *From the Boardroom to the War Room* (Rochester, NY: Rochester University Press, 2005), p. 30.

60. Bruce Ackerman, *We the People, Vol. 2: Transformations* (Cambridge, MA:

Harvard University Press, 1998), pp. 260, 263, 270–1, 279.

61. Cited in Klein, *For All These Rights*, p. 115.

62. Zygmunt Bauman, *Modernity and Ambivalence* (Cambridge: Polity Press, 1991), p. 20.

63. Etymologically, 'garden' originates in the same root as the Old English *geard*, meaning 'fence' and hence 'enclosed space'. The *geard* developed into Modern English 'yard' while 'garden' came into the language as *gardyne* via the Old Norman French *gardin* – see Anne van Erp-Houtepen, 'The Etymological Origin of the Garden', *Journal of Garden History*, Vol. 6, No. 3, 1986, pp. 227–31. On the metaphor see Simon Pugh, *Garden-Nature-Language* (Manchester: Manchester University Press, 1988), pp. 2–7, 55, 125; Eve Darian-Smith, *Bridging Divides: The Channel Tunnel and English Legal Identity in the New Europe* (Berkeley: University of California Press, 1999), pp. 51–3.

64. Franklin D. Roosevelt, 'Annual Message to the Congress', 4 January 1939, in *The Public Papers and Addresses of Franklin D. Roosevelt, 1939: War and Neutrality* (London: Macmillan, 1941), p. 5.

65. Earle, 'American Security', p. 189.

66. See here Michael S. Sherry, *In the Shadow of War: The United States since the 1930s* (New Haven: Yale University Press, 1995), pp. 22, 31, 47.

67. Franklin D. Roosevelt, 'State of the Union Address', 11 January 1944, in *The Public Papers and Addresses of Franklin D Roosevelt, 1944–5, Victory and the Threshold* (New York: Harper and Brothers, 1950), pp. 33–4, 41. On this link see Franz Schurman, *The Logic of World Power* (New York: Pantheon Books, 1974), p. 42.

68. Schurman, *Logic of World Power*, p. 67.

69. On 'Dr. New Deal' and 'Dr. Win-the-War' see Franklin D. Roosevelt, 'Press Conference', 28 December 1943, in *The Public Papers and Addresses of Franklin D Roosevelt, 1943: The Tide Turns* (New York: Harper and Brothers, 1950), p. 569. For a critique of such organic metaphors see my *Imagining the State*, chap. 1.

70. It is a sign of how the language of security has shifted since the Second World War that a series of pamphlets under the label 'collective security' could be so focused on the minutiae of social security issues. See, for example, H. Ladd Plumley, 'Budgeting the Costs of Illness', *Studies in Individual and Collective Security No. 1*, 1947; Walter Sulzbach, 'German Experience with Social Insurance', *Studies in Individual and Collective Security No. 2*, 1947; Elizabeth W. Wilson, 'Compulsory Health Insurance', *Studies in Individual and Collective Security No. 3*, 1947; Henry W. Steinhaus, 'Financing Old Age', *Studies in Individual and Collective Security No. 4*, 1948; William J. Shultz, 'Social Security and the Economics of Saving', *Studies in Individual and Collective Security No. 5*, 1948; Earl E.

Muntz, 'Growth Trends in Social Security', *Studies in Individual and Collective Security No. 6*, 1949.

71. See Paul Virilio, *Negative Horizon* (1984), trans. Michael Degener (London: Continuum, 2005), p. 170; Paul Virilio, *Speed and Politics: An Essay on Dromology* (1977), trans. Mark Polizzotti (New York: Semiotext(e), 1986), p. 123.

72. Robert A. Pollard, *Economic Security and the Origins of the Cold War, 1945–1950* (New York: Columbia University Press, 1985), p. 13.

73. Latham, *Liberal Moment*, p. 143; Pollard, *Economic Security*, p. 3.

74. Cited in Pollard, *Economic Security*, p. 13.

75. Roosevelt, 'Press Conference', 28 December 1943, p. 574.

76. Alan S. Milward, *The Reconstruction of Europe* (Berkeley: University of California Press, 1984). Also Pollard, *Economic Security and the Origins of the Cold War*, p. 65; Melvyn P. Leffler, *A Preponderance of Power: National Security, the Truman Administration, and the Cold War* (Stanford, CA: Stanford University Press, 1992), pp. 157, 160

77. Joyce Kolko and Gabriel Kolko, *The Limits of Power: The World and United States Foreign Policy, 1945–1954* (New York: Harper and Row, 1972), pp. 341–2, 35, 428.

78. This in part explains why CIA security agents acting covertly in France helped forge a split within European unionism around the issue of the Marshall Plan, hoping to sideline communist opposition to the project of American capital.

79. Latham, *Liberal Moment*, p. 175.

80. NSC-68, 14 April 1950, in Thomas H. Etzold and John Lewis Gaddis (eds), *Containment: Documents on American Policy and Strategy, 1945–1950* (New York: Columbia University Press, 1978), p. 401.

81. Richard J. Aldrich, *The Hidden Hand: Britain, America and Cold War Secret Intelligence* (Woodstock: Overview Press, 2002), pp. 342–70.

82. David Campbell, *Writing Security: United States Foreign Policy and the Politics of Identity* (Manchester: Manchester University Press, 1992), p. 159.

83. Allen W. Dulles, *The Marshall Plan* (Oxford: Berg, 1993), p. 4.

84. George Kennan, 'Overdue Changes in Our Foreign Policy', *Harper's Magazine*, Vol. 213, No. 1275, August 1956, pp. 27–33, p. 28; *The National Security Strategy of the United States of America* (Washington: The White House, 2002), p. 15.

85. Policy Planning Staff, 'Resume of the World Situation', 6 November 1947, in Etzold and Gaddis, *Containment*, p. 90.

86. NSC-68, pp. 397, 407.

87. To give just one example: in 1948 Stalin was of the view that the Greek uprising would have to be 'stopped . . . as quickly as possible'. Thus as

the Greek rebels fought to achieve the first democratic Republic of Greece the Soviets offered neither military nor ideological support. Cited in Milovan Djilas, *Conversations with Stalin*, trans. Michael B. Petrovich (Harmondsworth: Penguin, 1963), pp. 140–1.

88. NSC-68, in Etzold and Gaddis (eds), *Containment*, pp. 401, 412.
89. Hogan, *Cross of Iron*, pp. 23–68.
90. X (George Kennan), 'The Sources of Soviet Conduct', *Foreign Affairs*, Vol. 25, No. 4, 1947, pp. 566–82; George Kennan, 'The Long Telegram', in Etzold and Gaddis (eds), *Containment*, pp. 50–63.
91. Cited in David Caute, *The Great Fear: The Anti-Communist Purge under Truman and Eisenhower* (London: Secker and Warburg, 1978), p. 26.
92. George F. Kennan, *Memoirs, 1925–1950* (Boston: Little, Brown and Co., 1967), p. 358.
93. John Lewis Gaddis, *Strategies of Containment: A Critical Appraisal of Postwar American National Security Policy* (Oxford: Oxford University Press, 1982), pp. 37, 40, 63, 83, 85; Stephen E. Ambrose, *Rise to Globalism: American Foreign Policy Since 1938, Fourth Revised Edition* (New York: Penguin Books, 1985), p. 95.
94. Cited in Pollard, *Economic Security*, p. 150.
95. Arthur Krock in the New York Times, 5 October 1947, cited in Pollard, *Economic Security*, p. 148.
96. Dulles, *Marshall Plan*, p. 116. The book was ready to be submitted to the publisher in January 1948, but the smooth passage of the Foreign Aid Act rendered it redundant.
97. NSC-20/1, 18 August 1948, in Etzold and Gaddis (eds), *Containment*, p. 182; NSC-68, p. 408.
98. Cited in Pollard, *Economic Security*, pp. 227–8; Mastanduno, 'Economics and Security', p. 828.
99. Pollard, *Economic Security*, p. 223.
100. The UK Intelligence and Security Committee *Annual Report* for 2004–5 notes: 'We took evidence from Ministers, departments and the Agencies on the Agencies' work to support and safeguard the UK's economic well-being. This is an important topic, with a large number of departments and government organisations having an interest in it. We note that there is not a common definition across Whitehall of what constitutes economic well-being' – Intelligence and Security Committee [UK], *Annual Report, 2004–2005* (Cm 6510, April 2005), p. 29.
101. Latham, *Liberal Moment*, pp. 144–6; Anthony Burke, 'Aporias of Security', *Alternatives*, 27, 2002, pp. 1–27, p. 14.
102. Karl Marx and Frederick Engels, *Manifesto of the Communist Party* (1848), in Karl Marx and Frederick Engels, *Collected Works, Vol. 6* (London: Lawrence and Wishart, 1976), pp. 487–8.

103. Bradley S. Klein, *Strategic Studies and World Order: The Global Politics of Deterrence* (Cambridge: Cambridge University Press, 1994), pp. 90–1, 105.

104. The phrase was used by Clinton, 'President's News Conference with President Jiang in Beijing', 27 June 1998. Speaking on 19 November 1999, then-Governor Bush repeated the idea: 'we firmly believe that our nation is on the right side of history'. Condoleezza Rice also repeated the idea, cited in Andrew J. Bacevich, 'Different Drummers, Same Drum', *The National Interest*, Summer 2001, pp. 67–77, p. 70.

105. John Stockwell, *The Praetorian Guard: The U.S. Role in the New World Order* (Cambridge, MA: South End Press, 1991), pp. 70–1.

106. George W. Bush, 'Graduation Speech at the US Military Academy', West Point, New York, 1 June 2002. The extent to which the reference to '60 or more' countries was a rhetorical device can be seen in the way the actual number could never quite be pinned down. For Rumsfeld on 24 October 2001, it was '50 or 60 countries'.

107. 'In my 30-year history in the Drug Enforcement Administration and related agencies, the major targets of my investigations almost invariably turned out to be working for the CIA' – Dennis Dayle, former chief of an elite DEA enforcement unit, cited in Peter Dale Scott and Jonathan Marshall, *Cocaine Politics: Drugs, Armies, and the CIA in Central America* (Berkeley: University of California Press, 1998), pp. xviii–xix. For similar research on heroin and extending beyond Scott and Marshall's focus on Central America see Alfred W. McCoy, *The Politics of Heroin: CIA Complicity in the Global Drug Trade*, Revised Edition (Chicago: Lawrence Hill Books, 2003).

108. Noam Chomsky and Edward S. Herman, *The Political Economy of Human Rights, Vol. 1: The Washington Connection and Third World Fascism* (Boston: South End Press, 1979), pp. 252–3; Landau, *Dangerous Doctrine*, p. 107; Joel Kovel, *Red Hunting in the Promised Land: Anticommunism and the Making of America* (London: Continuum, 1997), p. 57.

109. Stockwell, *Praetorian Guard*, p. 81.

110. *The National Security Strategy of the United States of America* (Washington: The White House, September 2002), p. 15. The *Quadrennial Defense Review Report* of February 2006 then turns this preemptive logic on its head, by arguing that the problem with enemy states possessing weapons of mass destruction is that they might use those weapons preemptively (p. 32).

111. The *National Security Strategy of the United States of America*, 1988, under Reagan, held that part of the strategy was 'liberalisation', while Clinton's *National Security Strategy for a New Century* of May 1997 claimed (pp. 14–15) that 'economic and security interests are inextricably linked', and

in its Preface conflates security and prosperity.

112. As Donald Rumsfeld noted of the attacks on the World Trade Center in September 2001: they 'created the kind of opportunities that World War Two offered, to refashion the world' – *New York Times*, 12 October 2001. Tony Blair also liked to talk about the new opportunities for 'reordering the world' created by the attacks.

CHAPTER 4: SECURITY, IDENTITY, LOYALTY

1. Kevin Baker, 'We're in the Army Now', *Harper's Magazine*, October 2003, pp. 35–46; John Lewis Gaddis, *Surprise, Security, and the American Experience* (Cambridge, MA: Harvard University Press, 2004), p. 10; Richard Jackson, *Writing the War on Terrorism: Language, Politics and Counter-Terrorism* (Manchester: Manchester University Press, 2005), pp. 59, 76.

2. Benedict Anderson, *Imagined Communities: Reflections on the Origin and Spread of Nationalism*, Revised Edition (London: Verso, 1991).

3. Mark Neocleous, *The Monstrous and the Dead: Burke, Marx, Fascism* (Cardiff: University of Wales Press, 2005).

4. R. D. Laing, *The Divided Self: An Existential Study in Sanity and Madness* (Harmondsworth: Penguin, 1959); Anthony Giddens, *The Constitution of Society: Outline of the Theory of Structuration* (Cambridge: Polity Press, 1984); Zygmunt Bauman, *Globalization: The Human Consequences* (Cambridge: Polity Press, 1998).

5. Most notably David Campbell, *Writing Security: United States Foreign Policy and the Politics of Identity* (Manchester: Manchester University Press, 1992). But also see G. M. Dillon, 'The Alliance of Security and Subjectivity', *Current Research on Peace and Violence*, Vol. 13, No. 3, 1990, pp. 101–24; Bradley Klein, 'How the West was One: Representational Politics of NATO', *International Studies Quarterly*, Vol. 34, No. 3, 1990, pp. 311–25; Ole Waever, Barry Buzan, Morten Kelstrup and Pierre Lemaitre, *Identity, Migration and New Security Agenda in Europe* (London: Pinter, 1993); Jef Huysmans, 'Migrants as a Security Problem: Dangers of "Securitizing" Societal Issues', in Robert Miles and Dietrich Thranhardt (eds), *Migration and European Integration: The Dynamics of Inclusion and Exclusion* (London: Pinto, 1995); Michael C. Williams, 'Identity and the Politics of Security', *European Journal of International Relations*, Vol. 4, No. 2, 1998, pp. 204–25; Jutta Weldes and Diana Saco, 'Making State Action Possible: The United States and the Discursive Construction of the "Cuban Problem"', *Millennium*, Vol. 25, No. 2, 1996, pp. 361–95; Lene Hansen, 'Slovenian Identity: State Building on the Balkan Border', *Alternatives*, Vol. 21, No. 4, 1996, pp. 473–95; Bill McSweeney, *Security,*

Identity and Interests: A Sociology of International Relations (Cambridge: Cambridge University Press, 1999); Astrid von Busekist, 'Uses and Misuses of the Concept of Identity', *Security Dialogue*, Vol. 35, No. 1, 2004, pp. 81–98; Maria Stern, *Naming Security – Constructing Identity: 'Mayan-Women' in Guatemala on the Eve of 'Peace'* (Manchester: Manchester University Press, 2005).

6. Harry S. Truman, 'Special Message to Congress on Greece and Turkey', 12 March 1947, in Harry S. Truman, *Public Papers, 1947* (Washington: US Government Printing Office, 1963), pp. 176–80; 'The President's Special Conference With the Association of Radio News Analysts', 13 May 1947, in *Public Papers, 1947*, p. 238.

7. Marshall had offered aid to Eastern Europe and the Soviet Union as a means of either incorporating them into the system of global capital if they accepted or isolating them from it if they declined – George F. Kennan, *Memoirs, 1925–1950* (Boston: Little, Brown and Co., 1967), p. 341.

8. NSC-48/2, 30 December 1949, suggested that the US should as a security measure aim to exploit any rift between the Chinese and the USSR, and between Stalinists and other elements in China – in Thomas H. Etzold and John Lewis Gaddis (eds), *Containment: Documents on American Policy and Strategy, 1945–1950* (New York: Columbia University Press, 1978), pp. 269–76.

9. The comment was from Harry Rositzke, the CIA's head of secret operations inside the USSR, interviewed by Christopher Simpson, *Blowback: America's Recruitment of Nazis and Its Effects on the Cold War* (New York: Weidenfeld and Nicolson, 1988), p. 159. This use of Nazis had been planned for by key players in the national security state such as Kennan and the Dulles brothers, as Simpson shows in *Blowback* and *The Splendid Blond Beast* (New York: Grove Press, 1993). Since Simpson's research the 1998 War Crimes Disclosure Act requiring the CIA, FBI and Army to declassify operational information has made clear the extent to which being a fascist did not bar a person from working within the national security state. Between late-1946 and December 1952 over 600 German scientists were brought from Germany to the US and placed in major universities and corporations. See Richard Breitman, Norman J. W. Goda, Timothy Naftali and Robert Wolfe, *U.S. Intelligence and the Nazis* (Cambridge: Cambridge University Press, 2005).

10. David Caute, *The Great Fear: The Anti-Communist Purge under Truman and Eisenhower* (London: Secker and Warburg, 1978); Joyce Kolko and Gabriel Kolko, *The Limits of Power: The World and United States Foreign Policy, 1945–1954* (New York: Harper and Row, 1972); Abbot Gleason, *Totalitarianism: The Inner History of the Cold War* (Oxford: Oxford

University Press, 1995).

11. Kennan, *Memoirs, 1925–1950* , p. 319.

12. For example, the HUAC, *Report of Un-American Activities and Propaganda, 3 January, 1939* (Washington, 1939), in David Brion Davis, *The Fear of Conspiracy: Images of Un-American Subversion from the Revolution to the Present* (Ithaca: Cornell University Press, 1971), pp. 279–82.

13. NSC-68, 14 April 1950, in Etzold and Gaddis (eds), *Containment*, p. 413.

14. See Richard Longaker, 'Emergency Detention: The Generation Gap, 1950–1971', *Western Political Quarterly*, Vol. 27, No. 3, 1974, pp. 395–408; Robert Justin Goldstein, 'An American Gulag?', *Columbia Human Rights Law Review*, Vol. 10, 1978–9, pp. 541–73.

15. US Commission on National Security/21st Century, *Road Map for National Security: Imperative for Change*, 15 February 2001, p. viii.

16. NSC-20/4, 23 November 1948, in Etzold and Gaddis (eds), *Containment*, p. 210.

17. Joint Chiefs of Staff, 'Review of the Current World Situation', 15 January 1951, in *Foreign Relations of the United States, 1951, Vol. 1*, p. 70; also pp. 71 and 74.

18. Melvyn P. Leffler, *A Preponderance of Power: National Security, the Truman Administration, and the Cold War* (Stanford, CA: Stanford University Press, 1992), p. 107.

19. W. Scott Lucas, 'Mobilizing Culture: The State-Private Network and the CIA in the Early Cold War', in Dale Carter and Robin Clifton (eds), *War and Cold War in American Foreign Policy, 1942–1962* (Houndmills, Basingstoke: Palgrave, 2002), p. 85; Michael Williams, *Culture and Security: Symbolic Power and the Politics of International Security* (London: Routledge, 2007), pp. 7, 77.

20. Walter L. Hixson, *Parting the Curtain: Propaganda, Culture, and the Cold War, 1945–1961* (Basingstoke: Macmillan, 1997), p. 11; David Caute, *The Dancer Defects: The Struggle for Cultural Supremacy During the Cold War* (Oxford: Oxford University Press, 2003), p. 24.

21. Policy Planning Staff Memorandum, 4 May 1948, in *Foreign Relations of the United States, 1945–1950: Emergence of the Intelligence Establishment* (Washington: US Government Printing Office, 1996), p. 670.

22. Richard M. Fried, *The Russians are Coming! The Russians are Coming! Pageantry and Patriotism in Cold-War America* (Oxford: Oxford University Press, 1998), p. 33.

23. Cited in Stuart J. Little, 'The Freedom Train: Citizenship and Postwar Political Culture, 1946–1949', *American Studies*, Vol. 34, No. 1, 1993, pp. 35–67, p. 42.

24. Cited in Michael Kammen, *Mystic Chords of Memory: The Transformation of Tradition in American Culture* (New York: Alfred A. Knopf, 1991), p. 573.

25. He was speaking to a Congressional Committee in 1949, cited in James Gregory Bradsher, 'Taking America's Heritage to the People: The Freedom Train Story', *Prologue*, Vol. 17, 1985, pp. 229–46, p. 229.

26. Nancy E. Bernhard, *U.S. Television News and Cold War Propaganda, 1947–1960* (Cambridge: Cambridge University Press, 1999); Emily S. Rosenberg, 'U.S. Cultural History', in Ernest R. May (ed.), *American Cold War Strategy: Interpreting NSC 68* (Boston: Bedford Books, 1993); Lucas, 'Mobilizing Culture', p. 95; Eva Cockcroft, 'Abstract Expressionism, Weapon of the Cold War', *Artforum*, Vol. 12, No. 10, 1974, pp. 39–41; Frances Stonor Saunders, *Who Paid the Piper? The CIA and the Cultural Cold War* (London: Granta, 2000); Caute, *Dancer Defects*, pp. 539–68; Jean-Michel Valantin, *Hollywood, The Pentagon and Washington: The Movies and National Security* (London: Anthem Press, 2005).

27. Leffler, *Preponderance of Power*, pp. 107, 145.

28. NSC-20/2, 25 August 1948, in Etzold and Gaddis, *Containment*, p. 298.

29. Carl Schmitt, *The Concept of the Political* (1932), trans. George Schwab (Chicago: University of Chicago Press, 1996), p. 65.

30. Committee on the Present Danger, 'Common Sense and the Common Danger: Policy Statement of the Committee on The Present Danger', 11 November 1976, in *Alerting America: The Papers of the Committee on the Present Danger* (Washington: Pergamon-Brasseys, 1984), p. 3; *Taking the Stand: The Testimony of Lieutenant Colonel Oliver L. North* (New York: Pocket Books, 1987), p. 12.

31. Kennan, *Memoirs, 1925–1950*, p. 294.

32. NSC-68, p. 389-91; NSC-20/4, p. 208, emphasis added; Policy Planning Staff Memorandum, 4 May 1948, pp. 668–9; NSC-20/1, 18 August 1948, in Etzold and Gaddis (eds), *Containment*, pp. 174–6, 178.

33. Joint Chiefs of Staff, 'Review of the Current World Situation', p. 72, citing a memorandum from the Joint Chiefs of Staff to the Secretary of Defense in April 1950.

34. Eyal Weizman, *Hollow Land: Israel's Architecture of Occupation* (London: Verso, 2007), pp. 106–7.

35. Lori Lyn Bogle, *The Pentagon's Battle for the American Mind* (College Station: Texas A & M University Press, 2004), p. 84.

36. Arthur M. Schlesinger, Jr, *The Vital Center: The Politics of Freedom* (London: André Deutsch, 1970), pp. 1, 52.

37. Christopher Thorne, *Border Crossings: Studies in International History* (Oxford: Blackwell, 1988). One is also reminded here of Ronald Reagan's pronouncement that America really needed to be on full alert as the Sandinistas were only 48 hours' drive from Texas.

38. Donald E. Pease, 'Hiroshima, the Vietnam Veterans War Memorial, and the Gulf War', in Amy Kaplan and Donald E. Pease (eds), *Cultures of*

United States Imperialism (Durham: Duke University Press, 1993), p. 564. Also Michael Paul Rogin, *The Intellectuals and McCarthy: The Radical Specter* (Cambridge, MA: MIT Press, 1967), p. 33; Jerry W. Sanders, *Peddlers of Crisis: The Committee on the Present Danger and the Politics of Containment* (London: Pluto Press, 1983), pp. 23–50.

39. Richard Hofstadter, 'The Paranoid Style in American Politics' (1963), in *The Paranoid Style in American Politics and Other Essays* (New York: Vintage Books, 1967), pp. 4, 26, 29; E. H. Gombrich, *Myth and Reality in German War-Time Broadcasts* (London: Athlone Press, 1970), p. 14.

40. Gilles Deleuze and Félix Guattari, *Anti-Oedipus: Capitalism and Schizophrenia* (1972), trans. Robert Hurley, Mark Seem and Helen Lane (London: Athlone Press, 1984), p. 193; Kenneth Dean and Brian Massumi, *First and Last Emperors: The Absolute State and the Body of the Despot* (New York: Autonomedia, 1992), p. 100.

41. See Mark Neocleous, *Imagining the State* (Maidenhead: Open University Press, 2003), pp. 32–6.

42. John Lewis Gaddis, *Strategies of Containment: A Critical Appraisal of Postwar American National Security Policy* (Oxford: Oxford University Press, 1982), pp. 91–2.

43. Mary Kaldor, *The Imaginary War: Understanding the East-West Conflict* (Oxford: Blackwell, 1990); Guy Oakes, *The Imaginary War: Civil Defense and American Cold War Culture* (Oxford: Oxford University Press, 1994).

44. George Kennan, 'Comments on the General Trend of U.S. Foreign Policy', Draft Paper, 20 August 1948, cited in Gaddis, *Strategies of Containment*, p. 27.

45. Cited in Walter LaFeber, *America, Russia, and the Cold War 1945–1996, 8th Edition* (New York: McGraw-Hill, 1997), p. 53.

46. David Campbell, 'Violent Performances: Identity, Sovereignty, Responsibility', in Yosef Lapid and Friedrich Kratochwil (eds), *The Return of Culture and Identity in IR Theory* (Boulder, CO: Lynne Rienner, 1997), p. 167.

47. Diana Johnstone and Ben Cramer, 'The Burdens and the Glory: U.S. Bases in Europe', in Joseph Gerson and Bruce Birchard (eds), *The Sun Never Sets: Confronting the Network of Foreign U.S. Military Bases* (Boston: South End Press, 1991), pp. 199–200.

48. On arguments along these lines, but with two very different perspectives, styles and approaches, see Francoise Hall, 'The United States' Search for Security: A Psychotherapist's Viewpoint', *Journal of Peace Research*, Vol. 20, No. 4, 1983, pp. 299–309; and Gore Vidal, 'How to Take Back Our Country', *The Nation*, 4 June 1988, pp. 781–3.

49. 'Think hard about it. I'm running out of demons. I'm running out of villains. I'm down to Castro and Kim Il Sung' – Colin Powell, interview

in *Air Force Times*, 15 April 1991.

50. Franz L. Neumann, 'The Concept of Political Freedom' (1953), in *The Rule of Law Under Siege: Selected Essays of Franz L. Neumann and Otto Kirchheimer*, ed. William E. Scheuerman (Berkeley: University of California Press, 1996), pp. 223–4; Schmitt, *Concept of the Political*, pp. 26–37.

51. See the debates among Policy Planning Staff on the early draft of the document in February 1950, in *Foreign Relations of the United States, 1950, Vol. 1* (Washington: US Government Printing Office, 1977), pp. 168–72.

52. Rosenberg, 'U.S. Cultural History', p. 161; David Ryan, 'Mapping Containment: The Cultural Construction of the Cold War', in Douglas Field (ed.), *American Cold War Culture* (Edinburgh: Edinburgh University Press, 2005), p. 59; Bradley S. Klein, *Strategic Studies and World Order: The Global Politics of Deterrence* (Cambridge: Cambridge University Press, 1994), pp. 114–18.

53. The theme of God was to be reasserted and consolidated in June 1954 with the addition of the words 'one nation under God' to the pledge of allegiance, and then again in July 1956 with the formal ratification of 'In God We Trust' as the nation's motto. This of course was in part designed to offer a contrast to the atheist movement of communism.

54. John Higham noted how the myth of consensus heavily influenced the writing of history books during these years – see 'The Cult of "American Consensus"', *Commentary*, Vol. 27, No. 2, 1959, pp. 93–100. Also see Sacvan Bercovitch, *The American Jeremiad* (Wisconsin: University of Wisconsin Press, 1978), pp. 132–75, and Bercovitch, *Rites of Assent: Transformations in the Symbolic Construction of America* (New York: Routledge, 1993), pp. 29–67. One might add that 'American studies' has peddled the same myth of American exceptionalism. The place of American studies in the security complex is taken up in Chapter 5.

55. X [Kennan], 'Sources of Soviet Conduct', *Foreign Affairs*, Vol. 25, No. 4, 1947, pp. 566–82, p. 582.

56. Kennan, *Memoirs, 1925–1950*, pp. 304–5; George F. Kennan, *Memoirs, 1950–1963* (New York: Pantheon, 1972), pp. 66–70.

57. NATO's foundation myths portray the Alliance as first and foremost a security arrangement, but this obscures NATO's political and cultural function in constituting and maintaining political identity. In a major radio address on 18 March, 1949, the day on which the text of the North Atlantic Pact was made public, Secretary of State Acheson called for a recognition of the deeply cultural 'affinity and natural identity of interests' between the two sides of the Atlantic founded on common institutions, morals and values – 'Radio Address by the Secretary of State (Acheson) on the North Atlantic Treaty, 18 March 1949', in *Documents*

on American Foreign Relations, Vol. XI, 1949 (Princeton University Press, 1950), p. 601. As an embodiment of a certain geopolitical space, NATO presupposed a singular identity of/for members of the 'West', an identity which needed to be secured. This helped shape the political identity of its members in the US and Europe through a celebration of the 'freedom' of the West set against the 'unfreedom' of the Soviet bloc. Thus NATO was never simply an instrumental device for securing a specific geopolitical space and/or the individual and collective interests of its members, but, rather, has played a direct part in articulating and constituting a cultural and political identity of and for its members. See Dillon, 'Alliance of Security and Subjectivity', pp. 118–21; Klein, *Strategic Studies*, pp. 121, 128.

58. Reflecting on his seven-year stint as Secretary of Defense, Robert S. McNamara commented that the reason Canada and the US are at peace is 'because of the vast fund of compatible beliefs, common principles and shared ideals . . . our mutual basis for peace has nothing whatever to do with military hardware' – *The Essence of Security: Reflections In Office* (New York: Harper and Row, 1968), p.143.

59. Campbell, *Writing Security*, p. 33; Campbell, 'Violent Performances', p. 167; Klein, *Strategic Studies*, pp. 114–17.

60. One can trace the theme of 'our values' and 'our way of life' on 11 September 2001. Bush made three statements or proclamations on that day. In his first speech Bush is simply concerned to state his overall control of the situation. But by the third, and longest, statement, delivered as an 'Address to the Nation' just twelve hours after the attacks, Bush iterates in the very first sentence the idea that the attacks were on 'our way of life'. See 'Statement by the President in his Address to the Nation', 11 September 2001. Read in this way, Bush's 'Remarks at National Day of Prayer and Remembrance' of 14 September read as much like a eulogy for America as for the dead, a hymn to the 'national character' and 'national unity'. By 20 September the theme had been developed into a rhetorical question: 'Why do they hate us?'. Answer: they hate our way of life – Bush, 'Address to a Joint Session of Congress and the American people', 20 September 2001. On the other hand, the theme had been central to much of the rhetoric about 'humanitarian intervention' in the previous decade. For example, commenting on the Kosovo campaign, Tony Blair said that the British actions 'are guided by a more subtle blend of mutual self interest and moral purpose in defending the values we cherish', adding, of course, the necessary link with security: 'the spread of our values makes us safer' – 'Doctrine of the International Community', Speech to the Economic Club of Chicago, 22 April 1999.

61. Michael J. Shapiro, *The Politics of Representation: Writing Practices in Biography, Photography, and Policy Analysis* (Madison, WI: University of Wisconsin Press, 1988), pp. 101–2, 123; Campbell, *Writing Security*, pp. 7–8, 69, 99–101; McSweeney, *Security, Identity and Interests*, p. 73.

62. Edmund Burke, *Reflections on the Revolution in France* (1790), ed. Conor Cruise O'Brien (Harmondsworth: Penguin, 1968), pp. 170–1.

63. Cited in Athan Theoharis, *Seeds of Repression: Harry S. Truman and the Origins of McCarthyism* (Chicago: Quadrangle Books, 1971), p. 104, emphasis added. For the figures see Francis H. Thompson, *The Frustration of Politics: Truman, Congress, and the Loyalty Issue 1945–1953* (Cranbury, NJ: Associated University Presses, 1979), p. 22.

64. Cited in Thomas I. Emerson and David M. Helfeld, 'Loyalty Among Government Employees', *Yale Law Journal*, Vol. 58, No. 1, 1948, pp. 1–143, p. 66, emphasis added.

65. Executive Order 9835, Prescribing Procedures for the Administration of an Employees Loyalty Program in the Executive Branch of the Government, 1947.

66. Carey McWilliams, *Witch Hunt: The Revival of Heresy* (Boston: Little, Brown and Co., 1950), pp. 16–17; Philip Jenkins, *The Cold War At Home: The Red Scare in Pennsylvania, 1945–1960* (Chapel Hill: University of North Carolina Press, 1999); M. J. Heale, *American Anticommunism: Combating the Enemy Within, 1830–1970* (Baltimore: Johns Hopkins University Press, 1990), p.150.

67. Robert Justin Goldstein, *Political Repression in Modern America: From 1870 to the Present* (Cambridge, MA: Schenkman Publishing Co., 1978), pp. 351–2.; Caute, *Great Fear*, p. 22.

68. Walter Gellhorn, *Security, Loyalty, and Science* (Ithaca: Cornell University Press, 1950), p. 128.

69. 'Statement by the President on the Government's Employee Loyalty Program', 14 November 1947, in Truman, *Public Papers, 1947*, p. 490. In an interview in 1961 Truman was still unable to appreciate any of the complex political, philosophical and personal issues surrounding loyalty: 'You're either loyal to the United States, or you're not!' – cited in Alan D. Harper, *The Politics of Loyalty: The White House and the Communist Issue 1946–1952* (Westport, CT: Greenwood Publishing, 1969), p. 233.

70. For contemporary comments on the inability to define loyalty see Francis Biddle, *The Fear of Freedom* (New York: Doubleday, 1951), p. 13, and Harold W. Chase, *Security and Liberty: The Problem of Native Communists, 1947–1955* (New York: Doubleday and Co., 1955), pp. 43–5.

71. Gellhorn, *Security, Loyalty, and Science*, p. 131–4; Alan Barth, *The Loyalty of Free Men* (London: Victor Gollancz, 1951), p. 104; Goldstein, *Political Repression*, p. 300–1; Thompson, *Frustration of Politics*, pp. 50, 172.

72. J. Edgar Hoover, 'The Disloyalty of Communists and Fellow Travelers', [Testimony before the Committee on Un-American Activities, House of Representatives, 26 March 1947], in John C. Wahlke (ed.), *Loyalty in a Democratic State* (Boston: D. C. Heath and Co., 1952), pp. 102–7.

73 . This was just one question of many asked about reading materials. One senses here a precursor to the surveillance of the reading habits of US citizens under the PATRIOT Act.

74. One employee had joined the Baltimore Bookshop. Although the Bookshop was not listed by the Attorney General, the Washington Bookshop was and so, since they were both 'Bookshops', a member of the Loyalty Board sought to question the employee about this. 'Why was that organization called the Bookshop?', he was asked. Because 'they sold books', was the not unreasonable answer. Cited in Biddle, *Fear of Freedom*, p. 224.

75. Cited in Harper, *Politics of Loyalty*, pp. 48–9.

76. Cited in Gellhorn, *Security, Loyalty, and Science*, p. 152. There's a lovely little story of the questioning of anthropologist Gene Weltfish by McCarthy's Government Operations Permanent Subcommittee chaired by McCarthy himself. Weltfish had published with Ruth Benedict *The Races of Mankind* (1943), which, using Army intelligence tests, had shown that the intelligence scores of Southern whites were in fact lower than those of Northern blacks. After trying to get Weltfish to admit to being a communist or associated with communists, McCarthy himself tried to change tack by raising the question of race and picking up Weltfish and Benedict's book.

> Sen. McCarthy: Just opening at random, I find something on page 18 of the book entitled *The Races of Mankind*, which should interest my southern colleagues to some extent. It shows the intelligence tests of the Southern Whites: Arkansas: 41.55 [and] Northern Negroes: Ohio: 49.50.
> Miss Weltfish: May I state that this came from Army records?
> Sen. McCarthy: Pardon?
> Miss Weltfish: That this material came from Army records.

The air of panic as the Committee sensed its loss of control of the hearing was widely appreciated. But what the hearing shows is that *any* discussion of race was out of bounds; just trying to *think* about the question was considered suspect, even if one was doing so using knowledge gathered by the state itself. The story is told in David H. Price, *Threatening Anthropology: McCarthyism and the FBI's Surveillance of Activist Anthropology* (Durham: Duke University Press, 2004), pp. 126–31.

77. For this background see Mary L. Dudziak, *Cold War Civil Rights: Race and the Image of American Democracy* (Princeton, NJ: Princeton University Press, 2000).

78. Cited in David K. Johnson, *The Lavender Scare: The Cold War Persecution of Gays and Lesbians in the Federal Government* (Chicago: University of Chicago Press, 2004), p. 114.

79. The Senator, Republican Kenneth Wherry, is cited in Johnson, *Lavender Scare*, p. 2.

80. Cited in Johnson, *Lavender Scare*, pp. 108–9.

81. Jack Lait and Lee Mortimer, *Washington Confidential: The Lowdown on the Big Town* (New York: Crown Publishers, 1951), pp. 90–8.

82. Schlesinger, *Vital Center*, pp. 126–7. For Schlesinger's interest in 'desire' see K. A. Cuordileone, '"Politics in an Age of Anxiety": Cold War Political Culture and the Crisis in American Masculinity', *Journal of American History*, Vol. 87, No. 2, 2000, pp. 515–45.

83. Lionel Trilling, 'The Kinsey Report', in *The Liberal Imagination: Essays on Literature and Society* (London: Secker and Warburg, 1964), pp. 223–42.

84. Cited in William N. Eskridge, Jr, 'Privacy Jurisprudence and the Apartheid of the Closet, 1946–1961', *Florida State University Law Review*, 1997. http://www.law.fsu.edu/journals/lawreview/frames/244/eskrfram. html.

85. Johnson, *Lavender Scare*, pp. 115–17, 131–4.

86. Hugh Wilford, *The CIA, the British Left and the Cold War* (London: Frank Cass, 2003), p. 218.

87. Michel Foucault, commenting on the supposed political problem of a purported passivity in sexual relations in ancient Greece – *The Uses of Pleasure: The History of Sexuality, Vol. 2* (1984), trans. Robert Hurley (London: Penguin, 1987), p. 220.

88. Cited in Louise S. Robbins, 'The Library of Congress and Federal Loyalty Programs, 1947–1956: No "Communists or Cocksuckers"', *Library Quarterly*, Vol. 64, No. 4, 1994, pp. 365–85, p. 367.

89. McCarthy cited in David Halberstam, *The Fifties* (New York: Fawcett Columbine, 1993), p. 54; North cited in Bob Woodward, *Veil: The Secret Wars of the CIA, 1981–87* (London: Headline, 1988), p. 443.

90. Johnson, *Lavender Scare*, pp. 16, 30, 34. Robert Corber, *In the Name of National Security: Hitchcock, Homophobia, and the Political Construction of Gender in Postwar America* (Durham: Duke University Press, 1993), p. 8; Geoffrey Smith, 'National Security and Personal Isolation: Sex, Gender, and Disease in the Cold-War United States', *International History Review*, Vol. 14, No. 2, 1992, pp. 221–40.

91. Michel Foucault, *Abnormal: Lectures at the College de France 1974–1975*, trans. Graham Burchell (London: Verso, 2003), p. 50.

92. Cited in Caute, *Great Fear*, p. 324.
93. Cited in Johnson, *Lavender Scare*, pp. 136–7.
94. These questions and those on previous pages can be found in a variety of sources, but most usefully in Adam Yarmolinsky (ed.), *Case Studies in Personnel Security* (Washington: Bureau of National Affairs, 1955), and Biddle, *Fear of Freedom*, pp. 219–45. For other examples and discussion see Eleanor Bontecue, *The Federal Loyalty-Security Program* (Ithaca: Cornell University Press, 1953), pp. 137–42; Ralph S. Brown, Jr, *Loyalty and Security: Employment Tests in the United States* (New Haven: Yale University Press, 1958); Caute, *Great Fear*, pp. 280–2, 383; Emerson and Helfeld, 'Loyalty Among Government Employees', pp. 70–5; Goldstein, *Political Repression*, p. 303; L. A. Nikoloric, 'The Government Loyalty Program', in Wahlke (ed.), *Loyalty in a Democratic State*, p. 55; Philip M. Stern, *The Oppenheimer Case: Security on Trial* (London: Rupert Hart-Davis, 1969), pp. 472–3, 486–7.
95. Johnson, *Lavender Scare*, p. 36; Laura Belmonte, 'Selling Capitalism: Modernization and US Overseas Propaganda, 1945–1959', in David C. Engerman et al. (eds), *Staging Growth: Modernization, Development, and the Global Cold War* (Amherst: University of Massachusetts Press, 2003), pp. 114–15.
96. Alan Nadel, *Containment Culture: American Narratives, Postmodernism, and the Atomic Age* (Durham: Duke University Press, 1995), p. 117; Elaine Tyler May, *Homeward Bound: American Families in the Cold War Era* (New York: Basic Books, 1988), p. 14; Corber, *In the Name of National Security*, pp. 6–10; Johnson, *Lavender Scare*, p. 123.
97. In his lectures on psychiatric power Foucault situates the loyalty oath in the regime of sovereignty. And yet it is quite clear that in terms of how they fabricate subjectivity, they are also, in his terms, 'disciplinary' – *Psychiatric Power: Lectures at the Collège de France* (2003), trans. Graham Burchell (Basingstoke: Palgrave, 2006), pp. 43–7.
98. Jean-Paul Sartre, *Critique of Dialectical Reason, Vol. 1* (1960), trans. Alan Sheridan-Smith (London: Verso, 1991), p. 421.
99. Henry Steele Commager, 'Who is Loyal to America?', *Harper's Magazine*, Vol. 195, No. 1168, September 1947, pp. 193–9, p. 195.
100. Barth, *Loyalty of Free Men*, p. 125.
101. Elmer Davis, *But We Were Born Free* (London: André Deutsch, 1955), p. 22.
102. Allen Weinstein, 'The Symbolism of Subversion: Notes on Some Cold War Icons', *Journal of American Studies*, Vol. 6, No. 2, 1972, pp. 165–79, p. 174.
103. Carl Bernstein, *Loyalties: A Son's Memoir* (London: Macmillan, 1989), pp. 189–90.

104. Nikoloric, 'The Government Loyalty Program', p. 57. Also Biddle, *Fear of Freedom*, p. 238; Brown, *Loyalty and Security*, p. 54; Chase, *Security and Liberty*, pp. 2, 51; Emerson and Helfeld, 'Loyalty Among Government Employees', pp. 55, 60, 66; Gellhorn, *Security, Loyalty, and Science*, p. 160; McWilliams, *Witch Hunt*, p. 16; Stern, *Oppenheimer Case*, pp. 489–91; Frank J. Donner, *The Age of Surveillance: The Aims and Methods of America's Political Intelligence System* (New York: Alfred A. Knopf, 1980), p. 27

105. Hans Magnus Enzensberger, 'Towards a Theory of Treason' (1964), in *Raids and Reconstructions: Essays on Politics, Crime and Culture* (London: Pluto Press, 1976), p. 70.

106. Cited in Nadel, *Containment Culture*, p. 85.

107. Harold Garfinkel, 'Conditions of Successful Degradation Ceremonies', *American Journal of Sociology*, Vol. 61, No. 5, pp. 420–4, p. 421.

108. Victor S. Navasky, *Naming Names* (London: John Calder, 1982), p. 321.

109. Nadel, *Containment Culture*, p. 78.

110. Davis, *But We Were Born Free*, p. 23; Harper, *Politics of Loyalty*, p. 50; Campbell, *Writing Security*, p. 171.

111. Barth, *Loyalty of Free Men*, pp. 137–8. This might explain why much of the public seemed to have misunderstood the distinction between loyalty and security, as reported by Johnson, *Lavender Scare*, p. 31.

112. Enzensberger, 'Theory of Treason', p. 62.

113. Caute, *Great Fear*, pp. 273–4; Barth, *Loyalty of Free Men*, pp. 135–6; Goldstein, *Political Repression*, p. 338.

114. Sartre, *Critique of Dialectical Reason, Vol. 1*, pp. 430–1. Also James Der Derian, *On Diplomacy: A Genealogy of Western Estrangement* (Oxford: Blackwell, 1987), p. 41.

115. Joel Kovel, *Red Hunting in the Promised Land: Anticommunism and the Making of America* (London: Continuum, 1997), pp. 118, 281.

116. Barth, *Loyalty of Free Men*, p. 129.

117. Emerson and Helfeld, 'Loyalty Among Government Employees', p. 133; also Commager, 'Who is Loyal to America?', p. 198; McWilliams, *Witch Hunt*, p. 35; Navasky, *Naming Names*, p. 342. For an even earlier recognition of the comparison see Carl Joachim Friedrich, 'Teachers' Oaths', *Harper's Magazine*, Vol. 171, January 1936, pp. 171–7.

118. To give just one example to spell out the point: 'There are millions of good Americans who practice the Muslim faith who love their country as much as I love the country, who salute the flag as strongly as I salute the flag' – President Bush, 'Remarks Following a Meeting with Congressional Leaders', 19 September 2001.

CHAPTER 5: THE COMPANY AND THE CAMPUS

1. Interviewed for and cited in Joel Bakan, *The Corporation: The Pathological Pursuit of Power and Profit* (London: Constable, 2004), p. 111.
2. 'Mission Statement' and 'What we Do', both at http://www.bens.org/about-us.html.
3. *The National Security Strategy of the United States of America* (Washington: The White House, September 2002), p. 18.
4. Tony Blair, 'Seven Pillars of a Decent Society', Speech in Southampton, UK, 16 April 1997.
5. Steven Spitzer, 'Security and Control in Capitalist Societies: The Fetishism of Security and the Secret Thereof', in John Lowman, Robert J. Menzies and T. S. Plays (eds), *Transcarceration: Essays in the Sociology of Social Control* (Aldershot: Gower, 1987); George S. Rigakos, *The New Parapolice: Risk Markets and Commodified Social Control* (Toronto: University of Toronto Press, 2002).
6. Mark Neocleous, *Imagining the State* (Maidenhead: Open University Press, 2003), pp. 46–61.
7. For these details and those which follow see: Tim Shorrock, 'Selling (Off) Iraq', *The Nation*, 23 June 2003; Chalmers Johnson, *The Sorrows of Empire: Militarism, Secrecy, and the End of the Republic* (London: Verso, 2004); Rory Carroll and Julian Borger, 'Iraq Rebuilding under threat as US Runs out of Money', *The Guardian*, 9 September 2005, p. 14; Ed Harriman, 'Where Has All the Money Gone?', *London Review of Books*, 7 July 2005, pp. 3–7; Seymour M. Hersh, *Chain of Command* (New York: Harper, 2005); Oliver Morgan, 'All Eyes on Halliburton', *The Observer*, 11 September 2005, p. 5; Frances Fox Piven, *The War at Home: The Domestic Costs of Bush's Militarism* (New York: New Press, 2004); Julian Borger and David Pallister, 'Corruption: the "Second Insurgency"', *The Guardian*, 2 December 2006; Ed Harriman, 'Cronyism and Kickbacks', *London Review of Books*, 26 January 2006, pp. 14–16; Antonia Juhasz, *The Bush Agenda: Invading the World, One Economy at a Time* (London: Duckworth, 2006); Eliot Weinberger, 'What I Heard about Iraq in 2005', *London Review of Books*, 5 January 2006, pp. 7–14; Daniel Politi, 'Winning Contractors', *Center for Public Integrity* – http://www.publicintegrity.org
8. Just five months after the Report, BearingPoint was awarded a $9 million initial contract to facilitate Iraq's economic 'recovery', rising to just under $80 million and renewable annually for two more years – The Center for Public Integrity, 'The Windfalls of War', http://www.publicintegrity.org.
9. Donald Rumsfeld, 'Core Principles for a Free Iraq' [Speech in New York], 27 May 2003, *Wall Street Journal*, 27 May 2003.

10. Retort, *Afflicted Powers: Capital and Spectacle in a New Age of War* (London: Verso, 2005), pp. 41, 72.
11. War on Want, *Corporate Mercenaries* (London: War on Want, 2006).
12. Eric Hobsbawm, *The New Century* (London: Little, Brown and Co., 2000), pp. 11–15.
13. Anna Leander, 'Privatizing the Politics of Protection: Military Companies and the Definition of Security Concerns', in Jef Huysmans, Andrew Dobson and Raia Prokhovnik (eds), *The Politics of Protection: Sites of Insecurity and Political Agency* (London: Routledge, 2006), p. 29; Peter Singer, *Corporate Warriors: The Rise of the Privatized Military Industry* (Ithaca: Cornell University Press, 2003); Deborah D. Avant, *The Market for Force* (Cambridge: Cambridge University Press, 2005).
14. Or, as some prefer, private military companies (PMCs). Many firms calling themselves private security companies often perform military roles with military consequences, and in the zones of conflict in which such companies are usually engaged the line between policing and combat is often blurred. Moreover, calling them private military companies completely ignores the range of security companies that work solely in the domestic field, and thus could not reasonably be called 'military'. And yet calling them 'private' security companies is also a little misleading, since it presupposes that there are non-private security companies, when in fact the only real alternative is the state. For these reasons, I will avoid using 'PSC' as well as 'PMC', and stick to the far more straightforward 'security companies'.
15. War on Want, *Corporate Mercenaries*, p. 4; Max Hastings, 'We Must Fight Our Instinctive Distaste for Mercenaries', *The Guardian*, 2 August 2006; Jon Ronson, *The Men Who Stare at Goats* (London: Picador, 2005), p. 183; Singer, *Corporate Warriors*, p. 49; Leander, 'Privatizing the Politics of Protection', p. 20; Avant, *Market for Force*, pp. 8, 147–8; Eugene Gholz and Harvey M. Sapolsky, 'Restructuring the U.S. Defense Industry', *International Security*, Vol. 24, No. 3, 1999–2000, pp. 5–51; Johnson, *Sorrows of Empire*, p. 140; Ken Silverstein, *Private Warriors* (London: Verso, 2000), p. 182; Ben Hayes, *Arming Big Brother: The EU's Security Research Programme* (Amsterdam/London: Transnational Institute/Statewatch Briefing Series, No. 2006/1, 2006).
16. Singer, *Corporate Warriors*, pp. 7, 49, 55.
17. See, for example, Herfried Münkler, *The New Wars* (2002), trans. Patrick Camiller (Cambridge: Polity Press, 2005); Mary Kaldor, *New and Old Wars, 2nd Edition* (Cambridge: Polity Press, 2006).
18. Leander, 'Privatizing the Politics of Protection', p. 19.
19. Silverstein, *Private Warriors*, p. 143.
20. Dominick Donald, *After the Bubble: British Private Security Companies*

after Iraq (London: RUSI, Whitehall Paper 66, 2006); Jeremy Greenstock, 'Private Security Companies in an Insecure World', *RUSI Journal*, Vol. 151, No. 6, 2006, pp. 42–4.

21. For example: Clifford D. Shearing and Philip C. Stenning, 'Modern Private Security: Its Growth and Implications', *Crime and Justice*, Vol. 3, 1981, pp. 193–245; 'Reframing Policing', in Clifford D. Shearing and Philip C. Stenning (eds), *Private Policing* (Newbury Park, CA: Sage, 1987); Nigel South, *Policing for Profit: The Private Security Sector* (London: Sage Publications, 1988), pp. 9–11; Trevor Jones and Tim Newburn, *Private Security and Public Policing* (Oxford: Oxford University Press, 1998).

22. See the CoESS website at http://www.coess.org. For discussion of the trends and comparative figures see Les Johnston and Clifford Shearing, *Governing Security: Explorations in Policing and Justice* (London: Routledge, 2003), pp. 118–9; Les Johnston, 'Transnational Security Governance', in Jennifer Wood and Benoit Dupont (eds), *Democracy, Society and the Governance of Security* (Cambridge: Cambridge University Press, 2006), p. 37; Alison Wakefield, 'The Security Officer', in Martin Gill (ed.), *The Handbook of Security* (Houndmills: Palgrave, 2006), pp. 384–6; Mark Button and Bruce George, 'Regulation of Private Security: Models for Analysis', in Gill (ed.), *Handbook of Security*, p. 563.

23. See the SIA website at http://www.the-sia.org.uk .

24. Johnston, 'Transnational Security Governance', p. 36.

25. David J. Rothkopf, 'Business Versus Terror', *Foreign Policy*, 130, 2002, pp. 56–64.

26. Office of Homeland Security, *National Strategy for Homeland Security*, July 2002, p. 63.

27. Tim Starks, 'Security "Gold Rush" Yields Nuggets for Some', *Congressional Quarterly Weekly*, 22 January 2005 – http://www.globalsecurity.org/org/news/2005/050122-security-gold.htm.

28. Cited in Christian Parenti, *Lockdown America: Police and Prisons in an Age of Crisis* (London: Verso, 1999), p. 211.

29. The comment was Senator Phil Graham's cited in Parenti, *Lockdown America*, p. 230. Also see Charles Overbeck, 'Prison Factories: Slave Labor for the New World Order?', http://www.parascope.com/articles/0197/prison.htm; Eve Goldberg and Linda Evans, 'The Prison-Industrial Complex and the Global Economy', http://www.hartford-hwp.com/archives/26/152.html; Brian Jarvis, *Cruel and Unusual: Punishment and US Culture* (London: Pluto Press, 2004); Nils Christie, *Crime Control as Industry: Towards GULAGS, Western Style*, Second Edition (London: Routledge, 1994); Ruth Wilson Gilmore, *Golden Gulag: Prisons, Surplus, Crisis, and Opposition in Globalizing California* (Berkeley: University of

California Press, 2007).

30. Shearing and Stenning, 'Modern Private Security', p. 193; South, 'Private Security', p. 190; Clifford D. Shearing and Philip C. Stenning, 'Private Security: Its Implications for Social Control', *Social Problems*, Vol. 30, No. 5, 1983, pp. 493–506.

31. Jennifer Wood and Clifford Shearing, *Imagining Security* (Cullompton: Willan, 2007).

32. For example: 'The United States can defeat terrorists by drawing on the very attributes that inflame its enemies . . .: American enterprise, American capital, American technology, the hard work of the American people, U.S. reliance on the market-place, and the role of the individual' – Rothkopf, 'Business Versus Terror', p. 64.

33. George Rigakos, *Nightclub: Bouncers, Risk and the Spectacle of Consumption* (McGill-Queen's University Press, 2008).

34. Karl Marx, *Capital: A Critique of Political Economy* (1867), trans. Ben Fowkes (Harmondsworth: Penguin, 1976), p. 163.

35. Rigakos, *New Parapolice*, pp. 5, 13, 23.

36. Spitzer, 'Security and Control', pp. 45–6.

37. See Mike Davis, *City of Quartz: Excavating the Future in Los Angeles* (London: Vintage, 1990), pp. 223–50; Adam Crawford, 'Policing and Security as "Club Goods": The New Enclosures?', in Wood and Dupont (eds), *Democracy, Society and the Governance of Security*, pp. 111, 127.

38. Spitzer, 'Security and Control', p. 51.

39. Paul Virilio, *Speed and Politics: An Essay on Dromology* (1977), trans. Mark Polizzotti (New York: Semiotext[e], 1986), pp. 119–23; Ian Loader, 'Consumer Culture and the Commodification of Policing and Security', *Sociology*, Vol. 33, No. 2, 1999, pp. 373–92.

40. Adorno to Benjamin, 29 February, 1940, in Theodor W. Adorno and Walter Benjamin, *The Complete Correspondence 1928–1940*, trans. Nicholas Walker (Cambridge: Polity Press, 1999), p. 321.

41. The parallel is the culture industry – see Theodor Adorno and Max Horkheimer, *Dialectic of Enlightenment* (1944), trans. John Cumming (London: Verso, 1979), p. 139.

42. Karl Polanyi, *The Great Transformation: The Political and Economic Origins of Our Time* (Boston: Beacon Press, 1957), pp. 72–3.

43. Marx, *Capital*, p. 165.

44. Marx, *Capital*, pp. 164–5.

45. Marx, *Capital*, p. 176.

46. Marx, *Capital*, pp. 983, 1046.

47. Karl Marx, *Capital: A Critique of Political Economy, Vol. 2*, trans. David Fernbach (Harmondsworth: Penguin, 1978), p. 303.

48. Karl Marx, 'Debates on the Law on Thefts of Wood' (1842), in Karl Marx

and Frederick Engels, *Collected Works, Vol. 1* (London: Lawrence and Wishart, 1975), pp. 262–3.

49. G. A. Cohen, *Karl Marx's Theory of History: A Defence* (Oxford: Oxford University Press, 1978), p. 129.

50. Nick Dyer-Witheford, *Cyber-Marx: Cycles and Circuits of Struggle in High-Technology Capitalism* (Urbana: University of Illinois Press, 1999), p. 141.

51. 'Letter to Tatiana [Schucht]', 3 August 1931, in Antonio Gramsci, *Letters from Prison*, ed. Frank Rosengarten (New York: Columbia University Press, 1994), p. 52.

52. Robin Luckham, 'Armament Culture', *Alternatives*, Vol. 10, No. 1, 1984, pp. 1–44, p. 11. Also Andreas Behnke, 'The Message or the Messenger? Reflections on the Role of Security Experts and the Securitization of Political Issues', *Cooperation and Conflict*, Vol. 35, No. 1, 2000, pp. 89–105.

53. See Victor Marchetti and John D. Marks, *The CIA and the Cult of Intelligence* (1974), (New York: Dell Publishing, 1980), pp. 50–1; Sigmund Diamond, *Compromised Campus: The Collaboration of Universities with the Intelligence Community, 1945–1955* (New York: Oxford University Press, 1992), pp. 150–203; Jane Sanders, *Cold War on the Campus: Academic Freedom at the University of Washington, 1946–64* (Seattle: University of Washington Press, 1979); Ellen W. Schrecker, *No Ivory Tower: McCarthyism and the Universities* (Oxford: Oxford University Press, 1986). The CIA likes to claim that its Officer-in-Residence programmes are completely public and open. Yet when Daniel Brandt of Public Information Research attempted under the Freedom of Information Act to establish a list of participants he was denied the information. The letters can be viewed at http://www.cia-on-campus.org.

54. A full list of the books has never been issued, as the CIA has successfully fought all legal attempts to have them revealed. Former CIA Director John Stockwell estimates the books to number at least 1,200 – *The Praetorian Guard: The U.S. Role in the New World Order* (Cambridge, MA: South End Press, 1991), pp. 34, 101. Others have put the figure much higher.

55. John Phillips, Chief Scientist for the CIA, cited in Daniel Golden, 'After Sept. 11: CIA becomes a Force on Campus', *Wall Street Journal*, 4 October 2002 – http://www.mindfully.org/Reform/2002/CIA-Growing-On-Campus4oct02.htm.

56. The comment comes from a 1968 report written for the CIA by University of California administrator Earl Clinton Bolton, 'Memorandum for [deleted]; Subject: Agency-Academic Relations', 5 August 1968 – http://www.cia-on-campus.org/foia/ac01.html accessed 13 April 2005. Bush's comment comes from his tenure as CIA Director in the mid-1970s, in which he tried to help engineer a campus resurgence on

the part of the CIA – cited in John Trumpbour, 'Harvard in Service to the National Security State', *Covert Action Information Bulletin*, Fall 1991, pp. 12–16.

57. Bruce Cumings, 'Boundary Displacement: Area Studies and International Studies During and After the Cold War', *Bulletin of Concerned Asian Scholars*, Vol. 29, No. 1, 1997, pp. 6–26.

58. Diamond, *Compromised Campus*, pp. 12–13.

59. The US Commission on National Security/21st Century's *Roadmap for National Security: Imperative for Change* (February 2001) has sections on education as national security, while the US Higher Education Act, 2003, mandates the federal funding of international studies and foreign languages to overcome what many on the right thought had become the one-sided approach of Middle Eastern studies which gave too much sympathy to the Palestinian cause. Part of the rubric of the Department of Homeland Security is to 'engage' the academic community.

60. Diamond, *Compromised Campus*, pp. 65–8.

61. Robin W. Winks, *Cloak and Dagger: Scholars in the Secret War, 1939–1961* (New York: Quill, 1987), p. 384; Diamond, *Compromised Campus*, p. 55.

62. Diamond, *Compromised Campus*, p. 95.

63. David C. Engerman, 'The Ironies of the Iron Curtain: The Cold War and the Rise of Russian Studies', in David A. Hollinger (ed.), *The Humanities and the Dynamics of Inclusion since World War II* (Baltimore: Johns Hopkins University Press, 2006), p. 315.

64. Engerman, 'Ironies of the Iron Curtain', p. 315.

65. Stephen F. Cohen, *Rethinking the Soviet Experience: Politics and History Since 1917* (Oxford: Oxford University Press, 1985), p. 8.

66. See Carl Friedrich and Zbigniew Brzezinski, *Totalitarian Dictatorship and Autocracy* (New York: Praeger, 1956); Carl Friedrich (ed.), *Totalitarianism: Proceedings of a Conference held at the American Academy of Arts and Sciences 1953* (New York: Harvard University Press, 1954).

67. See Stephen White, 'Political Science as Ideology: The Study of Soviet Politics', in Brian Chapman and Allen Potter (eds), *W.J.M.M., Political Questions: Essays in Honour of W. J.M. Mackenzie* (Manchester: Manchester University Press, 1974), pp. 252–68; Ida Oren, *Our Enemies and US: America's Rivalries and the Making of Political Science* (Ithaca: Cornell University Press, 2003).

68. 'This was a time when we practiced a good deal of self-censorship . . . It was a period . . . when a neighbor of mine, a graduate student at MIT, upon learning that I was writing a dissertation dealing with Lenin, told me sternly that he disagreed with me a hundred percent' – Alfred G. Meyer, 'Coming to Terms with the Past . . . And with One's Older Colleagues', *The Russian Review*, Vol. 45, No. 4, 1986, pp. 401–8, p. 403.

69. Meyer, 'Coming to Terms with the Past', p. 402.

70. Robert F. Berkhofer, Jr, 'The Americanness of American Studies', *American Quarterly*, Vol. 31, No. 3, 1979, pp. 3405; Philip Gleason, 'World War II and the Development of American Studies', *American Quarterly*, Vol. 36, No. 3, 1984, pp. 343–58; Leila Zenderland, 'Constructing American Studies', in Hollinger (ed.), *Humanities and the Dynamics of Inclusion*, pp. 273–313.

71. Paul A. Bové, 'Can American Studies Be Area Studies?', in Miyoshi and Harootunian (eds), *Learning Places*, pp. 206–30.

72. The story is told in Leo Marx, 'Thoughts on the Origin and Character of the American Studies Movement', *American Quarterly*, Vol. 31, No. 3, 1979, pp. 398–401, p. 399.

73. Gene Wise, '"Paradigm Dramas" in American Studies: A Cultural and Institutional History of the Movement', *American Quarterly*, Vol. 31, No. 3, 1979, pp. 293–337, pp. 308–10; Michael Denning, *Culture in the Age of Three Worlds* (London: Verso, 2004), p. 172.

74. Gene M. Lyons and Louis Morton, *Schools for Strategy: Education and Research in National Security Affairs* (New York: Frederick A. Praeger, 1965).

75. Robert B. Hall, *Area Studies: With Special Reference to their Implications for Research in the Social Sciences* (New York: Social Science Research Council, 1947), pp. 82–3, cited in Immanuel Wallerstein, 'The Unintended Consequences of Cold War Area Studies', in Noam Chomsky et al., *The Cold War and the University: Toward an Intellectual History of the Postwar Years* (New York: New Press, 1997), p. 203.

76. Jerome S. Rauch, 'Area Institute Programs and African Studies', *Journal of Negro Education*, Vol. 24, Mo. 4, 1955, pp. 409–25; David Horowitz, 'Sinews of Empire', *Ramparts*, October 1969 – http://www.cia-on-campus.org; Gene M. Lyons, *The Uneasy Partnership: Social Science and the Federal Government in the Twentieth Century* (New York: Russell Sage Foundation, 1969), pp. 174–6; Theodore Draper, 'Intellectuals in Politics', *Encounter*, Vol. 46, No. 6, 1977, pp. 47–60; John Trumpbour, 'Harvard in Service to the National Security State', pp. 12–16; Lyons and Morton, *Schools for Strategy*, pp. 62–3; Ron Robin, *The Making of the Cold War Enemy: Culture and Politics in the Military-Industrial Complex* (Princeton, NJ: Princeton University Press, 2001), p. 35; Immanuel Wallerstein, 'Unintended Consequences', pp. 195–231.

77. Peter J. Seybold, 'The Ford Foundation and the Triumph of Behaviouralism in American Political Science', in Robert F. Arnove (ed.), *Philanthropy and Cultural Imperialism: The Foundations at Home and Abroad* (Boston: G. K. Hall, 1980).

78. Similarly, when a group of academics at the University of Michigan

established the *Journal of Conflict Resolution* the Michigan political science department refused to sponsor the journal because the topic of 'peace' was associated with the Left. See Deborah Welch Larson, 'Deterrence Theory and the Cold War', *Radical History Review*, 63, 1995, pp. 86–109.

79. McGeorge Bundy, 'The Battlefields of Power and the Searchlights of the Academy', in E. A. J. Johnson (ed.), *The Dimensions of Diplomacy* (Baltimore: Johns Hopkins Press, 1964), pp. 2–3.

80. Winks, *Cloak and Gown*, pp. 114–15.

81. See Horowitz, 'Sinews of Empire'.

82. Christopher Simpson, 'Universities, Empire, and the Production of Knowledge', in Christopher Simpson (ed.), *Universities and Empire: Money and Politics in the Social Sciences During the Cold War* (New York: New Press, 1998) p. xiv.

83. Cumings, 'Boundary Displacement', p. 8.

84. Cumings, 'Boundary Displacement', p. 8; Arif Dirlik (ed.), *What is in a Rim? Critical Perspectives on the Pacific Region Idea* (Lanham: Rowman and Littlefield, 1998). On the question of Zen see Andrew E. Barshay, 'What is Japan to Us?', in Hollinger (ed.), *Humanities and the Dynamics of Inclusion*, p. 358.

85. Harry Harootunian, 'Postcoloniality's Unconscious/Area Studies' Desire', in Masao Miyoshi and Harry Harootunian (eds), *Learning Places: The Afterlives of Area Studies* (Durham: Duke University Press, 2002), p. 151.

86. Neocleous, *Imagining the State*, pp. 46–61.

87. Cited in Allan A. Needell, 'Project Troy and the Cold War Annexation of the Social Sciences', in Simpson (ed.), *Universities and Empire*, pp. 4, 22.

88. Needell, 'Project Troy', p. 4.

89. Marchetti and Marks, *CIA and the Cult of Intelligence*, pp. 153, 196.

90. A debate took place during 1979 and 1980 concerning the origins of the term 'Third World', largely in the pages of the journal *Third World Quarterly*. Whatever the differences between the contributors about the first use of the phrase, the general agreement is that the term became important between 1949 and 1952.

91. Sidney W. Mintz, 'On the Concept of a Third World', *Dialectical Anthropology*, Vol. 1, No. 4, 1976, pp. 377–82; Carl E. Pletsch, 'The Three Worlds, or the Division of Social Scientific Labour, circa 1950–1975', *Comparative Studies in Society and History*, Vol. 23, No. 4, 1981, pp. 565–90.

92. Daniel Lerner, *The Passing of Traditional Society: Modernizing the Middle East* (New York: Free Press, 1958), p. 45.

93. Daniel Lerner, *Passing of Traditional Society*, pp. 46–7.

94. Irene L. Gendzier, 'Play It Again Sam: The Practice and Apology of

Development', in Simpson (ed.), *Universities and Empire*, pp. 57–95.

95. Bradley S. Klein, *Strategic Studies and World Order: The Global Politics of Deterrence* (Cambridge: Cambridge University Press, 1994), p. 92.

96. Geoffrey Kay, *Development and Underdevelopment: A Marxist Analysis* (London: Macmillan, 1975), pp. 2–5.

97. Max Millikan, Donald L. M. Blackmer et al., *The Emerging Nations: Their Growth and United States Policy* (London: Asia Publishing House, 1962), p. 23.

98. W. W. Rostow, *The Stages of Economic Growth: A Non-Communist Manifesto* (Cambridge: Cambridge University Press, 1960), p. 6. Though first published in 1960 the book is the culmination of work going back at least a decade if not more – see Mark H. Haefele, 'Walt Rostow's Stages of Economic Growth: Ideas and Action', in David C. Engerman et al. (eds), *Staging Growth: Modernization, Development, and the Global Cold War* (Amherst: University of Massachusetts Press, 2003).

99. Harootunian, 'Postcoloniality's Unconscious', p. 158. Also Ali A. Mazrui, 'From Social Darwinism to Current Theories of Modernization: A Tradition of Analysis', *World Politics*, Vol. 21, No. 1, 1968, pp. 69–83; Irene L. Gendzier, *Managing Political Change: Social Scientists and the Third World* (Boulder, CO: Westview Press, 1985), p. 27; Richard Barbrook, *Imaginary Futures: From Thinking Machines to the Global Village* (London: Pluto Press, 2007), pp. 206–18; Jennifer L. Beard, *The Political Economy of Desire: International Law, Development and the Nation State* (Abingdon: Routledge-Cavendish, 2007), p. 159.

100. Millikan et al., *Emerging Nations*.

101. Millikan et al., *Emerging Nations*, p. 24; also pp. 43–4.

102. Millikan et al., *Emerging Nations*, p. 22.

103. Michael E. Latham, *Modernization as Ideology: American Social Science and 'Nation Building' in the Kennedy Era* (Chapel Hill: University of North Carolina Press, 2000), p. 9; Gendzier, 'Play It Again Sam', p. 79.

104. James S. Coleman, 'Conclusion', in Gabriel A. Almond and James S. Coleman (eds), *The Politics of the Developing Areas* (Princeton, NJ: Princeton University Press, 1960), pp. 533, 536.

105. Gendzier, 'Play It Again Sam', pp. 60, 75; Gendzier, *Managing Political Change*, pp. 22–43, 54, 63; Latham, 'Ideology, Social Science, and Destiny', p. 204; Vinay Lal, *Empire of Knowledge: Culture and Plurality in the Global Economy* (London: Pluto Press, 2002), pp. 110–13.

106. See 'Memorandum From the Interagency Committee on Police Assistance Programs to President Kennedy', 20 July 1962, in *Foreign Relations of the United States, 1961–1963, Vol. VIII* (Washington: US Government Printing Office, 1996), p. 345–8. For discussion see D. Michael Shafer, *Deadly Paradigms: The Failure of U.S. Counterinsurgency Policy* (Princeton,

NJ: Princeton University Press, 1988), pp. 65, 87.

107. See Mark Duffield, *Global Governance and the New Wars: The Merging of Development and Security* (London: Zed Books, 2001); Wood and Shearing, *Imagining Security*, pp. 90–1; Mark Duffield and Nicholas Waddell, 'Securing Humans in a Dangerous World', *International Politics*, Vol. 43, No. 1, 2006, pp. 1–23.

108. Millikan and Blackmer (eds), *Emerging Nations*, p. 19; Lerner, *Passing of Traditional Society*, p. 405.

109. Lerner, *Passing of Traditional Society*, pp. 50–1, 64, 71–3, 89.

110. Oren, *Our Enemies and US*, pp. 135, 145; Herman, 'The Career of Cold War Psychology'; Gendzier, *Managing Political Change*, pp. 119–24.

111. Gabriel A. Almond and Sidney Verba, *The Civic Culture: Political Attitudes and Democracy in Five Nations* (1963), (London: Sage, 1989), p. 478.

112. Almond and Verba, *Civic Culture*, pp. 2–4.

113. Oren, *Our Enemies and US*, p. 134.

114. Timothy W. Luke, 'Political Science and the Discourses of Power: Developing a Genealogy of the Political Culture Concept', *History of Political Thought*, Vol. 10, No. 1, 1989, pp. 125–49; Gendzier, 'Play It Again Sam', p. 58.

115. Gendzier, *Managing Political Change*, p. 156.

116. Almond and Verba, *Civic Culture*, pp. 2–4, 13.

117. Gabriel A. Almond, *The American People and Foreign Policy* (1950) (Westport, CT: Greenwood Press, 1960).

118. Rostow, *Stages*, pp. 145–67.

119. Ellen Herman, 'The Career of Cold War Psychology', *Radical History Review*, 63, 1995, pp. 53–85.

120. Gabriel Almond, *The Appeals of Communism* (Princeton, NJ: Princeton University Press, 1954), pp. 245–7.

121. Lucian W. Pye, 'Political Culture and Political Development', in Lucian W. Pye and Sydney Verba (eds), *Political Culture and Political Development* (Princeton, NJ: Princeton University Press, 1965), p. 7.

122. Sydney Verba, 'Comparative Political Culture', in Pye and Verba (eds), *Political Culture and Political Development*, pp. 529–37, 542, 549.

123. Lerner, *Passing of Traditional Society*, p. 396.

124. NSC 4, *Coordination of Foreign Information Measures*, 9 December 1947, and NSC 4-A, *Psychological Operations*, 9 December 1947, both in *Foreign Relations of the United States, 1945–50: Emergence of the Intelligence Establishment* (Washington: US Government Printing Office, 1996), pp. 643–8.

125. Christopher Simpson, *Science of Coercion: Communication Research and Psychological Warfare 1945–1960* (Oxford: Oxford University Press, 1994), p. 39; also p. 36.

126. Simpson, *Science of Coercion*, pp. 53; also pp. 4, 9–10, 62.
127. Simpson, *Science of Coercion*, pp. 48–51, 106, 108.
128. Jack M. McLeod and Jay G. Blumler, 'The Macrosocial Level of Communication Science', in Charles R. Berger and Steven H. Chaffee (eds), *Handbook of Communication Science* (London: Sage, 1987), p. 284.
129. Robin, *Making of the Cold War Enemy*, p. 76.
130. Wilbur Schramm and John W. Riley, 'Communication in the Sovietized State, as Demonstrated in Korea', *American Sociological Review*, Vol. 16, No. 6, 1951, pp. 757–66; 'The Soviet Communist Theory', in Fred S. Siebert, Theodore Peterson and Wilbur Schramm, *Four Theories of the Press* (1956) (Urbana: University of Illinois Press, 1963), pp. 105–146.
131. Todd Gitlin, 'Media Sociology: The Dominant Paradigm', *Theory and Society*, Vol. 6, No. 2, 1978, pp. 205–53.
132. Simpson, *Science of Coercion*, p. 62; Simpson, 'Universities, Empire, and the Production of Knowledge', p. xx.
133. See Richard Lambert, 'DoD, Social Science, and International Studies', *Annals of the American Academy of Political and Social Science*, Vol. 502, 1989, pp. 94–107.
134. Michael A. Bernstein, 'American Economics and the National Security State, 1941–1953', *Radical History Review*, 63, 1995, pp. 9–26; S. M. Amadae, *Rationalizing Capitalist Democracy: The Cold War Origins of Rational Choice Liberalism* (Chicago: University of Chicago Press, 2003).
135. David H. Price, *Threatening Anthropology: McCarthyism and the FBI's Surveillance of Activist Anthropology* (Durham: Duke University Press, 2004); Laura Nader, 'The Phantom Factor', in Chomsky et al., *Cold War*, pp. 107–46; Montgomery McFate, 'Anthropology and Counter-insurgency: The Strange Story of their Curious Relationship', *Military Review*, March–April 2005, pp. 24–38.
136. Note the following: 'I surveyed the five top journals in political science that specialize in international relations during the period 1991–2000. I did not find a single article in any of these journals that focused on CIA covert operations. Mentions of covert operations were very rare and, when they occurred at all, they were confined to a few sentences or a footnote. In effect, an entire category of international conduct has been expunged from the record, as if it never occurred' – David N. Gibbs, 'The CIA is Back on Campus', *Counterpunch*, 7 April 2003, p. 13. The journals in question were *World Politics*, *International Organization*, *International Security*, *Journal of Conflict Resolution*, and *International Studies Quarterly*.
137. Larson, 'Deterrence Theory', p. 92.
138. See G. M. Dillon, 'The Alliance of Security and Subjectivity', *Current Research on Peace and Violence*, Vol. 13, No. 3, 1990, pp. 101–24, and Klein, *Strategic Studies*, pp. 124–5.

139. Michael Burleigh, *Death and Deliverance: 'Euthanasia' in Germany 1900–1945* (Cambridge: Cambridge University Press, 1994), pp. 4–5.

140. Christopher M. Hutton, *Linguistics and the Third Reich: Mother-Tongue Fascism, Race and the Science of Language* (London: Routledge, 1999), p. 57.

141. Kanishka Jayasuriya, '9/11 and the New "Antipolitics" of "Security"', *Social Science Research Council*. http://www.ssrc.org/sept11/essays/jayasuriya.htm – accessed 29 September 2004.

142. Simon Dalby, 'Contesting an Essential Concept: Reading the Dilemmas in Contemporary Security Discourse', in Keith Krause and Michael C. Williams (eds), *Critical Security Studies: Concepts and Cases* (London: UCL Press, 1997), p. 20.

143. In their 1979 song 'Return the Gift', Gang of Four tell 'a little tale of how an individual shrinks – how one becomes not a subject but merely an object of history – when he or she wins a radio give-away contest', writes Greil Marcus. 'It's a song about the way the winner exchanges the multitudes of a unique personality for capital's reductive prize: fear'. Having accepted the symbols of status and security as a substitute for a true self, the 'winner' in this game ceases to exist. But, of course, we know perfectly well that nothing in 'Return the Gift' is going back. Greil Marcus, sleeve notes to Gang of Four, *A Brief History of the Twentieth Century* (EMI, 1990).

INDEX

═══